Child Development

Made Simple

The Made Simple series
has been created
especially for self-education
but can equally well
be used as
an aid to group study.
However complex the subject,
the reader is taken
step by step,
clearly and methodically,
through the course. Each volume
has been prepared by experts,
taking account of
modern educational requirements,
to ensure the most
effective way of
acquiring knowledge.

D1395702

In the same series

Child Development

Made Simple

Richard Lansdown, MA, Dip Psych, PhD

MADE SIMPLE
B O O K S

HEINEMANN PROFESSIONAL PUBLISHING

Made Simple Books
An imprint of Heinemann Professional Publishing Ltd
Halley Court, Jordan Hill, Oxford OX2 8EJ

OXFORD   LONDON   MELBOURNE   AUCKLAND

First published 1984
Reprinted 1986
Reprinted 1988

British Library Cataloguing in Publication Data
Lansdown, Richard
    Child development made simple.—(Made
    simple books, ISSN 0265–0541)
    1. Child development
    I. Title   II. Series
    155.4   BF721

ISBN 0 434 98599 6

Made and printed in Great Britain by
Richard Clay Ltd, Bungay, Suffolk

Preface

This book has been written for anyone seeking an introduction to the study of child development, and will therefore be of interest to all students of childcare, education, medicine, nursing and social work as well as trainee teachers and, of course, also parents and parents to be. It would be both arrogant and contrary to the spirit of the book to exclude children themselves from such a list, and I hope that senior pupils in secondary schools will be able to use it as well.

In the last three decades there has been a rapidly expanding body of knowledge in this field, much of which is found only in books and journals written by and for specialists. In this book such sources have been drawn upon in order to provide an up-to-date commentary on what has become one of the fastest growing areas in the social sciences. Care has been taken to give details of all major references; my apologies go in advance to anyone whose work has not been acknowledged. My grateful thanks go to Pat Nicholson for her skill in working with the manuscript.

RICHARD LANSDOWN
The Hospital for Sick Children
Great Ormond Street

Contents

Part 5: The Baby becomes a Child: Personal Growth

Part 6: The Activities of Childhood

Part 7: Adolescence

Part 8: Developmental Disorders

Part 9: Technical Aspects of Study

Part 1
The Study of Child Development

1
An Introduction to Principles and Practice

Basic Themes of this Book

Consider the lives of two children, both born profoundly deaf. The first grows up in a poor country where there is no educational provision for the disabled. He is malnourished and can find only the most menial of occupations when he grows up.

The second grows up in a rich country, where educational facilities are well developed. She learns to communicate, does well at school and university and although much of her life is a struggle she is able to play a full part in her community.

These accounts illustrate the first basic theme of this book: **we are all products of both biology and the environment**. At birth children come into the world with certain biologically determined equipment and are thus programmed to cope with demands made on them. Some children are clearly programmed more adequately than others. But each child encounters a different set of demands and grows up in a unique environment. How one grows from childhood to adult status is the result of the interaction between heredity and environment.

The second basic theme is related to the first: **children are always part of a system**. At first this system is the simple one of child–mother (or mother substitute). Later it becomes child–family, then child–school and later still, child–community. The essential point of emphasising that these are systems is that the child affects the mother (or the aunt, teacher or friend, etc.) as much as he or she is influenced. Early texts on child development described a one-way process; now we are more confident in asserting that the process is two-way.

An extreme example of the two-way process operating early in life comes when we consider what happens when a baby is born blind. Because there is no vision there is no ordinary response when a significant adult approaches. The ordinary response that most parents expect is crowing and gurgling of delight with arms and legs being waved in all directions. Because the baby cannot see the adult, but can hear, the response is one of 'stilling'—that is, there will be a freezing of bodily movement, so that sounds can be attended to. Unfortunately this apparent lack of interest puts some parents off and they find themselves saying how difficult it is to respond to a baby who does not greet them.

As far as possible these themes will be developed within a scientific framework; that is, observations will be used to illustrate certain theoretical points. In this the view of Charles Darwin is acknowledged; he said that facts are of no use unless they support a point of view. On the other hand, of course, points of view are of little value unless they are supported by facts.

Darwin's dictum would be easier to apply to child development studies if there were one major theory encompassing all observations. Unfortunately such a theory does not exist in psychology at large, let alone in child psychology. Perhaps human behaviour is too complex for one theory ever to explain everything. (See Chapter 2 for an introduction to theories in general.) But do not jump to the conclusion that there is total disarray in the ranks of those who write about child development; there are coherent ways of fitting observations together to support firmly held points of view, and one of the points of studying child development rather than just watching children is to enable this coherence to emerge.

Chronological Age Groupings

So far there has been mention of baby and child. Many terms are used rather vaguely in some texts and the following list is included now to indicate what is meant in the book. The definitions are those currently in use in Britain.

Germinal	the first two weeks after conception
Embryonic	two to six weeks after conception
Foetal	from six weeks after conception to birth
Perinatal	around the period of birth
Neonatal	the first two weeks after birth
Infancy	the first two years of life
Early childhood	two to five years of age
Later childhood	six years to puberty
Adolescence	from puberty to adulthood

Principles of Child Development

The Study of Change

The first principle is that **development primarily involves change** and so the one major aim of the academic study of child development is to establish the characteristics of age-related changes in physique, abilities and behaviour from conception to maturity.

Many people use the words growth and development as though they were synonymous. Although neither occurs without the other they do not mean exactly the same thing. **Growth** refers to quantitative change—increases in size and structure. **Development** refers to qualitative change, occurring in an orderly and coherent manner. Implicit in the notion of development is an increase in complexity. As one author has put it: 'The mental filing system not only grows larger, but it is reorganised over time, with infinitely more cross-references.'

Types of Change

Changes can be grouped into four main categories, with some being inter-related.

1. **Changes in size** include physical changes in height and weight, for example, and mental changes in memory, perception and understanding.

2. **Changes in proportions.** Relatively, the neonate's head is much larger compared to his body than that of the grown adult and there are several quite dramatic changes in proportion during the years to late adolescence.

3. **Disappearance of old features.** With age certain physical features are no longer of use and they are discarded, first teeth being an example. Some psychological and behavioural traits go as well; think of the way that baby talk is discarded, or the way that the ability to crawl rapidly across a floor disappears.

4. **The acquisition of new features.** Some new features develop as a result of maturation and some from new learning. An example of the former is secondary sex characteristics associated with puberty and of the latter a knowledge of stamps of the world.

The Importance of Early Development

Long before scientific studies were published on child development Milton observed: 'The childhood shows the man as morning shows the day.' Current thought has tended to place less emphasis on the exclusivity of the influence of early experience, arguing perhaps that early morning showers can be replaced by sunny periods in the afternoon. (See Chapter 3 for a fuller discussion of this.) Despite this relatively recent shift in opinion there remains a powerful body of evidence pointing to the persistence of early behaviour patterns. (See, also in Chapter 3, the section on Temperament.)

Development is the Product of Maturation and Learning

In the introductory part of this chapter the point was made that children are the products of both their biological inheritance and environmental factors. **Maturation** refers to the biological, it is the unfolding of character-istics potentially present in the individual. **Learning** is a general term in this context, referring to influences on development that come through training and practice. One of the most heated areas of debate over the relative importance of maturation and learning is that to do with the development of intelligence (see Chapter 14).

The Developmental Pattern is Predictable

Every species follows a pattern of development peculiar to itself. Two laws relating to physical development in humans are:

1. **The cephalocaudal law:** development proceeds from head to foot.
2. **The proximodistal law:** development proceeds from near to far.

Applying these laws in human development leads us to expect that we

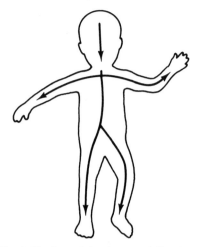

Fig. 1. The laws of developmental direction.

shall observe improvements in structure and function in the region of the head before the trunk, the legs and feet; and in the trunk before the arms and legs. Consideration of foetal development bears out both laws.

Characteristics of Development are Consistent

1. Development proceeds from the general to the specific. (See Chapter 10 on Perception for a further discussion and example of this rule.)
2. Development is continuous.
3. Different areas develop at different rates. A child may make rapid progress in talking and be very slow in walking; this is not necessarily a sign of abnormality.
4. There are developmental correlations. This is, in a way, a counter-balance to point 3 above: in general, a child who lags in walking as a baby is likely to be less than average in games and other gross motor skills as he grows up.

Individual Differences

This cannot be said strongly enough: even identical twins have some different experiences and no two people are completely alike. It is essential for parents to understand this principle when they are tempted to compare one child to the detriment of another.

The Developmental Pattern is Periodic

Although development is consistent and follows a pattern this does not mean that it is steady across all areas. There are periods of rapid growth, and periods when nothing seems to be happening, the latter being known as **plateaux**.

Child Development and Child Psychology

Psychology is a study of **the explanation and prediction of behaviour** and child psychologists are concerned with most if not all of the topics considered by students of child development. Nevertheless, the two disciplines are not identical. Child psychology is concerned with *particular aspects* of behaviour —language, perception, learning, for example—while crucial to child development is the *overall pattern of change in behaviour.*

Another way of expressing the difference is that child psychology looks primarily at **content**: child development at **process**. So, when language is being studied, psychology is primarily taken up with what children say; child development with how they learn to say it and what causes variation from one child to another. Note that this is a distinction of primary emphasis: there is much overlapping of the data studied by both.

The Value of Studying Child Development

The earliest students of children were interested mainly in discovering ways to improve educational techniques, an example being the seventeenth-century Slavic educational reformer **John Comenius.** This is still a major reason for acquiring an understanding of child development, along with other practical points related to health and emotional adjustment. But there are three other major incentives.

The Testing of Traditional Beliefs

Traditional beliefs have long influenced adults' attitudes towards children; they may have a basis of truth but they should always be questioned. An example of a traditional belief now being examined is the difference in learning abilities between the sexes. Boys have always been perceived as naturally better at maths and science than girls. This may be a correct view; it is clearly of crucial importance to investigate it.

The Development and Testing of Theories

Theories of child development, as opposed to traditional beliefs, need testing and elaborating (see Chapter 2 for a further discussion of theories). Freud put forward the view that the child's early experiences, especially his relations with his mother, are vitally influential on subsequent behaviour. Work by **John Bowlby** and **James Robertson** based on this theory has had widespread effects on popular views about, for example, the importance of parents being with children in hospital. More recent testing of this theory by sociologists has suggested that it lacks sophistication, that we need to consider factors within the family wider than the simple mother–child bond (see Chapter 3).

The Normal and the Expected

Finally, we need to have some grasp of *what can and cannot be considered normal or expected behaviour* and the conditions which facilitate both the normal and the deviant. It is a great help to the caregiver of a two-year-old to know that apparently irrational temper tantrums are the norm rather than the exception. It is a help to realise that many young children reverse **b** and **d** when they write. (See Chapter 25 for a further discussion of developmental disorders.)

What is more, a knowledge of normal development enables us to prepare both children and ourselves for future steps. The classical example of this is preparation for adolescence. Unfortunately there is so much misunderstanding of adolescence as a phase that many parents in Western cultures have an expectation that the years 14 to 19 must bring turmoil. The result is possibly that turmoil may come simply because it is expected. An appreciation of the observed events of adolescence, as outlined in Chapter 24, is likely to lead to a different set of expectations.

Note that this book confines itself to child development—that is, its subject matter is the person up to about 18 years of age. In recent years there has been a growing interest among psychologists in psychological development into adulthood and old age. Anyone wishing to study this further is advised to read *Developmental Psychology: A Life-Span Approach* by James Birren and others (Houghton Mifflin Company, USA, 1981).

Methods of Studying Child Development

The Treatise and the Biographical Record

Following the pioneering work of Comenius, one of the first people to study children as individuals, there came two distinct types of approach. One was the **philosophical treatise**, an example being found in the work of **Jean-Jacques Rousseau** (1712–78). Although they played a major part in determining thought, these writers were no more than indirect in their references to children themselves.

More familiar to present-day readers was the technique adopted by those who followed the other approach, that of the **biographical record**. **Johann Pestalozzi** (1746–1827), a Swiss, is credited with being among the first to publish data of this kind; his record of his 3½-year-old son was produced in 1774. Almost a hundred years later, in 1877, **Charles Darwin** published *A Biographical Sketch of an Infant*, noting there that he began his recordings even during the baby's first few days for he felt convinced 'that the most complex and fine shades of expression must all have a gradual and natural origin'.

Darwin, however, was primarily interested in **phylogenesis**—the evolution of the species through many centuries. More concerned with **ontogenesis**, the evolution of the individual organism, was **Wilhelm Preyer** who published *The Mind of the Child* in 1881. This book earned Preyer the title Father of Modern Child Psychology for he departed from earlier biographical recorders who had confined themselves to general observations and anecdotes, focusing instead on careful measurements of behaviour beginning with the development of reflexes from birth. Diary-type accounts such as these have been relatively rarely published, yet they have obvious value: they enable one to study change in minute detail, over time, with recording being done on the spot, virtually at the same time as the event. Both a comment and an explanation for their rarity was given by the American psychologist **J. B. Watson** in 1928:

'Would you believe the most astonishing truth that no well trained man or woman has ever watched the complete and daily development of a single child from its birth to its third year? Plants and animals we know about because we have studied them, but the human child until very recently has been a mystery.'

The key phrase in this quotation is 'no well trained man or woman'. Observations by people who do not really know what they are looking for result in little more than a string of ill-digested anecdotes. Ultimately the most fruitful use of this technique is the generation of hypotheses for more general, more systematic study.

Questionnaires, Surveys and Interviews

Once a hypothesis has been generated the obvious way to find out whether it is likely to be generally true is to go out and ask people questions. Say one is interested in the effects on children's language development of living in a high-rise flat, the assumption being that such conditions lead to isolation and in turn to impoverished language. The next stage is to find such children and, having assessed their language development, to ask questions of their parents about where they played and who they talked to (see also Chapter 27).

A pioneer in this approach was the American **G. Stanley Hall**, who introduced the questionnaire to child psychology and who is now best known for his work on adolescence. The questionnaire remains an invaluable tool for research workers, but it is not without its drawbacks. If it is sent by post there is often a poor return, as low as 35–40 per cent is not uncommon. Even if arrangements are made to collect it there is usually an inflexibility about the format of the questions which either annoys people or leads to false answers.

Consider the following, which might be given to the parents of a six-year-old:

To the child's father:

How often do you kiss your child good night?

Every night ☐   Most nights ☐   Rarely ☐   Never ☐

Is this a question likely to yield useful information? The commercial traveller, away three nights a week, might want to give a qualified answer, as would the father on shift work.

The Structured Interview

A more flexible approach is the structured interview in which a series of questions are put, more or less formally, in person by the interviewer. This technique yields much richer information and can be seen put to good use in the work of **John** and **Elizabeth Newson** of Nottingham University (see, for example, their book *Four Years Old in Urban Community*, Allen and Unwin, 1968).

But even the best trained interviewers, or the most sophisticated questionnaires, rely on people answering truthfully and correctly. There is no sure way of establishing the honesty of a respondent, although the interviewer may have a hunch that all is not well. Rather than telling wild untruths—'All our children could speak eight languages by the time they were six'—it is possible that some people, parents and teachers being no exception, will feel that they are being examined when asked about their children. The result can be a slight distortion in the truth to allow the respondent to be shown in a good light.

The correctness of answers depending on memory is another matter. With the best intentions towards honesty in the world some people distort in their remembering. In an article published in the *Journal of Abnormal and Social Psychology* in 1963, **L. C. Robbins** found that parental answers to questions about their children in the past were rarely more than 80 per cent accurate. One question, which might have been thought easy to remember, was 'when did the child first stand alone?' Fewer than 20 per cent of mothers and fewer than 10 per cent of fathers gave an accurate answer.

Laboratory Studies and Experimental Techniques

Some researchers prefer to use a technique as close as possible to that employed by other scientists—that is, they use a laboratory-like setting with children's responses the main outcome of their experiments. An example of this method is a study on children's honesty. They are brought to a laboratory where there is either a hidden camera or a one-way screen. There they are given a task and are told, incidentally, that the answers are in the examiner's book. After five minutes the examiner is called from the room and the children are observed to see if they look up the answers.

The experimental approach need not be confined to a laboratory. It can be transported almost anywhere. One might be interested in discovering the effects on children's behaviour of their being told that they have done badly on a task. One way to do this is to ask children to fill in a simple scale to indicate how tense or relaxed they feel. All children are then given a task but half are told they have done well, half that they have done badly. Then all fill in a tense–relaxed scale again.

The **advantages** of these methods are that many of the variables which might affect the child's performance can be controlled. For example, instructions can be tape-recorded so that every child hears exactly the same words said in the same way.

The **disadvantage** is that one is not always sure that one can generalise from an experimental result to real life. An inherent weakness, which can be seen to apply to many other techniques as well as this, is the enormous difficulty of holding all relevant factors constant. Because of the complexity of humans it may even be that the experimenter is not aware of what factors are relevant. An example of this last point is found in the work of **Tom Bower**, who has spent many years studying babies' visual perception. He found that there is a difference in their responsiveness according to whether or not they are on their back or propped up. In the latter position they are much more alert, a finding that earlier workers appeared to have overlooked.

Observations in a Natural Setting

There are certain objections to treating children as though they can be manipulated like bunsen burners. It is better, argue some, to return to Preyer and observe certain selected behaviours in the home, school or neighbourhood in much the same way that ethologists study monkeys.

This has its attractions but it should not be imagined that it is either easy or necessarily reliable; so much depends on the observer, who must be carefully trained. If this is done, then the technique has much to offer.

If, for example, we are interested in the different responses to Father Christmas in three-, four- and five-year-olds, one way to find out is to watch them when Father Christmas comes into the room. Indeed, there are some questions that can be answered only by these means. The use of video cameras has given a great fillip to systematic observation of these types, for several observers can watch the same film over and over again until they all agree on their interpretation.

But that last word, *interpretation*, reveals a fundamental weakness. No matter how many video films are taken, ultimately behaviour has to be interpreted and this is no easy matter. Take a child who quarrels with another. Was that action a push, or a smack? Was it accidental? Was it intentional but was the force used accidental? When one adds the possibility of something happening off-camera, or out of the view of the observer, the problems multiply. Nevertheless, if one is researching into relatively discrete, easily definable behaviour—for example, how many times a child gets off a chair in a 30-minute period—personal observation is invaluable.

Talking to Children: the Clinical Method

The American psychologist **George Kelly** once said words to the effect: 'If you want to know what's wrong with someone, ask him.' In the same vein some investigators have approached the problem of finding out about children simply by asking them questions. Much of our understanding of children's concepts has been achieved in this way (see Chapter 9).

This approach has much to commend it. By varying the inflection of one's voice, by use of repetition, by pausing, by changing vocabulary one can tailor questions to individual children and really get to each of them.

But it, too, has its drawbacks. It is **time-consuming**; some children take a very long time to relax sufficiently to talk freely and even if one can establish rapport quickly there is a limit to the number of personal interviews that can be conducted by any one enquirer. More serious is the limitation on the **range of children available**; the pre-verbal are obviously not accessible.

What is more, the **validity of the findings** is often questionable for one can never always be certain that the child is not giving answers that he feels the adult is looking for.

Cross-sectional and Longitudinal Studies

If one is seeking information about differences between certain ages one can approach the task in two ways. The first is cross-sectional—that is, a group of children of different ages is looked at. An example of this approach is work recently carried out in Europe and America to investigate the relationship between lead and intelligence. By measuring the amount of lead in the body conclusions can be drawn about the changes that occur between, say, the ages of six and 12.

A longitudinal study is one in which a group of children is followed through several years to monitor their progress. An example of this technique is the National Child Development Study which followed thousands of children all born in 1958 and reported on how they had fared up to the age of 22. (For details consult the National Children's Bureau, 8 Wakeley Street, London, EC1.)

The advantages and disadvantages of the two approaches may be summarised as follows:

Cross-sectional studies

Advantages are that they are	time saving
	relatively cheap
	can be carried out by one person.
Main **disadvantage** is that	they may give a distorted picture of the developmental process, since different factors could affect each age group.

Longitudinal studies

Advantages are that they	allow for each child's progress to be analysed
	enable growth and change within children to be measured
	give an opportunity to consider both maturational and environmental factors.
Disadvantages are that	different experimenters may be required because of the time involved
	they are more expensive than cross-sectional work
	data may be cumbersome to analyse.

Ethics

Whatever is done with or to a child should, ethically, be in his or her best and direct interest. It should also be done with the informed consent of either the child or the child's parents.

This can raise some difficult questions. If one informs a child, or parents, about an observational study, this might affect the child's behaviour and thus invalidate the work. At what age should one assume that children can have sufficient understanding to give informed consent? If it is uncertain whether or not a research student's results will be of value can that student say that asking a child to spend time being tested is in *that* child's direct interest? Similarly, is it ethical for a child to be made uncomfortable during an experiment? Can one legitimately ask questions of children about their families and friends?

There are no pat answers to any of these ethical problems. Nevertheless, they cannot be ignored and each study has to be considered on its merits.

The Value of Replication

The obstacles to a scientific study of human development are daunting. No one method is flawless and children themselves are so complex, living in a multi-variegated environment, that it may seem all too much. One partial solution lies in the value of replication. If one research study suggests that children behave in a certain way under certain conditions then it is essential that the study be repeated to see if the same results pertain.

A recent failure to replicate results can be found in studies on the effects of mothers' behaviour according to their experience with their baby during the so-called 'sensitive period' immediately after birth. When early results appeared in the 1970s, it seemed that early skin-to-skin contact, for example, was a prime determinant of subsequent maternal behaviour. However, more recent attempts at repeating these studies have produced negative or inconsistent results and the early enthusiasm has been tempered (see also page 156).

On the other hand, the value of replication has also been shown positively: it can be said with some certainty that birth order has some relationship to intelligence, for many studies have shown that the youngest of a large family tends towards being the least intelligent.

Conclusion: Matching the Technique to the Question

One of the skills of the developmental psychologist is that of choosing the appropriate technique for each question. Cost and time should not be constraints, although unfortunately they often are. Sometimes different techniques can be used to answer different aspects of the same overall question; this is particularly the case in certain educationally related topics when the complexity of the subject dictates a complex investigatory design.

Questions

1. Discuss the statement: The best way to find out about children is to watch them.
2. Give three examples of change that would be considered proper for the study of child development.
3. How might a biographical record of an infant kept today differ from one made in the eighteenth century?
4. Explain the meaning of 'replication' and give two examples in the study of child development.

Exercises

1. Design a questionnaire to yield information on students' attitudes to methods of disciplining young children.
2. With one two others, observe a child in a natural setting for 15 minutes and compare observations.

2
Theories of Child Development

The Nature of Theories in Science and in Child Development

It can be argued that we do not need a theory of child development since everything can be explained by common sense. Indeed, there are some who dismiss all psychology as common sense dressed up in statistics. But one need consider only the history of opinions on the shape of the world to be made wary of common sense. For thousands of years it was self-evident that the world is flat; just look and you will see. A proper wariness of the self-evident has led to the development of theories in natural science based on two major features:

1. **Hypotheses must be testable.** A statement must be capable of *disproof* if it is to be incorporated into a scientific system. Thus I can say that my Aunt Mabel is a bad cook. This statement can be tested by getting her to cook several dishes and trying them out. In theory it would be possible to imagine her producing a stunning meal which would show me to be wrong. On the other hand, if I were to say that my Aunt Mabel will never win the football polls I cannot devise an experiment that will show this to be wrong because one day she may win. A popular saying, 'The exception proves the rule', is actually a shortened version of the more correct 'The possibility of an exception supports the rule'. This point is discussed further in Chapter 27.

2. **Observed phenomena must be repeatable.** Anyone carrying out research in the natural sciences must describe the work so that another person may repeat it and thus verify it. Behind this insistence on repeatability is a search for general laws leading to experiments that can be carried out at will. To take an example: there is mild interest in the story of someone who has a dream about another person who subsequently dies; there would be tremendous scientific interest in anyone who could have such a dream repeatedly. Scientific laws might be generated if the dreams could be experienced on command.

Is a Science of Child Development Possible?

The answer to this question is a qualified 'yes'. One can certainly make coherent statements which are testable. It is possible to carry out experiments or other investigations in a way that enables others to repeat them. But there are some aspects of child psychology and therefore of child development which are less suitable for this rigorous approach. The work of the psychoanalytic school of psychology, discussed below, is seen by some commentators as falling outside the boundaries of science because so many of its statements are untestable.

Even if untestable theories are rejected one is left with a choice between several others. The would-be scientist has two choices open: either to select from the range of alternatives that which seems the most plausible and most far reaching in its application and to reject all others, or to take here and there from several, selecting those aspects of theories that seem most helpful. In either case it will be necessary to become aquainted with as many approaches as possible.

Why have a Theory?

At this point the reader may wonder why theorising is necessary. Why do we not collect and record observations rather in the same way that we collect stamps. We can then watch our collection of observations grow richer and richer. An answer to this point was touched on in Chapter 1: without a theoretical backing to one's observations there is no coherence to the thoughts that arise. The stamp collection analogy is not quite irrelevant: consider how much difference there is between a collection of stamps put into a book haphazardly and one with the same stamps arranged first by country and then by set.

The Nature of a Theory of Child Development

First an acceptable theory must provide **explanations for events**. A logical problem can arise in distinguishing between *explanations* and *descriptions*. For example, one might consider a table of word acquisition as a function of the child's age. Does such a table explain or simply describe how many words a child is likely to have at a given age? In general such distinctions are rarely made—more important is the second point of whether or not a theory can accurately predict.

The predictive power of a theory is seen by some as central. Prediction here is not related to foretelling the future in a crystal ball sense: it means using observable data within a framework of a theory to predict the occurrence of other observable phenomena. For example, take a three-year-old child who has never before been parted from his mother and watch as he becomes an in-patient in a hospital which restricts visiting. Our observed data are related to his age and experience. Using attachment theory one can predict that he will be upset by this experience and will show signs of distress. This prediction can be checked. It is not likely to be confirmed in every single case because humans are so complex that few if any such predictions are 100 per cent correct. Rather, though, we can speak of probabilities of the prediction's validity (see Chapter 26 for a further discussion of the statistical use of the term probability).

A theory becomes more powerful when it predicts what is not already known to be true, when it *generates* predictions rather than merely confirms them. Piagetian theory, for example, allows us to generate many hypotheses about children's ability to learn.

Third, a theory must use **clear language**. Only if the basic theory is clearly expressed can one carry out experiments to test what is said. Clarity of language leads to **operational definitions**, operational here meaning that the definition is sufficiently clear that one investigator knows exactly what another meant. It is no use describing a child as 'fretful' unless one says what signs are to be observed in a fretful child.

Fourth, the theory must be capable of **disproof**. This point about testable hypotheses has already been noted above, and it applies as much to child development as to any other field if the theory is to regard itself as scientific.

Pre-Twentieth-Century Concepts of Child Development and Contributions to Theory

Science as we know it today expanded during the nineteenth century. Before then most concepts about children were derived from religious teaching. Little thought was expended on wondering why children behaved in a certain way, much more went on working out ways of disciplining them and moulding their characters. **Lloyd de Mauser**, in *The History of Childhood* (Souvenir Press, 1974), states (some would say overstates) the case thus:

'The history of childhood is a nightmare from which we have only recently begun to awaken. The further back in history one goes the lower the level of childhood and the more likely children are to be killed, abandoned, beaten, terrorised and sexually abused.'

But eventually thoughts did turn to topics related to how children *do* grow up rather than how they *should*. A major contribution to the field was made by **Lambert Quetelet**, a Belgian mathematician-astronomer who published *On Man and the Development of His Faculties* in 1859, a book that so caught the public imagination that it sold out in one day. Darwin's work, plus that of **Gregor Mendel** (discussed in Chapter 4), paved the way for the consideration of humans as influenced both by environment and heredity—two theoretical standpoints which seem set to continue generating research for evermore.

An offshoot of Darwinian theory was a view, particularly popular during the nineteenth century, that **ontogeny recapitulates phylogeny**—that is, the development of an individual repeats the stages of the evolution of the species. Some evidence was given to support this view by observations that the human foetus does appear to develop much as other mammals but the whole notion of recapitulation is now seen as a gross oversimplification. Few psychologists today would agree with early theorists that children should, in order to be well adjusted later, go through animal-like stages of behaviour when very young.

Towards the end of the nineteenth century **Francis Galton**, sometimes known as the first British developmental psychologist, supervised measurements of nearly 10,000 visitors to the 1884 London Exposition. To manipulate these data Galton developed a number of statistical techniques, including that of correlation (see Chapter 28).

By the end of the nineteenth century the field was set, with tools available, for the explosion of theory that has taken place since then. Four major theories are considered in some detail in the next section.

Four Major Theories of Child Development

Jean Piaget

For some the work of Piaget (1896–1980) is synonymous with developmental psychology. In an obituary published in 1982 W. D. Hall wrote that Piaget's work provided '. . . the most self-consistent, enveloping and thoroughly tested body of theory that we have concerning human cognitive growth in the first two decades of life'.

The amount of his work is vast; he published getting on for 20,000 printed pages. It is rarely easy to understand in the original French and is often opaque in translation. It has generated hundreds of studies, influenced generations of teachers and in the last few years has been subjected to heavy criticism. In this section an outline will be given first of his life and thought as it influenced his work, to be followed by a description of his approach in general and some of his basic concepts. More detailed discussions of his notion of the development of understanding and some of the criticisms of his work are given in Chapter 9.

First, Piaget himself: born in Switzerland, he showed early promise and his first scientific work, on the albino sparrow, appeared when he was 10. So high was his standard that he was offered the post of curator of the mollusc collection at the Natural History Museum in Geneva on the strength of his writing; he had to decline because he was still at school. He received a doctorate at the age of 21.

While an adolescent he became fascinated by philosophy and had hoped to work in a field combining both philosophy and mathematics. However, he continued his studies in zoology at university and his approach to the problems of psychology reflect his biological background. His attachment to biology is graphically illustrated in his own words. While still a student he conceived the idea of identifying God with life. This notion '. . . . stirred me almost to ecstasy because it enabled me to see in biology the explanation of all things and of mind itself. . . . Between biology and the analysis of knowledge I needed something other than philosophy. I believe it was at that moment that I discovered a need that could only be satisfied by psychology.' (From Piaget's autobiography, 1952.)

While studying psychology in Paris he observed that a child's answers to standard questions can give rise to further, more probing questions. His earliest work, on the sparrow, had been a careful description based on observation and now he began to employ the same technique to psychology: the child became the source of data.

The main body of his work fell into three phases. The first, up to 1929, saw the statement of his theory of intellectual development with the publication of four major books: *Language and Thought of the Child*, *Judgement and Reasoning in the Child*, *The Child's Conception of the World* and *The Child's Conception of Physical Causality*. It is important to note that a number of critics of Piaget have based their views on this early phase; in later years his views were modified.

During the second phase he drew heavily upon observations of his own children and studied perceptual development, play, dreams and—most important of all in his eyes—the notion of groupings.

The third phase, from the beginning of the Second World War to his death, saw the development and refinement of his work. He has been described by Henry Maier as comparable with an explorer who sets out to investigate unknown territories, but who ends up discovering a new continent.

For a large part of his professional life he was Director of the Institut J. J. Rousseau in Geneva but he was also the first non-Frenchman to hold a chair at the Sorbonne since 1530.

Piagetian Theory

A key question for zoologists is how organisms adapt to their environment. As a zoologist Piaget was continuously intrigued by this process and he studied the development of human intelligence within this framework. In his own words, 'My theory of development ... is impossible to understand if one does not begin by analysing in detail the biological presuppositions from which it stems.' He was not concerned with the physiological underpinning of behaviour: rather he took from biology the central interest in *the ways that organisms adapt and develop*. It is biological adaptation that provides the core of his approach.

Equilibrium. An essential characteristic of a living organism is its system of **self-regulation**. No matter how warm or cold the air may be our body temperature is more or less maintained at an even level, unless of course illness interferes with the process. If our body tissue is damaged, say we graze a knee, there is a system of self-repair.

The more efficient and flexible the self-regulating system, the better the organism will be at adapting to environmental change. When a satisfactory relationship with the environment has been attained this is, in Piagetian terms, a state of equilibrium. It is not a state of non-activity—far from it, it is one in which the system is constantly working on a checks-and-balance principle.

When this stability is upset, because there is introduced some element which the existing checks and balances cannot cope with, a state of **disequilibrium** occurs. One can think back to the first time that one went to a new school, or college, or job: previous experience was not sufficient to enable one to cope and there was an uneasy period lasting until one could cope—until, in short, equilibrium returned.

The schema. In biology a structure adapts to the environment; in Piagetian terms the **human equivalent of this biological structure** is called a schema. It may be simple and unitary or it may be a whole system. Another way of conceptualising the idea is to see the schema as an **organised pattern of behaviour**. This, though, can lead to oversimplification for Piaget used schema as a complex concept encompassing both overt motor behaviour and internalised thought processes. He was, after all, primarily interested in the development of thought and his work set out to investigate how the primitive schemas of the neonate gradually broaden, differentiate and merge, becoming increasingly internal and sophisticated.

Assimilation and accommodation. The schema represents what it is that adapts; assimilation and accommodation explain *the system* by which adaptation takes place. At a simple level:

Assimilation is used to describe how the organism can handle new problems with existing mechanisms.

Accommodation is the process by which the organism changes in order to handle new problems which the existing system cannot manage.

The two should be seen as complementary processes.

At a more complex level one can consider the sequence of the two. **A. L. Baldwin** gives an example in his *Theories of Child Development* (John Wiley, 1967), a book from which I have drawn heavily in the writing of this chapter. His example is of the schema of grasping. An eight-month-old child will be able to grasp certain objects, say a finger, but not something very small or very large. The gradual acquisition of the ability to grasp other-sized objects can be seen as an example of accommodation. But before accommodation can take place the object must in some sense *seem to be graspable*, i.e. the schema must to some degree assimilate the object before accommodation occurs. Since this process is so central to Piaget's work and since it often provides a stumbling block to students of his work, it will be approached more descriptively, as shown in Fig. 2.

The model shown in Fig. 2 can go some way to explaining motivation:

Fig. 2. The process of accommodation.

if something is either too easy or so difficult that there is no possibility of accommodation the organism will give up. What is required is that the new situation is sufficiently recognisable to allow some initial assimilation but also sufficiently novel to maximise accommodation. It is reasoning of this kind that has led Piaget's work to have such an impact on educational theory.

Stages of development play an important part in Piagetian theory and are illustrated further in Chapter 9, which deals in some detail with the way in which he sees a child's understanding passing through certain stages. Here it should be noted that while Piaget perceived development as being continuous, this does not imply that there is a simple, linear path from the neonate to the fully mature. Rather certain structures underly behaviour at certain times, so one may assert that a child is at a certain stage according to what he is capable of at that time. These structures are developed in sequence, each building on the one that went before.

Sigmund Freud

Everyone has heard of Piaget but most people cannot understand him; everyone has also heard of Freud but most do not believe him. This is a somewhat flippant but not totally untrue statement, for no other theorist on child development can have met the same degree of disbelief becoming hostility that Freud encountered. In his *History of the Psychoanalytic Movement* Freud himself noted how a former colleague (Breuer) '.... showed the reaction of distaste and repudiation which was later to become so familiar to me, but which at that time I had not yet learned to recognise as my inevitable fate'.

Sigmund Freud (1856–1939) was born in Moravia, now in Czechoslovakia, then part of the Austro-Hungarian Empire, the first-born son of a superstitious mother who saw the fact that he entered the world covered in a growth of black hair as a portent that he would become a great man. Freud himself was aware of the influence that his mother's faith in his greatness had: 'A man who has been the undisputed favourite of the mother keeps for life the feeling of a conqueror.....'

His father, however, was less indulgent. Previously married, financially insecure, he was stern, insisting that the traditional Jewish injunction about honouring the father be obeyed.

The young Sigmund intended to be a lawyer but found himself with what he later described as an urgent necessity to understand something of the riddles of this world. So he chose the path of science and after a diversion into physiology finally qualified in medicine in Vienna in 1881. After a spell in neurology he moved to the study of nervous diseases, then in its infancy, and went to Paris where he studied under the greatest psychiatrist of the time, Jean Marie Charcot. Charcot had made hypnotism a respectable practice, at least in some circles, and used it to investigate hysteria, long thought to be the result of a malfunctioning uterus. When Freud returned to Vienna and spoke of men suffering from hysteria he met immediate opposition and then, having demonstrated that such a possibility was to be observed, he was ignored.

Finding that hypnosis was not always adequate for his needs, he developed the technique of free association to uncover thoughts. He became even more isolated from respectable scientific circles by the publication of his theories of sexuality which he derived from what his patients said when in a completely relaxed state.

By 1902, however, he had gained sufficient acceptance to enable him to become the centre of a small group of doctors and writers including **Alfred Adler** and **Wilhelm Stekel**. Professionally he was 'professor extraordinary' at the university in Vienna, a post given for his earlier work in neurology, far from the recognition that some have seen in it. But he and his circle continued in their assertion that there was more to medicine than the body. The First World War marked a rough dividing line in Freud's work, for it was in the post-war years that he devoted himself to theoretical formulations and their application to society as a whole.

Such was their success that psychoanalytic notions and vocabulary began to permeate the thinking of the western world. In 1929 he was granted the freedom of Vienna and on his seventy-fifth birthday he was made an honorary member of the Vienna Medical Society. He received these and other honours with little enthusiasm, attending none of the celebrations and accepting nothing in person.

In 1938 he left Vienna for London. The Nazis had burned his books five years earlier but they let him go on payment of a quarter of a million Austrian schillings. In London he soon settled to a regular work routine, including seeing patients, but in 1939 he succumbed to the cancer which had afflicted him for sixteen years. He died of cancer of the mouth, greatly exacerbated if not caused by excessive smoking. He fitted neatly into his own formulation of an 'oral' personality: ambitious, envious, with a tendency to self-punishment.

Psychoanalytic Theory: Basic Principles

The central assumption of psychoanalytic theory is that much of what we do is governed by forces buried in our **unconscious**. The forces are conceptualised as being like physical energy which come from the primitive part of our personality and have to be expressed somehow. The process of socialisation leads to a need to repress or to channel these forces and the way this is done leads to personality formation. Problems of **anxiety and neurosis** can be traced to **conflicts** between the forces which need expression and the more policeman-like part which forbids this expression.

A further assumption is that all behaviour can be explained in this way— we never do anything by accident. Thus when we are late for an appointment we do not, at some level, really want to keep it; when we say something which is apparently a slip of the tongue we really do mean to say what we did. The phrase 'Freudian slip' comes from this notion. (See Freud's *The Psychopathology of Everyday Life*, 1901.)

Much of psychoanalytic writing is concerned with treatment. This will largely be ignored in the following part of this chapter not because it is not important to the theory but because it is not central to an understanding of the theory's explanation of child development.

Instinctual drives

One of the fundamental concepts of psychoanalytic thought is the instinctual drive, not to be confused with instinct in the sense that it is used in, for example, nest-building in birds. Drives in the psychoanalytic sense are seen to be the root of an almost limitless variety of human behaviour.

The assumed mechanism is thus: **instinctual energy is psychological energy**. As energy becomes accumulated in specific areas of the body, organs become tense; when the tension increases the energy breaks through as a desire—to eat, scratch, drink or have sex. Gratification occurs when the desire is met, the origin of the whole process being the paramount need to maintain life. Unfortunately Freud used terms like 'sexual' or 'erotic' to cover such pleasurable gratification, which leads to much misunderstanding of his basic point.

Libido is a word that exemplifies both much of his thought and much of the misunderstanding. 'I give the name of libido to the energy of the sexual instincts and to that form of energy alone,' he wrote. But he also wrote that he saw sexuality as 'divorced from its too close connection with the genitals ... as a more comprehensive bodily function having pleasure as its goal and only secondarily coming to serve the ends of reproduction'. He went on to note that the term also covered 'all those merely affectionate and friendly impulses to which usage applies the exceedingly ambiguous word love'.

Nevertheless, it is hardly surprising that some of his ideas related to libido shocked the good doctors of Vienna. It must have been difficult for them to contemplate the notion that little boys are afraid that their fathers will castrate them or that farming is a symbolic rape of the mother.

Ego instincts is a term covering a number of other drives seen as less important than the libidinal. They included hunger, thirst and the escape from pain.

As with the theories of others, that of Freud was not static and he revised ideas on instinctive drives. Later on in his life, in 1920, he speculated on whether or not one could trace them all to a few basics. After what he described as 'long hesitancies' he concluded that all could be reduced to two: **Eros**, or the life instinct, and its counterpart, **Thanatos**, the death instinct. The latter was an inevitable part of the theory for if he was asserting that all behaviour is explicable it was essential that he invoke some mechanism to account for suicide, masochism and self-destructive acts.

Cathexis is the notion which links the instinctual drive to actual behaviour. Once one has conceived of a drive almost as though it were physical energy then that energy can be attached in varying quantities to different objects, people and ideas: this particular form of attachment is called cathexis. One can observe a child and his mother and see how important she is to him; one can then argue that for him she is cathected. An important corollary to this idea is that the greater the cathexis in any one direction the less there is to go round to others. A child who remains fixated on his mother is unlikely ever to reach sexual maturity.

The Unconscious

Consciousness, defined by **David Stafford Clark** as '... an immediate, constantly changing reflection of everything of which we are aware at a given instant in time', was seen by Freud as no more than a relatively small part of an individual's mental life.

Preconsciousness is the storehouse of memory: everything that is available to us when we try to recall.

The **unconscious** contains both the more primitive drives and impulses influencing our behaviour without our ever being aware of their influence, plus every set of ideas or memories which have a strong emotional charge and which have been repressed so that they are no longer available to the conscious process. It is important to avoid falling into the trap of thinking that unconscious refers only to that of which we are unaware; by definition it is referring to that of which we *cannot* be aware.

The Id, the Ego and the Superego

Freud saw the development of socialisation from child to adult not in terms of different instinctual drives or even different amounts of drives but in the pattern of cathexis or other regulating mechanisms, which determine how those drives are satisfied. The pattern of cathexis he described in three more terms:

1. **The id.** To understand the concept of the id one must first be aware of what Freud called **primary process**. The young child knows what he wants and he wants it now and he is not prepared to wait and no matter how often he is told that he cannot have it he will stamp his feet and have a tantrum because he wants it now and he really does not care what other people think about him. This is primary process functioning and it governs one structure of the personality known as the id.

Another way of characterising the id is to see it as governed by the **pleasure principle**: only immediate pleasure, which can include relief from pain, is taken into account. It is no use telling a young child that treatment in the dentist's chair will lead to less pain in the future: what counts is the pain the dentist is inflicting now this minute.

2. **The ego** is the second system to develop within the child's personality system. The id remains within the unconscious; the ego is that part of the unconscious which has been separated in order to make contact with the external world. Above all else, the ego is realistic, it delays and inhibits drives, representing the role of enlightened self-interest. Gratification is still the goal, but gratification gained in a more mature way than is found if one follows only the id, for the ego is capable of delaying gratification to make it the greater.

3. **The superego** is a rather different matter. There is no direct conflict between the id and the ego, they differ only on how to attain their ends. The superego, on the other hand, has somewhat different aims.

The superego is that part of the personality which restricts totally rather than modifying the drives of the id. Freud saw the superego as playing a policeman-like role, acting to serve the good of society as a whole by curbing the self-seeking energy of the other two aspects. Freud emphatically did not, however, see the superego as being culturally determined, no matter what its function. Rather, he saw the child develop a superego as he interpreted *parental injunctions* on sexuality. In this way the restrictions imposed by a superego may be out of all proportion violent and extreme. In such cases the ego can be seen as an intermediary between the id and the superego.

The Freudian Theory of Psychodynamics

The concepts given above form the bricks of Freudian theory; they operate together in a psychodynamic system.

A cornerstone to the theory at work is that action is controlled by consciousness. Thus although much may come from the unconscious it can never directly influence behaviour. A crucial area of study then is **the conditions which determine access to consciousness.**

One condition is that the nature of consciousness is such that its content must be **perceptible**. Some content is obviously so—what is seen, heard or smelt, for example. Most mental events are not so easily perceived and so become attached to verbal labels. One theory of why we cannot easily remember events of our first couple of years of life is that they happened during our pre-verbal phase.

The second condition is the level of cathexis, which must be sufficiently high. In everyday language one can say that we tend to think more about things that are important to us than those which are not.

Defence mechanisms exist to prevent the overwhelming of consciousness by thoughts which, if allowed to remain, would be too painful to bear. Guilt at remembering something we would rather not have done, anxiety in the face of some dreaded event, sorrow at the thoughts of loss—all bring pain if allowed to run riot in the mind. The following are some ways of dealing with them:

Repression: the idea is relegated to the unconscious and 'forgotten'.

Displacement: replaces one item with another, more acceptable. Thus excessive hand washing can be seen to replace masturbation if the latter is thought of as guilt-laden.

Reaction formation: changes one motivation to the exact opposite, so hatred can be manifest as kindness.

Projection: involves the attribution of the dangerous drive to another. We always see in others our own greatest faults.

Denial: The last and in some ways the simplest to understand. When we deny in a Freudian sense we see the world as we want to, not as it really is.

These defence mechanisms have been described individually but to some commentators they fall together in certain patterns or styles in individuals, reflecting the style with which the person deals with his environment as a whole, not just with the unpleasant aspects.

One word of warning: it is sometimes assumed that defence mechanisms are somehow bad and that the mentally healthy person does not need them. This is a misunderstanding; there are times when only a well-functioning defence keeps a person sane.

The Application of Freudian Theory

Just as Piagetian theory has a main area of interest in the development of understanding, so psychoanalytic theory is most relevant to an understanding of the way the personality is formed. For a further discussion of the part of the theory in the development of personality see Chapter 18.

Criticisms of Psychoanalytic Theory

As Freud himself discovered, it is very easy to be critical of his theory, especially when points are taken out of context. Apart from isolated sniping there are three major areas of weakness.

The first is the relative inaccessibility of the main data of the theory— namely thoughts and feelings. Thoughts and feelings do not readily lend themselves to operational definition and so one of the basic requirements of a scientific theory noted in Chapter 1 cannot be met.

Second is the tendency of some psychoanalysts to ascribe opposition to their ideas to resistance and repression on the part of their opponents. 'If you do not agree with what I am saying you must be repressing the truth' is as near an untestable hypothesis as one can get.

Third is the undoubted fact that most of Freud's patients on whose free associations he based his work were middle-class Europeans brought up in a society where sexual matters were not openly discussed.

In Chapter 18 readers will have an opportunity to consider the way in which psychoanalysis deals with the development of personality. Such a task is perhaps as good a test as any if one is seeking to come to conclusions on the value of a theory. They will also be able to examine the work of **Erik Erikson**, one of Freud's followers who has developed certain aspects of the approach in a way that may be more acceptable to the modern reader.

Learning Theory

Learning theory, sometimes referred to as **Stimulus-Response** theory, or **S-R** for short, stands in stark contrast to the two approaches already mentioned in this chapter. One characteristic is that it is not associated with one person; instead three major figures have contributed to the approach.

Ivan Pavlov (1849–1936) was an almost direct contemporary of Freud and shared an interest in physiology. He studied medicine in St Petersburg and after a spell in Leipzig returned there as professor at the Institute of Experimental Medicine. While conducting experiments on digestion he noticed that the dogs he used in his laboratory sometimes salivated in anticipation of the food they received. This observation led directly to a study of the way in which the dogs' responses of salivation were learned or conditioned.

He summarised his findings in five laws which became known as **classical conditioning theory** (see below), thus becoming the father of S-R psychology.

J. B. Watson (1878–1958) followed Pavlov in his interest in a study of stimulus-response relationships but rejected the Russian's idea that behaviour is maintained by reward, arguing instead for the power of **frequency**

and **recency**. He also rejected all notions of the unconscious and any other so-called mentalistic concepts like sensation and will. His contribution to academic psychology was curtailed as he had to resign from his post at Johns Hopkins University, USA, in consequence of a liaison which led to his divorce. He moved to advertising, where he became even more successful in the practical application of his theories than he had been in their academic exposition.

B. F. Skinner (1904–   ) was born in the USA and has been at Harvard University since 1948. He built on the ideas of both Pavlov and Watson but distinguished between two types of behaviour: **respondent**, when an organism responds in a simple way to a stimulus from the environment, and **operant**, when the organism behaves in a goal-directed way to change the environment (see below for a further discussion of this).

He applied this ultra objective approach to a very diverse range of behaviour including children's learning from machines and pigeons playing ping-pong.

Basic Principles of Learning Theory

Although the first person to be mentioned as influential in the development of learning theory was Pavlov, the roots of associationism and the role of learning in child development can be traced to the eighteenth- and nineteenth-century British empiricists Locke, Hume, Mill and others. A characteristic of the eighteenth-century view, however, was that it was two *ideas* that became associated, whereas Watson asserted that only *behaviour* was the proper study of psychology. Although this extreme view is no longer held by some behaviourists—indeed, there is now a growing school which deals in thoughts and ideas calling itself **cognitive behaviourism**—for many years and to some extent still psychologists who followed the S-R tradition ignored everything except behaviour. Their argument is simply that we can observe and measure behaviour objectively, we cannot do either with what goes on inside someone's mind. It is better, therefore, to take a 'black box' approach to thoughts; if we came across a black box with a lot of wires and gauges coming out of it we could watch the gauges and make up rules to predict what they will do without ever opening the box or without knowing what is inside it.

In the first and last analysis, argue these theorists, **behaviour is the result of learning**. We do something because we have been reinforced for doing it, or some very similar act, in the past. We refrain from doing something because we have found either that it brings no reward or that the consequences of such an act are unpleasant. Put like that the theory seems so simple that it is hardly worth stating, yet there has been built on this simple foundation a complex edifice which has had an enormous effect not only on the way children are brought up but in the assumptions that many people have about the way life should be led. If psychoanalytic views have passed into the accepted way of thinking of many writers and artists, if Piagetian views have become part of the wallpaper of many educational systems, learning theory has had its influence on political thought, particularly in the years since the end of the second world war.

Classical Conditioning

In Pavlov's original observations he noted a sequence: a dog is given food and immediately salivates. The food is called an **unconditioned stimulus**; the salivation is an **unconditioned response**.

Conditioning occurs when the unconditioned stimulus is paired with some other stimulus. In Pavlov's case a bell was rung just before the food was presented; the ringing became the conditioned stimulus since the dogs salivated to the sound of the bell. Salivation to the bell became known as the conditioned response. We can bring the picture nearer home by considering how a school bell, heralding the end of a lesson, can bring immediate relaxation, or excitement, depending on the age of the child and the nature of the lesson. The point is that it is not the sound of the bell itself that brings the change of behaviour, it is the fact that the bell has in the past been associated with relief from tension or boredom. The sound of the bell has become a conditioned stimulus.

The timing of the pairing of stimuli is crucial: the longer the interval that elapses between them the weaker the effect. Some would argue that this is why imprisonment so often fails to stop people committing further crimes—there is too great a period between the crime and the imprisonment. The general state of the organism is also of importance. A hungry dog is likely to condition more quickly than one that is satiated; a child must reach a certain level of understanding before conditioning will take place, although the behaviour of very young infants reveals that they can respond to some conditioning.

Operant Conditioning

Sometimes called **instrumental conditioning**, the operant principle can also be illustrated by an animal experiment. A rat is put into a box with a lever in it. At first the rat will explore the box but may not do anything with the lever. Eventually the lever will be pressed and a pellet of food drops into a nearby tray. The rat eats the food and sooner or later presses the lever again and has more food. Eventually the rat presses the lever frequently and becomes satiated, when he stops the lever activity.

The difference between the two approaches is that in operant conditioning the reinforcement comes after the response, i.e. the rat has to do something to get the reward, whereas in classical conditioning the response comes second (salivation comes after the bell rings).

A difference in outcome between the two approaches is that operant mechanisms can be used to link any two bits of behaviour if the reinforcement is sufficiently strong. In this way randomly occurring actions can be selectively reinforced and behaviour shaped over time. This is how Skinner taught his pigeons to play ping-pong; it is an explanation for much human behaviour, including speech. (Think of the shouts of joy that greet a baby's first 'word'.)

The **nature of the reinforcement** is tricky. For some it is anything that leads to an increase in behaviour. Others prefer the notion of drive reduction; it is anything that leads to the reduction of uncomfortable drives like hunger or thirst. More recently it has been noted that even turning on a light in a cage will increase behaviour of some sort and the theory has grown up that any stimulus change is reinforcing. Certainly one should be aware that there is far more complexity and subtlety to the concept of reinforcer than just 'something obviously pleasurable'. One interpretation of children's bad behaviour is that the resulting smack is reinforcing because it is more rewarding than being ignored.

Extinction occurs when the conditioning becomes undone. If a bell sounds but there is no food the dog will eventually stop salivating to the bell; if the lever pressing produces no food the rat will stop that activity.

It might be worthwhile at this stage to pause to consider ways in which children's behaviour becomes extinguished either at home or at school. Perhaps there is a lesson to be learned which might with value be applied to the often asked question on why there is such a change in attitude to school between the ages of 10 and 14. 'Adolescence' can explain some of the change but it is possible that there is also, for many children, a different pattern of rewards.

Inhibition is not the same as extinction; this distinction is of vital importance to anyone working with children. Inhibition occurs when a behaviour is punished, i.e. the inclination to do something may be there but it is overlaid by the anticipation of punishment. Thus there is a crucial difference between inhibition and extinction; if a piece of behaviour is extinguished it is unlikely to occur in *any* circumstances, whereas if it is inhibited it *will* occur if it is thought that the result will escape punishment. This distinction also helps partly to explain the relative failure of our penal system, and perhaps says something about discipline in schools.

Partial reinforcement is an aspect of the theory that at first glance appears to make no sense at all but which, on reflection, explains a great deal. The theory is simple: any behaviour which is consistently rewarded will extinguish more easily than that which is rewarded inconsistently. There is no printing error in that statement; for once a psychological argument is put forward advocating *inconsistency* as a powerful weapon in determining behaviour. An everyday example of the power of partial reinforcement is gambling: the gambler is rewarded from time to time. When he has a losing run he is buoyed up by the memory of that big win he had ten races ago, and there was always the little win he had five races ago and so there is always the chance of another big win in a couple of races or so, because after all, one knows that one cannot win every time. Another everyday example, closer to home for the student of child development, is the child who learns that constant, whining demands will eventually bring the ice cream or the extra bar of chocolate that has once or twice been refused.

There is, of course, another side to this coin: that the adult who can manage to be completely consistent in dealing with children will not be in the position of having given partial reinforcement and will, therefore, be far more in command of the situation.

Secondary conditioning. Think back to the dogs salivating to the sound of a bell. If a light is paired with the bell, then the light can become a **secondary conditioned stimulus**. In the experiment with pressing a lever it is possible to pair tokens with lever pressing, the token being exchanged for food pellets. It does not take a very large conceptual leap to get to *money as a secondary reinforcement*: the actual value of any single coin is generally very small yet the power of money to influence behaviour is incalcuable.

Generalisation is a further, valuable concept when one is trying to apply learning theory to everyday life. The basic point is that if a response has been conditioned to a *particular stimulus* then the organism is likely to respond to *similar stimuli*. In other words, there will be a generalisation curve which can be traced according to the similarity of the presented stimulus to the original one. One of the earliest examples of this is the response of the very young baby to being picked up and held by anyone: there is usually a quieting of behaviour. When the baby becomes older and able to discriminate the mother from other people the generalisation no longer pertains because the presented stimulus (the stranger) is not sufficiently similar to the original (the mother).

Criticism of Learning Theory

One of the fundamental criticisms of learning theory has to do with the **definition of a reinforcer**. A reinforcer is whatever leads to an increase in behaviour, and whatever leads to an increase in behaviour is a reinforcer, and so one goes round and round in a circle without ever really being able to come to a proper definition.

A criticism based on **historical observation** is that the original, hard-line theorists have been forced gradually to retreat from their position of S-R and nothing else and have had to admit that there are more things in heaven and earth to be included in any account of human behaviour. The purist, for example, dealt only with muscular movements as responses, the brain being seen as a static mediator of nerve impulses. It is now acknowledged that there is more complexity to behaviour and to neural mechanisms than was originally postulated. What is more, notions of expectancy and intention have to be incorporated into the system if it is adequately to explain behaviour.

Perhaps most important of all, the black box referred to above has been opened, and thoughts are now seen as important for some theorists. Indeed, thoughts are seen as bits of behaviour. To early thinkers this is heresy; to more recent workers it is an inevitable modification of an approach that promised much but did not always provide all the answers.

Sociobiology

Spiders spin webs, birds migrate, cats, even when fed out of tins, chase small moving objects. These examples of behaviour are properly seen as genetic in origin, owing nothing to environmental pressures. Sociobiology is **the systematic study of the biological** basis of all social behaviour, to quote **Edward Wilson's** book *Sociobiology: The New Synthesis* (Harvard University Press, 1975), which marked the beginning of a study of human nature based on Darwinian theories of natural selection and an understanding of contemporary genetics. Natural selection argues essentially that our genes are selfish, that behaviour leading to further reproduction of the species will continue while other behaviour will, by definition, wither. It will wither by definition because if it does not lead to the furtherance of the species then that species will die out.

An example of sociobiological theory in humans is the **incest taboo** claimed by Wilson to be among the universals of human social behaviour. There are immediately obvious reasons why this taboo should be practised so widely: offspring from incestuous relationships are biologically weaker, so it is arguable that any society accepting incest as a norm would very soon weaken itself. There is further support for the notion from a study of kibbutzim in Israel: children brought up together as though they were siblings show little if any interest in each other sexually.

The argument is taken a step further in considering attitudes towards the disabled or deformed. Animals rarely if ever rear such young—even the weakest in a litter, although not deformed, may be left to die. Similarly, the predominant human response throughout the ages has been one of rejection. In parts of Britain it was not unknown for a disabled baby to be buried alive with the mother (see *Child Life and Health*, edited by R. G. Mitchell, J. & A. Churchill, 1970).

Sociobiologists trace *the origin of all behaviour, animal and human, to the gene.* They admit that cultural differences exist between groups of humans but they see in human universals far more powerful similarities than differences, universals which, in the words of D. P. Barach, provide 'our strongest evidence for the legitimacy of human sociobiology'.

Specific aspects of the biological debate, particularly that related to intelligence, are discussed later in this book. There it will become clear that a wholly or even mainly biologically based explanation for human behaviour is not without its critics. Two groups of critics have been some behavioural psychologists, notably B. F. Skinner, and sociologists.

Skinner, as was outlined above, sees all behaviour as determined by patterns of reinforcement. Although in a 1981 paper entitled 'Selection by Consequences' he tacitly admits that evolutionary pressures can affect behaviour, his fundamental position is that 'a person is not an originating agent: he is a locus, a point at which many genetic and environmental conditions come together in a joint effect'. In other words, all that we do is a result of conditioning, we are not free agents.

Sociobiologists, and others, argue that Skinner is basically wrong. A fundamental flaw is that he rests his case solely on empirical evidence—that is, evidence based on observation and experiment. As **Roger Trigg** has pointed out in his book *The Shaping of Man* (Blackwell, 1982), 'the view that the whole of human nature lies open to scientific investigation ... can never itself be empirically proved'. What is more, discoveries *about man* are being made *by man* and while it may, just, be possible for man to treat other men as objects he cannot take this approach towards himself. If all scientists were as Skinner describes all men, they would all be constantly at the mercy of prior conditioning and would be dealing in the consequences of conditioning rather than possible truths. (I have drawn heavily on Trigg's work in writing this section.)

Sociologists, those who study societies rather than individuals, see man as shaped by society and not by anything else. An extreme statement of this position can be found in **Durkheim**: 'Every time that we find that a social phenomenon is directly explained by a psychological phenomenon we may be sure that the explanation is false.' A man, to such sociologists, is only a man to the extent that he is civilised. While allowing that biology places limits on behaviour—neither elephants nor man can fly—sociologists see man reproducing not as biological but as social beings and they point to the enormous diversity of human cultures as support for their view. As one biologist has noted, only about 100 generations have passed since the Roman Republic. This time span is too short to have allowed very much genetic variation, yet human societies have changed to an extraordinary extent.

The sociobiological response to sociologists is one of flat contradiction. What is extraordinary, they assert, is that human societies are so similar, as the quote from Barach on universals bears out.

Roger Trigg, although seeing much to support in a sociobiological view, writes from the standpoint of a philosopher and sees a fundamental weakness in the biological explanation of all human behaviour. His point is that man, uniquely, has consciousness. This sets him aside from animals and so arguments about birds migrating are interesting but not wholly relevant for man. A consequence of consciousness is **religious thought** and **moral behaviour**, neither of which is satisfactorily explained, to Trigg at least, by invocations of selfish genes. He anticipates the assertion that religiously based self-sacrifice is really based on a form of selfishness with the point that loving others for one's own ends is not the Christian definition of love and does not lead to salvation. He could have added that other major religions make the same point.

Genes or Society?

So far this section has been written as though all those concerned think only in black and white terms. Unfortunately, the argument about the place of genetics so easily becomes political that polarisation seems inevitable. In fact, as so often happens, extreme positions soften. This process has occurred among sociobiologists. **Edward Wilson**, in a book published with **Charles Lumsden**, *Genes, Mind and Culture* (Harvard University Press, 1981), admits that sociobiology 'has not taken into proper account either the human mind or the diversity of cultures'.

One compromise is to see *genes setting the stage and society writing the play*. In other words, biology sets limits but environmental factors determine how a person will develop within those limits. This is an attractive compromise but it merely avoids the real issue. The real question admits both biology and environment but asks: which is *more* important?

Questions

1. Piaget was a biologist, not a psychologist. Consider ways in which his biological training affected his work.
2. Psychoanalytic theory cannot be tested, therefore it is worthless. Is this a reasonable statement?
3. Give three examples of the selfish gene.
4. What is meant by the incest taboo? How can it be explained in terms of the history of the human race?

Exercises

1. Observe any interaction between two or more people and predict what behaviour is likely to be repeated as a result of positive reinforcement. Specify the reinforcers.

2. Devise a questionnaire on any aspect of child rearing and ask three groups of people to reply to it. Choose groups likely to be different, e.g. by age or social class. Draw conclusions on the theoretical views of each group.

3
Influences on Development

Introduction

It is very easy to fall into the trap of citing a single cause for a complex situation. People who argue that children's problems are 'all the parents' fault' or that 'bad blood' explains all delinquency are grossly oversimplifying. In this chapter some examples of different types of influence are given, mainly to illustrate this crucial point.

The chapter is not meant to cover all possible influences; indeed, it could be seen that the whole book is devoted more or less to this topic of explaining why children do certain things at certain times. Included here are those topics which do not have a chapter to themselves but which are, nevertheless, of sufficient importance to be noted at some length.

Temperament

Temperament is generally taken to refer to the child's **persistent prevailing mood**, that which determines the characteristic adjustment to life. Everyday words used within this context are cheerful, apprehensive, miserable and the like. **C. I. Sandstrom** sees the word as describing the 'characteristic pattern of the development of energy'.

The seventeenth-century student cited **four humours** to explain differences in temperament: blood, phlegm, choler and melancholy, four 'liquid or fluent parts of the body' according to Robert Burton. The word humour remains in our vocabulary, in the same context but with a very different meaning. It can be seen that two characteristic approaches of the seventeenth century were (1) a desire to classify and (2) an assumption that the origin of temperament can be found in constitutional factors. These two characteristics can still be found in the work of twentieth-century writers.

The present approach to temperament addresses itself to **behavioural style**. Most of the work has been done in America, although corroborative studies have been carried out in Norway and Britain. An early example of a study was that of **Wagner Bridger** who observed hundreds of babies and found that they showed widely differing responses to stimuli. One would flinch at a loud noise, another would respond to the same sound in quite a different way. Science was confirming what parents have always known: babies are different one from another. What is more, Bridger noted that there was a certain consistency within babies in their pattern of response; perhaps science was showing something else that parents have always known: babies are 'born that way'.

The largest body of work in this area is that of **Alexander Thomas** and **Stella Chess**, both American, who have been studying the development of temperament since 1956. One of their best-known pieces of work is their longitudinal study of 136 babies who were followed from infancy to early adolescence. Thomas and Chess assert that three basic temperamental patterns are established within the first three or four months. They are:

1. **Easy babies** respond positively to new situations, adapt easily to new food, have regular patterns of sleeping and eating and take readily to school.

2. **Difficult babies** have irregular habits, protest when confronted with anything new and have tantrums when frustrated. On the other hand, they are not all bad, since once they have adapted to something new they can be quite agreeable.

3. **Slow to warm up babies** withdraw at first and then adapt slowly. When given something new to eat they are liable not to spit it out but to let it dribble slowly from their mouth. When first at school they will stay on the sidelines for the initial week or so.

Of their 136 babies, two thirds were clearly in one or other category, the rest showing mixed patterns. Of the two thirds who could be put into one group, 40 per cent were easy, 10 per cent difficult and 15 per cent slow to warm up. Similar patterns have been found in children from quite different backgrounds, subjected to culturally determined different handling, one example being working-class children from Puerto Rico who were also studied by Thomas and Chess.

Nine characteristics were found to delineate one type from another:

1. Level of anxiety
2. Rhythmicity or regularity of biological functions (feeding, sleeping and eliminating)
3. Approach or withdrawal
4. Adaptability
5. Intensity of reaction
6. Threshold of responsiveness, i.e. the level of stimulation needed to evoke a response
7. Quality of mood
8. Distractability
9. Attention span and persistence

The Origins of Temperament

Evidence for a **genetic component** in the origin of temperamental differences comes from studies of twins. Working in Norway, **Anna Marie Torgersen** found greater similarities between identical than non-identical twins on all nine traits noted above. (It is unlikely that all the parents were aware in this study whether the twins were identical or not.) British work has confirmed this, although it was found that the similarities became less marked after the first 12 months of life. Negative support for the genetic theory is found in the conclusions of Thomas and Chess that they could detect no general differences between the parents of their groups of babies.

Thomas and Chess studied babies from mainly middle-class families; one investigation of working-class children came up with the conclusion that there is some evidence that mothers who are rated as anxious before the birth of the baby are more likely to have difficult children.

Studies carried out after a baby has been born are beset with the ever-present methodological problem of teasing out the direction of influence. As had been mentioned above (page 3), there is often an interaction between infants and their caretakers and if we find a difficult child and an anxious mother it is possible either that the mother has made the child difficult or the other way round—or both.

Given the paucity of evidence in this field it is difficult to come to more than a tentative conclusion. The drift of the evidence currently available suggests that temperamental characteristics *are* constitutional in origin, but that their expression can be modified according to the child's experience. Perhaps the most important point in this context is one made by **Julius Segal** and **Herbert Yahraes** when they assert that we should not be so influenced by accounts of environment shaping individuals that we are deluded into thinking that any change can be induced in any child. As they conclude: '... the fact is that the child's future has been determined in part before he or she has been brought from the womb.'

The Consistency of Temperament

Temperamental traits have been found to be reasonably stable over time. This, however, contributes little to the debate on origins, since it is more than likely that the environmental influences that have shaped a child will remain in operation for most of the formative period. At the least it does not contradict the genetic hypothesis.

Temperament and Behaviour

Since most of the work that has been done on tracing the relationship between temperament and behaviour has focused on behaviour problems this topic is discussed in Chapter 25.

Sex Differences

It would take a foolhardy person to assert that there are no observable differences between boys' and girls' behavioural characteristics. In some circles it would take a brave person to argue also that these differences are due entirely to genetic factors for many feminists are categorical in their ascribing much sex-related variation to the way people are treated rather than the way they are born. People are undoubtedly treated differently according to their sex, yet there are observably different characteristics in *all* mammals, not just in humans.

Observable Differences

These are relatively uncontroversial: clear differences exist between males and females soon after conception. They can be grouped as follows:

Vulnerability

On average, 120 males are conceived for every 100 females but the ratio of live births is only 106 : 100. Throughout life males are more vulnerable to a variety of disorders, including cerebral palsy, ulcers, mental retardation and some reading difficulties. The sex-linked recessive disorders like colour-blindness affect males more (see Chapter 4) and women outlive men.

Developmental Milestones and Early Physical Characteristics

Boys are heavier and longer than females at birth and develop larger hearts and lungs. The male hormone facilitates protein synthesis, the female hormones have no such action directly. The male, then, seems better equippped for an active, strenuous life.

Boys are, however, developmentally retarded on a number of counts: they walk later, they talk later, some dentition is later. Puberty is, on average, some 2½ years later.

Behavioural Differences

In infancy there have been reports of differences in **motor activity** and **sensory capacities**. Boys have been noted to exhibit more spontaneous motor activity, particularly of the gross motor type, while girls exhibit more finer movements, particularly of the facial area.

The **visual acuity** of males is superior to that of females from adolescence and there is some evidence that females have better **auditory discrimination**. Several studies have suggested that these differences are present in infants; for example **T. S. Watson** found that boys responded better to a visual reinforcer and girls to an auditory one when the subjects were as young as 14 weeks. Moreover, there have also been reports that these visual/auditory comparisons can validly be made in monkeys as well as humans, and that in the latter at any rate the differences persist into adulthood.

But the most often noted behavioural difference is related to **aggression**: the males of most mammalian species display more overt aggression than females. What is more, boys not only show aggression, they elicit more, and they retaliate more. Studies of aggression in children usually depend on observations of arguments over toys but the same pattern has been noted in older children as well as adults. One often quoted study of adults involved their giving what they thought were electric shocks to volunteer subjects in a learning experiment. As the giving of a shock could be seen as an example of behaviour which is compliant to an authority figure it might be assumed that females would be more prepared than males to give larger shocks; in fact the reverse was the case.

The other side of the aggression coin is the tendency of girls to show more **nurturant behaviour**, especially to younger children; boys have frequently been reported as indifferent to the manifest suffering of others.

Play has also been noted as having different qualities according to the sex of the child, boys being more creative and exploratory. Such observations raise questions about possible differences in thinking.

Thinking

Along with aggression, differences in the nature of the sexes' cognitive powers and characteristics have been the centre of much study, much speculation and much heat, especially in the last five or ten years. **David Wechsler**, the originator of the most widely used intelligence tests in the world, concluded: 'Our findings do confirm what poets and novelists have often asserted, and the average layman long believed, that men not only behave but *think* differently from women.'

The way in which males and females are said to differ are as follows:

Boys are said to be more **creative thinkers** than girls. **Corinne Hutt**, reviewing the evidence on this point, notes that it is equivocal—the most that can be said is that no study has shown girls to be more original. Boys are widely reported as being better at **maths** but this is not a simple picture. The difference does not begin to show itself until the age of about 11; before that the two sexes are about equal. Yet twice as many boys as girls take advanced level maths examinations. Maths has been associated with spatial ability, the kind of ability that enables people to do jigsaws and puzzles with bricks. People who are good at maths are also often good at chess. From this it can be argued that boys' superior mathematical attainment is related to spatial skills: there is evidence that males are better at tests using spatial items and also evidence that relatively few girls play chess.

Girls acquire **language** earlier than boys, and read more easily but their verbal reasoning has been reported as less good.

The measured IQ of girls is more stable than boys; that is, if a group of children are given a test and then given another several years later the correlation between the girls' scores is likely to be higher than that for the boys.

Differences in Variation

This pattern could be predicted from the points made above: with many normally distributed characteristics boys show greater variation than girls; that is, they appear more at both the top and the bottom ends of the distribution. An example is intelligence. The average IQ of the sexes is the same, but there are more subnormal and more very high scoring boys than girls.

A Warning against Exaggeration

The above may read like a handbook for the male chauvinist. Before beginning a discussion on the causes of the observed differences two general points should be borne in mind. The first is that the studies noted already deal with averages; there is no suggestion that all boys are more creative, or more aggressive, or better at chess than all girls. The second is that there are degrees of relativity as a function of societal factors. Thus Scottish men appear to be more sexually aggressive than Scottish women but Scottish women are likely in turn to be sexually more aggressive than Japanese women.

Why do Differences Exist?

Powerful support for the view that biological factors underlie observable differences in behaviour and thinking is found in the evidence on mammals other than humans. **Harry Harlow**, for example, watched monkeys and found that males spent proportionately more time in rough and tumble play, while the female counterpart was grooming. There are plausible explanations for this approach when one considers hormonal activity. Not only is behaviour affected by circulating hormones, the hormones themselves have a formative and organisational influence on brain function and structure.

An intriguing and fortunately rare opportunity to study both biological and environmental factors comes with the 'natural experiment' that occurs in **inter-sex children**—that is, those who are born of ambiguous sex. Several have been studied in the Dominican Republic. Some, brought up as girls, subsequently become male. Relevant to the present debate is the finding that from the age of five or six, before any physical changes had taken place, these children seemed to think like boys. The implication from this is the brain is 'wired' from birth in a certain way.

But biological factors are only part of the story. There is a mass of evidence to suggest that there are consistent differences in the way boys and girls are spoken to, played with and shaped in any number of ways from the earliest moment throughout their lives. Mothers in Western cultures play with their infants according to the baby's sex: boys receive more rough-and-tumble play, girls have more face-to-face talking. Girls are warned more readily than boys of physical dangers, and children are given toys which fit the sex-based stereotype of the culture. In one study tape-recordings were played to mothers, some of whom thought that the four-year-old they heard was a boy, others a girl. When asked to make statements about how they would respond to that child they replied differently according to the perceived sex.

A striking piece of evidence supporting environmental determinants comes from observations carried out in Kenya by **C. R. Ember**. Boys who had been given work perceived as feminine in the home were more feminine outside the home—that is, they were less dominant, more nurturing.

The **environmentalist** answer to the questions raised by differences in maths and chess, and to the fact that there have been few if any great women painters or composers, is found in the realm of expectations. Girls, they assert, learn that they are not expected to excel in such activities and so they feel more comfortable not doing so. In the case of maths this results in a vicious circle, for women maths teachers are less good because of society's expectations of girls generally.

An interesting test of this hypothesis was carried out in America in 1968 when students were asked to write essays concerned with success following medical training. The women students tended far more than the men to tell stories in which the successful woman was afraid of social rejection because she was deviating from the expected role for women. **Sheila Tobias**, in her book *Overcoming Math Anxiety* (W. W. Norton, 1978), is forthright: 'You're not dumb; you've just been intimidated by poor schooling, murky texts and mythologies about mathematical minds.'

Biology and Environment: a Possible Synthesis

Eleanor Maccoby and **Nancy Jacklin** concluded a survey of the literature on psychological sex differences by considering the view that whenever there are biological differences society tends to socialise individuals so as to emphasise the differences. In other words, we behave differently to boys and girls because they are different: it is the biologically based difference which comes first. Maccoby and Jacklin maintain that in some cultures this may be a wise course but it is not the only one. As they point out, in Western society leadership is being exercised through persuasion, inspiration and task competence rather than sex-stereotyped brute force. If it so wishes, society can train its boys to be nurturant, its girls to be aggressive. In their words: 'A variety of social practices are viable within the framework set by biology, and human beings, being less driven by predetermined behaviour patterns than lower animals, are in a position to select those socialisation processes that foster the life style they most value.'

Early Experience and the Notion of the Critical Period

Early Experience

The idea that experience gained as a young child is all-important in determining adult behaviour has a long history. Plato (428–348) wrote: 'And the first step, as you know, is always what matters most, particularly when we are dealing with those who are young and tender.' In 1975 the British psychiatrist **Anthony Storr** wrote: 'But, if we want our children to grow up happy, there is little doubt that the experience of the first few months and years of life is crucial.'

Support for the Early Learning Hypothesis

Powerful support for the idea has come from several quarters. **Freud**, for example, asserted that adult behaviour is determined by structures created in childhood: the way a child is managed at three can lead to neuroses at 23. The work of **John Bowlby** on attachment is still most influential in determining certain attitudes—for example, those to do with parental visiting in hospitals. Bowlby's thesis was that children under the age of about six need to maintain a warm, continuous and mutually satisfying relationship with their mother. If this is not done, later mental health is jeopardised. (See Chapter 15 for further discussion of attachment.)

    Piaget, too, with his insistence on one stage building on another, lent weight to the idea, as did the psychologist **Donald Hebb**, who although not a well-known figure outside somewhat limited academic circles, has exerted an enormous influence on psychological thought since the Second World

War. Hebb's view was that early learning is fundamental, providing a framework on which all else is built.

Questions on the Importance of Early Experience

Work carried out in the past thirty years has produced fundamental questions about the whole idea of the early experience hypothesis. The essence of the argument against is that early experience may be of crucial importance at the time but its effects are reversible. Two leading authors contributing to the debate are **Ann** and **A. D. B. Clarke**. In their book *Early Experience: Myth and Evidence* (Open Books, 1976) they maintain that:

1. Any experience which has more than a transitory effect must involve learning.
2. Learning theory asserts that any effect that lasts must be reinforced, otherwise it will fade. An everyday example is the child who learns that her mother gets cross if she dirties her clothes while playing. If the mother stops reprimanding the girl for dirty clothes the original learning will fade (see Chapter 2).

So, the Clarkes argue, if we are to test the theory of the crucial and irreversible nature of early experience we should see *what happens when reinforcements change*. They point out that most people do *not* have major changes in much of their lives; it is rare for a rich New York child to move to a Bombay slum.

A dramatic test of the Clarke view is found in the story of 'Isabelle' who was discovered in 1938 aged six, having spent most of her life shut up in a darkened room with her deaf-mute mother. She behaved towards men like a wild animal and her only utterances were 'a strange croaking sound'. Many of her actions were those of a deaf child and she appeared to be, developmentally, at no more than a six-month level in many ways. Her subsequent history was a lot happier than her first six years. She was well cared for and given careful and intensive teaching. Within two years she had attained a normal level of development in language and academic skills. By the time she was 14 she was described as 'seeming to be a bright, cheerful, energetic little girl'.

Michael Rutter added to the debate in his consideration of the evidence put forward by John Bowlby in his book *Maternal Deprivation Reassessed* (Penguin, 1972). He pointed out that one should consider the *nature* of the separation experience, not just the *fact* of separation. Often the whole experience is suffused with suffering: for example, if a baby is separated from the mother because she has to go to hospital there is likely to be distress expressed by the father and by other members of the family, the normal routine of the family will be upset and so on. Bowlby himself had noted, in 1956, that 'some of the workers who first drew attention to the dangers of maternal deprivation ... have tended on occasion to overstate their case'.

The Critical Period

Closely related to the idea of the importance of early experience is the concept of the critical period. The original formulation came from biology: certain organisms are seen to be particularly sensitive to outside stimuli at certain times. Some writers prefer to use the term **sensitive periods**, since this implies less rigidity of boundaries than the original.

Evidence on Critical Periods

Evidence in this field has come largely from animal experiments. Strictly speaking one should identify several types of critical, or sensitive, period:

1. **Foetal development.** The crucial nature of the critical period here is illustrated by the thalidomide tragedy. Pregnant women taking this drug were likely to produce a defective child and studies have been able to pinpoint just when the foetus was vulnerable, as Table 1 demonstrates. The general rule is that systems are most vulnerable when they are developing at their quickest rate.

Table 1. Foetal vulnerability to the effects of thalidomide.

Days after last period when thalidomide was taken	Organ in which malfunction appeared
34–38	Thumb, cranial nerves, external ear
39–44	Upper limbs
40–45	Heart, gall bladder, duodenum
42–45	Lower limbs
44–48	Femur or tibia (bones of thigh or calf)
50	Rectum

From W. Lenz (1964), *Proceedings of the Second International Conference on Congenital Malformations*, International Medical Congress Ltd.

2. **Brain development.** The process of brain development is enormously complex and far from fully understood. From what is known it seems that there are different peaks of critical development for different processes. The peak for the production of neurones comes first, myelination coming later. (See Chapter 7 for an explanation of these terms.) So interference with brain development will have differential effects depending on when it occurs.

3. **The establishment of social relationships.** This is not far from the work of Bowlby but in this context is much more precise and limited. The evidence often put forward is the phenomenon of imprinting, a pioneer in this work being **Konrad Lorenz**, who has worked notably with birds. Normally ducklings will follow their mother soon after hatching; Lorenz isolated greylag goslings from their mother and found that as soon as they were ready to follow anything they followed him. When subsequently given the opportunity to follow their mother, they continued to waddle after him. They had imprinted onto a human. The critical period for imprinting goslings seems to be the first day or two.

4. **Infantile stimulation.** An example comes from experimental work with rats. It had been noted that handling them before they are weaned had a much greater effect than later handling.

5. **Learning.** Another example from birds is the observation that a chaffinch isolated for the first 12 months after hatching will produce only an incomplete song. There appears to be a critical period for the learning of bird song which might be seen as similar to the phenomenon of language learning in the human. A child put in an environment where a foreign language is spoken will learn, usually, not only quickly but with a perfect accent. Once the age of 13 or 14 or so has passed, the accent will never be perfect.

Conclusion on the critical period. The evidence for this notion seems considerably stronger than that for the crucial importance of early learning in general. It is important that the two are not confused.

The Family

The family in the context of this chapter will be taken to mean, generally, the **nuclear family** of child or children and two parents, since this is the norm in Western society and has been for hundreds of years. There is a powerful myth that the nuclear family is a by-product of the Industrial Revolution, that before that grandparents and aunts and uncles all tended to be together in **extended families** similar to those widely found in India and Africa today. While there is no doubt that extended families did exist, and still do, there is equally no doubt that the nuclear family was the most common form as far back as the sixteenth century in England at least. (See Peter Laslett's *The World We have Lost*, published by Methuen (1971) for a full discussion of this point: he notes that English household size was constant at 4.75 at all times from the late sixteenth to the early twentieth centuries.)

It can, of course, be argued that the increase in the divorce rate and in the number of unmarried mothers in the last ten years or so has meant that in some parts of Western society one should no longer see the conventional nuclear family as the norm. Divorce rates have undoubtedly risen (see Table 2).

Table 2. Divorce in England and Wales, 1940 to 1980.

Year	Decrees made absolute
1940	7,555
1950	30,870
1960	23,868
1970	58,239
1980	148,301
1982*	146,700

From the Registrar General's *Statistical Review*.*: estimated figure

If the present rate continues one in five children in England and Wales will experience the divorce of their parents before they reach 16 years of age.

But to go from such figures to dismissing the nuclear family as a powerful influence today is to miss the point of much of this chapter. One cannot argue in a simple, one-to-one relationship fashion. The nuclear family remains the model that society appears to expect, it is the one extolled in popular fiction and in children's literature. Try, as an exercise in estimating the place of both parents in current opinion, analysing one week's television commercials. Count the number of families portrayed and see what proportion include both rather than one parent.

Cause and Effect: the Family and the Child

A very common diagnosis of deviant behaviour in children is to ascribe all blame to the family: 'It's all the parents' fault.' Closer analysis of family factors shows that this is rarely totally the case. **Robert Hinde**, in a chapter in Michael Rutter's *Scientific Foundations of Developmental Psychiatry* (Heinemann, 1980), from which I have drawn heavily, summarises some of the reasons for the complexity in relations between families and the outcome measured by children's behaviour.

1. Children differ at birth as a result of **genetic and prenatal factors** and are, therefore, **differentially susceptible** to environmental influences. (See above for a further discussion of temperamental differences between children.)

2. Children are born into different **environments**. Even those who have more or less similar traumas around the time of birth may experience different outcomes; the effects of some traumas are dissipated in high socioeconomic families and amplified in poor environments.

3. Any single bit of behaviour is likely to be dependent on **multiple influences** which may interact in complex ways. It is likely that behaviour is governed more by a **pattern of events** rather than one; for example, the loss of a parent in early childhood may have an effect only if associated with low social status.

4. Many of the most important influences depend on **relationships within families**. But such relationships are not all one way, the child can influence the parent as well as the other way round.

5. All individuals, relationships and families **change over time** and people are more susceptible to influence at certain times in their lives than at others.

6. All individuals and all families are influenced by **factors outside the family**.

7. An outcome may not appear until **well after the event**; for example, the death of a parent may have its effect several years later.

Family Separations

An extreme theory of separation is that which gained ground following the work of **Marshall Klaus** and **J. H. Kennell** in the mid-1970s. They observed a number of baby–mother pairs who maintained close, i.e. skin, contact during the first few hours of the baby's life and compared them with couples where the baby was separated from the mother for a few hours. They argued that the close, continuous relationship even at this age affected subsequent mother–child relationships for at least two years. This finding caused a stir in academic circles and subsequent attempts to replicate the finding have not all been successful; it is possible that the Klaus and Kennell finding can be explained by maternal expectations being changed as a result of paediatric intervention. However, the work opened up a whole new field and revived an old one in that attention was once more focused on the value of early, continuous relationships between the mother and the neonate. (See also Chapter 15 for a fuller discussion of this topic.)

The names most commonly associated with studies of the effects of separations lasting a few weeks or even a few days in some cases are **John Bowlby** and the **Robertsons**. Bowlby, best known in this context for his work on attachment, put forward the theory and James and Joyce Robertson produced evidence in their observations of children in hospital. There is a general agreement that short-term separation of children aged roughly 6 months to four years can have adverse short-term affects. However, if one is considering the influence of separation on child development rather than the immediate well-being of the child evidence is relatively sparse.

A powerful study was published in Britain in 1975 by **James Douglas**. He followed up a group of children who had been separated from their families by hospitalisation some twenty years or so before and found that either prolonged or repeated hospital admissions were associated with later behaviour disturbance in many although not all children for several years to come. It must be noted that these children were in hospital in the late 1940s and early 1950s when visiting was still restricted. Subsequent consideration of this finding by **Michael Rutter** and **David Quinton** confirmed Douglas's conclusion, although the point was made that separation of this kind does not *necessarily* lead to disturbance. Indeed, disturbance is more likely to occur when the separation experience takes place against a background of family discord (see point 3 above).

Another cause of separation is the need to send a child to some form of day-care because the mother is working. Here the evidence is equivocal: there is some to show that underprivileged children going to good day-care facilities are likely to benefit from the experience. On the other hand, not all day-care provision is good and adverse effects have been found. Yet a further complicating factor is the finding that mothers who stay at home with young babies are more likely to be depressed than those who go out to work, so perhaps one must balance this point in the equation if one is considering whether or not being separated for a period of each day is likely to have long-term adverse effects.

Parental Disharmony

The most commonly reported association between parental disharmony and subsequent behaviour is that delinquency appears to be an outcome, particularly in boys. Even if one looks at families which do not contain a child formally labelled delinquent there remains an association between marital disharmony and lower 'socialisation' scores, as was found in a study of American adolescents by **E. I. Mergargee** and colleagues in 1971. As usual when one is faced with associations, one must question the direction of the effect; perhaps the presence of an antisocial child caused the disharmony rather that the other way round? Epidemiological evidence from studies in the Isle of Wight and London suggest that the disharmony comes first.

Girls are less susceptible to this form of stress, it seems, although it is always possible that they manifest their disturbance in ways other than the delinquent. The age of the child is another variable to be kept in mind when trying to make predictions about the effect of disharmony. **Judith Wallerstein** found that young children were bewildered following parental separation and showed signs of regression. As the children got older they 'underwent early superego development' (see Chapter 2 for an explanation of this term) and the oldest group of children seemed relatively unaffected.

Divorce

Parental disharmony and divorce are sometimes discussed as though the latter was always preceded by the former. While this is so in many cases, it should not always be assumed that parents who divorce must have gone through a period of severe disharmony, nor that all children of divorced parents are psychologically harmed by the event. It is conceivable that, as with hospitalisation effects, one should look for an interaction between divorce and the atmosphere in the home before the formal separation. What is more, one should look also at the atmosphere immediately after the separation. The assumption that divorce brings an end to all conflict is mistaken: both parents tend to be inconsistent. Mothers tend to be depressed, self-involved and erratic. Fathers begin by being indulgent but become restrictive. The immediate post-divorce relationships within a family play a major role in determining the effects of the separation on children.

One should also note the finding of Wallerstein's study carried out in California in the late 1970s and early 1980s. One might imagine that divorce is so common in that State that children would come to expect it as normal behaviour, yet Wallerstein noted that even there 90 per cent of the children she interviewed showed acute distress and a wish that parents would reunite. This wish was observable immediately after the break-up. Five years later there was evidence that children could recover, psychologically, providing the post-divorce family they found themselves in was able to sustain them. Ten years later, as they entered adulthood, they were very concerned lest they, too, repeat the pattern and made unhappy marriages themselves.

Fostering and Adoption

The number of adoptions granted annually in Great Britain rose from about 3000 in 1927 (the year after a legal adoption as we know it was made possible in England and Wales) to a peak of nearly 27,000 in 1968. Since then there has been a sharp decline.

There is no hard evidence to answer the general question: how do adoptions turn out? The British Agencies for Adoption and Fostering report that more than three quarters of adoption placements turn out 'very well' and the National Children's Bureau report *Growing up Adopted* (1972) showed that at the age of seven adopted children were doing well in the community, and were certainly faring better than many children in single-parent families.

A more complex picture is presented in long-term studies of the effects of adoption carried out by **Barbara Tizard** and colleagues in London in the 1970s. They compared a group of children living in nursery care with working-class controls and found that *at two years* there were no differences in non-verbal IQ although the nursery group were behind in language development. Those who stayed in the nursery for *two more years* were no different from the controls in IQ or behaviour disturbance but they showed many of the signs of the institutionalised child, e.g. they were more demanding and formed more shallow relationships. Those adopted by *middle-class families before four* showed increased IQ but they, like those who remained in the nursery, gave evidence of a tendency to abnormal overt friendliness to strangers. Children left in the institution *after the age of four*, and those restored to their natural mothers, showed a decrease in IQ over the next four years, while *those adopted before four* had, generally, IQs above the average score. But although this presents an encouraging picture for the possible ameliorating effects of family life, there were continuing problems of a social nature, with the previously institutionalised children showing some of the same demanding, shallow relationship pattern that was noted above.

Other studies on the effects of adoption on intelligence are discussed by **Ann** and **A. D. B. Clarke** in *Early Experience: Myth and Evidence*. In particular they discuss the finding from adoptions in the Lebanon that two years seems a critical period; children adopted after two did not catch up in IQ. Clarke and Clarke argue that there are several possible explanations for this finding, one of which is a selective preference of adopters so that in comparing the children adopted before two with those adopted later one is not comparing like with like.

The Influence of the Family on Intellectual Development

A crude generalisation is that the **first-born child** is likely to be more intelligent and materially more successful than siblings, with IQs diminishing with larger families. There are, of course, exceptions to this generalisation and it would be unwise to assume that all first-borns are cleverer and more driving than all subsequent children.

There have been many explanations put forward for the relative success of the first-born. Biologically one might say that the mother is, by definition, younger when she has the first-born and perhaps is physically more capable. Culturally one can point to the premium put on the first-born, especially in some circles if it is a boy. Parents are, perhaps, more anxious about the first-born and therefore pay far more attention to it. **Judy Dunn** and colleagues have studied the effects of the birth of a sibling and in papers published in 1980 and 1981 show that following the birth of a second child mothers are more punitive towards the first-born, playing with them less. It is possible that this change in maternal behaviour pushes the first child into seeking higher levels of achievement.

An ingenious mathematical formula has been devised following a study of about 800,000 participants in the US National Merit Scholarship Qualification Test. This study showed a decrease in IQ with birth order, the exceptions being twins and only children who scored lower than would be expected. The formula is that the intellectual growth of each child depends on the intellectual status of all other members, and one needs to arrive at an average of the total membership to make predictions. Thus a child born first to parents of average intellectual level will find himself in an environment where the 'family level' is average adult. However, the second child will be born to a family where the average of the other three, i.e. the father, mother and the first-born, is less than adult average, since the first-born child will not have reached adult status and will, therefore, bring the average down. This model makes two assumptions. The first is that a newborn has an intellectual level of zero, the second that the apparent anomaly of the only child not being as clever as the first of several is due to the only child's lack of being able to act as a teacher to younger sibs.

Some attempt has been made to tease out the different contributions to intellectual development made by either parent. Thus in one study it was noted that mothers of language-delayed children compared to mothers of normal children scored lower on measures of enjoyment of the child's company, active encouragement of development and pride in their achievements. We remain in doubt about the direction of causality following work of this kind, for a language-delayed child is far less rewarding than one of normal development. Several studies have shown that children with father and mother present do better than children with mothers alone. There remains some uncertainty about the interpretation of these data, however, since the pressures on a single mother are greater than on one with a supportive husband. Father absence due to separation is, according to one study, most deleterious in terms of subsequent IQ if it occurs during the first two years of the child's life. The death of a father seems to have its greatest effect if it takes place during the ages of six and nine.

The Family and the Development of Sex Roles

The development of sex roles, or **gender identity**, is often seen as a direct result of family influences, sometimes seen as largely biological in origin and sometimes as a combination of the two. Here only the first of these views will be put forward (see the section on Psychobiology in Chapter 2 for a discussion of the second).

Both mothers and fathers have been shown to treat babies differently as a function of their sex. Mothers are said to talk more to girls and to encourage independence in boys. Toys are consistently chosen to fit the stereotype: guns for boys and dolls for girls. It remains an open question whether or not the stereotype has grown up and been maintained not on environmental but on biological origins.

Father absence has been a fruitful area of study. Boys in particular seem more affected in terms of gender identity, with most studies showing boys with absent fathers veering towards femininity and female cognitive style. (See the section above on Sex differences for a discussion of the nature of sex-related cognitive styles.) The age of separation is an important complicating variable, and another is related to the perception within the family of the absent father. An example of this last point is the finding that daughters of divorcees behave differently from daughters of widows. The former tend towards promiscuity and early heterosexual behaviour while the latter are more likely to be inhibited and frigid.

Summarising evidence on sex role typing and socialisation, **J. Block** and others put forward four main points:

1. *Well socialised individuals with socially appropriate sex roles* tend to come from families where the parents have clearly differentiated roles themselves, are available to their children throughout their adolescence and where the same sex parent provides a powerful model.

2. *Well socialised individuals with inappropriate sex roles* have parents who present more complex, ambiguous models.

3. *Unsocialised individuals with appropriate sex roles* tend to have a neurotic, rejecting same-sex parent and a seductive opposite-sex parent.

4. *Sex inappropriate, unsocialised individuals* tend to come from families evidencing conflict and psychopathology.

School Influences

In 1979 **Michael Rutter** and three colleagues published a book entitled *Fifteen Thousand Hours* (Open Books), drawing attention to the length of time that the average child in the UK spends in school. For many years the influence that school attendance can have on the development of individual children was ignored or minimised. Surveys of the attainment of children seemed to suggest that the quality of education received in school had little effect on attainment. For example, *The Equality of Educational Opportunity Survey* (1966) in America examined the education offered to children from ethnic minorities and concluded that differences in attainment could be explained by **family and personal characteristics** more readily than by school differences.

In Britain the picture was confirmed by the **Plowden Report** published in 1967 on primary education. A national survey was carried out for the Committee and the conclusion was that *parental attitudes and home circumstances were by far the most powerful contributors* to variation in educational performance. (See Table 3 below.)

However, in 1972 came the results of a study which began to raise serious questions about such general conclusions. The study was carried out by **Michael Power** and colleagues looking at delinquency in a London borough over an 11-year period. This work suggested that *a few schools accounted for most of the delinquents*, care having been taken by the investigators to ensure that they were not confused by the possibility that some schools drew on 'bad' areas. What is more, there was a marked similarity in the pattern of school associations over the whole period.

The question of *adequate controls for intake* is one that has received attention in work that followed Power. A study of nine secondary schools in South Wales carried out by **D. Reynolds** and colleagues ascertained first that the pupils were comparable on a non-verbal intelligence test and came from similar social classes. Significantly different results in attainment were found, enabling the authors to entitle one of their publications, *Schools do make a difference*.

The book referred to above, by Rutter and others, came to similar conclusions on attainment, attendance rates and delinquency, with added data based on primary school records to show that children who were difficult

Table 3. Percentage contribution of parental attitudes, home circumstances and state of school to variation in educational performance.

		Between schools		
	Infants	*Lower juniors*	*Top juniors*	*All pupils*
Parental attitudes	24	20	39	28
Home circumstances	16	25	17	20
State of school	20	22	12	17
Unexplained	40	33	32	35
		Within schools		
	Infants	*Lower juniors*	*Top juniors*	*All pupils*
Parental attitudes	16	15	29	20
Home circumstances	9	9	7	9
State of school	14	15	22	17
Unexplained	61	61	42	54

Source: *Children and their Primary Schools: A Report of the Central Advisory Council for Education (England),* HMSO, 1967.

Note. The Report states in a footnote to this table that the size of the variation unexplained is due in part to the simplicity of the test used to measure educational performance (a reading comprehension test).

in their secondary schools were *not* necessarily the same as those who had been difficult in earlier years, and vice versa. In other words, there appeared to be a response to the ethos of the school.

Fifteen Thousand Hours has not been without its critics. In an article in *The Guardian*, 22 July 1980, Maureen O'Connor noted that its publication had sparked off an academic row of 'classic nastiness', with the authors being accused of statistical inexactitude, philosophical incoherence and even of cheating in their interpretation of the results. Rutter has replied to these points, standing by what is said in the book. Readers interested in following the debate should start with the 1980 volumes of the National Foundation for Educational Research journal *Educational Research*.

School-based Factors

If one accepts what might be called the post-1972 view that schools do matter, the next question reasonably to be asked is why? What is it about one school that differentiates it from another?

Several factors have produced either negative or conflicting results. The **financial support** given to a school as a whole seems to have little effect, although it is possible that subgroups within a school might quite seriously be influenced. Work on **school size** is difficult to generalise from since most large towns tend to have only large schools and it is virtually impossible to control for intake variables. **Class size** has been looked at and the suggestion is that children do better in larger classes. There is an obvious objection to the ready generalisation from such results: in most schools remedial classes are kept smaller deliberately, so there is an in-built distortion of figures. **Streaming** has received a good deal of attention. There is some indication that children in lower streams tend towards delinquency but little to show that streaming or non-streaming produces dramatic differences when attainment is taken as an outcome measure.

Fifteen Thousand Hours attempted to analyse the classroom ethos and teachers' behaviour to try to answer questions on what leads to success. The results, although not totally unexpected, bear repetition. In short, what produced better results academically was teaching which was well prepared and geared to achieving success. Children in the more successful schools were taught in more attractive classrooms, given more responsibility and encountered teachers who themselves worked in cooperation with one another.

Expectations

One of the most widely read studies of streaming, by **Joan Barker-Lunn**, produced an interesting commentary on **self image**. More boys of below average ability in streamed classes had good self image compared to a comparable group in non-streamed schools, presumably because the former could still expect to be top, or near the top, in their group.

Expectations can, of course, work two ways: the child can have expectations of himself and the teacher can have expectations of the child. It is possible that the former is crucially influenced by the latter, a point that has not gone unnoticed by researchers.

One of the few pieces of educational research to gain wide readership was concerned with just this topic. In 1968 **R. Rosenthal** and **J. Jacobson** published *Pygmalion in the Classroom* (Holt, Rinehart and Winston). This study looked at the effect of telling teachers that some children had been identified by psychological tests as 'late bloomers'. When the children's attainments were looked at later, it was found that these 'late bloomers' registered greater gains than their peers, although the names had actually been taken at random.

While the work raises many pertinent questions, it must be noted that there are a number of criticisms of the method used, with a degree of doubt about the validity of the tests used, the validity of the statistical analysis and the extent to which the teacher paid any attention to the original predictions. More seriously, attempts to repeat the experiment have led to a failure to obtain the same effect.

A much more subtle, thorough and more convincing study was carried out in British schools by **Roy Nash**, published as *Classrooms Observed* (Longman) in 1973. Nash followed a group of children from their primary to secondary schools and made detailed observations of the relationship between teacher attitudes towards individual children and the subsequent performance of these pupils. Not only did he look at attitudes, he also made an analysis of the behaviour both of the children and the teachers, linking both to the attitudes that he had elicited. He argued that teacher expectations are a *self-fulfilling prophecy*, having a more important bearing on pupils' attainment than the social class from which the child comes. He argues strongly against broad generalisations about teachers or children, seeing the interaction between the two as all important.

Conclusions. Evidence from work carried out in the years since 1972 strongly suggests that schools do influence children, not only in what they learn but also in how they think of themselves and how they behave. The school has emerged from the shadow of the family and must merit consideration in its own right as a serious determinant of behaviour.

Cultural and Community Factors

Included in this section are those factors which might properly be seen as the province of the sociologist or the anthropologist rather than the psychologist. In one country children spend large parts of their earliest years strapped to their mother's back, in another they are picked up only when they cry; within a country child-rearing patterns vary widely as a function of the social class of the parents; within a town there seem to be differences from one street to another in the rate of delinquency. All these phenomena have been observed but there remains great uncertainty on the precise relationship between such factors and developmental patterns, as one recent summary of the literature by David Quinton concluded: 'At present ... the evidence presents challenges rather than solutions and indicates the complexity of the problems which are yet to be tackled.'

Social Class Differences

In Great Britain social class is a term based on classification of occupation— in families the father's occupation is always used. The classification most commonly employed is that found in the Registrar General's list used for census purposes, with occupations falling into six broad categories (see Table 4).

These categories are not perfect. They are crude in being based on an arbitrary division; the emphasis on the father's occupation is seen by some as unrealistic and difficulties arise when one has to place a label on a family where the father is absent and the mother is an out-of-work teacher. If she is on social security she may be classified as class VI; two days later she may get a job and jump up to class II. Nevertheless, they have been widely used and have repeatedly been shown to discriminate children in a number of ways which suggests that they have some validity.

The most consistent findings have been related to measured intelligence and attainment. Thus the **National Child Development Study** (1972) reported that parental social class was the variable most strongly related to reading at the age of seven. Children's behaviour, incidentally, seems much less related to social class differences than IQ and attainment.

The generally accepted view is that these differences are based largely on variations between classes in two areas: **language** and expectations concerning **conformity**.

Table 4. Social class groupings.

Social class		Approximate expected percentage (*not counting the unemployed*)
I	Higher professional (usually requiring a university degree or equivalent, e.g. doctors, university teachers)	4
II	Other professional and technical (schoolteachers, some civil servants, middle managers in industry or commerce)	15
III (non-manual)	Other non-manual (foremen, shop assistants)	21
III (manual)	Skilled manual occupations (bricklayers, electricians)	34
IV	Semi-skilled manual (bus conductors)	19
V	Unskilled manual (labourers)	7
VI	Unemployed or no male head of the household	

Language differences have been most studied. **John and Elizabeth Newson** reported that working-class mothers of four-year-olds played with and talked to their children less often than did parents in non-manual occupations. **Basil Bernstein** has suggested that there is a crucial difference in language use which is relevant here: middle-class children hear an elaborated code; those from the working classes hear a code described as restricted. (See Chapter 13 for a fuller discussion of this point plus definitions of the terms.)

Differences in values and attitudes have been less often studied but could be equally powerful. An argument is that middle-class parents come from a milieu where they expect that they can affect their environment, whereas working-class families feel themselves in the grip of 'them'. This difference is communicated to children with conformity being highly valued in the lower social groups.

Area Differences

Large and consistent differences between areas have been shown in a number of studies—for example, those examining delinquency and disturbance among children. The pattern is that of a downward trend, from the highest rates in inner city areas, through smaller towns to country areas. However, there are obvious variations between families in rural parts of the country and the more depressed inner parts of an industrial town and it is likely that one is picking up the effects of family factors rather than geographical location per se.

Poverty and Malnutrition

Looking at the world child population the most critical adverse influence on child development is **malnutrition**. A study carried out in Uganda in 1976 found that about 50 per cent of children in three districts showed signs of protein imbalance, growth retardation or both. Extrapolating to all developing countries, it was estimated that up to **300,000,000** people alive today have suffered some form of malnutrition in early life.

Poor food intake is not confined to developing countries although it is closely associated with **poverty**. In America, for example, many Navajo children living in Arizona suffer from the effects of poor food along with poor housing, poor sanitation, poor educational levels and unemployment.

The most striking effects of severe malnutrition are visible changes of emaciation or bloating of tissue as a result of water retention. The most serious effect is retardation of growth, especially possible *permanent* stunting of the brain. What is more, malnourished children are less responsive to their environment, more likely to be apathetic and irritable.

Some hope of the possibility of partially reversing the effects of malnutrition comes from a study carried out in 1975 on nearly 150 Korean girls who were adopted by American families by the age of two. About one third had been severely malnourished and one third marginally nourished. On adoption the girls' average height and weight were well below normal but by seven years of age they had all caught up with Korean averages. Their IQs were:

Severely malnourished group	102
Marginally nourished group	106
Well nourished group	112

From this one can conclude that although some of the effects on intelligence of poor food intake remain there can be some catching up, and one can expect that height and weight will respond fully.

The Korean girls were adopted into middle-class American families. Even if wholesale adoption were thought advisable it simply will not happen and millions of children are caught in a vicious circle, the so called **cycle of deprivation**. Mothers in poor cultures tend themselves to be less well fed, less well grown and less well cared for when they are pregnant. They use antenatal services less than they might and they have more children more frequently than their better off counterparts. Children of such families have lower birth weights, die more frequently in infancy and if they do survive have more illness.

In developed countries there is less severe poverty, less severe malnutrition, but the cycle of deprivation is evident nevertheless.

Cross-Cultural Studies

The wide and easily observed variation in child-rearing practices and family patterns from one culture to another provides a tempting natural experiment for anyone wishing to examine the effect of early experience on subsequent development.

Unfortunately, problems arise in interpreting the data available. In the first place most studies look only at two variables. They might look at child-rearing patterns and subsequent voting behaviour, for example, without considering possibly influential third variables which might be affecting both those under study. (See Chapter 27 for a fuller consideration of the problem of the confounding variable.)

In the second place it is far from easy to disentangle relatively stable personality characteristics in individuals from the effects of child rearing practices, so there is an inherent difficulty in tracing the influence of the latter on subsequent adult behaviour. **Margaret Mead** and colleagues warned against such cross-cultural assumptions in the 1920s and 1930s, arguing that both child-rearing habits and adult personality patterns are reflections of general cultural themes. These themes, asserted Mead, are communicated to children through all sorts of media, including art and drama, and it is going beyond the evidence to draw a simple line from child-rearing to adult behavioural outcomes. (While this statement by Mead is still acceptable much of her work has recently been questioned by another anthropologist, **Derek Freeman**, in his book *Margaret Mead and Samoa: The Making and Unmaking of an Anthropological Myth*, Harvard University Press, 1983.)

Despite these criticisms, there are some lessons to be learned from cross-cultural work. For example, parents operating within a culture which depends on agriculture and herding for its livelihood seem to rear more conforming, socially responsible children compared to those who live in a society where hunting is the main occupation. One large-scale comparison considered theft and crimes against the person in 48 different societies. The authors, **M. K. Bacon** and colleagues, concluded that theft was significantly more common in societies which were low in indulgence towards the children and person-related crime and more common in those communities which were characterised by using abrupt and punitive methods of socialisation of the young. Against this, one can place another study which argued that there is no relationship between the amount that a child is punished and subsequent adult aggression.

Two Worlds of Childhood: the USA and USSR

This is the title of a book by **Urie Bronfenbrenner** published in 1970 by Simon and Schuster. Bronfenbrenner set out to examine two nations in terms of 'what each country does for and with its children both intentionally and unintentionally.... We shall ask what are ... the consequences of the modes of treatment that we observe.' An American citizen, he visited the USSR seven times between 1960 and 1967 and came up with the conclusion that one of the main differences evident to him was that the Russian child was brought up firmly within a family framework, with parents who followed a tradition of seeing it as their primary duty to foster the child's development.

In contrast to this he found that the typical American child was exposed to a largely accidental process of development in which peers rather than parents played a major role. In an aside he writes that of the six countries in which he and his colleagues were working only one, England, exceeded the USA in 'the willingness of children to indulge in anti-social behaviour'. And only England had lower levels of parental involvement with children.

Although Bronfenbrenner's work refers to a previous generation of parents the theme and the message are still alive.

Migration

Migration can carry with it any one of several effects on children, depending on the nature and extent of the changes that are experienced. Among the possibilities are:

1. A move involving a change of language but with other cultural factors remaining similar. This is conceivable, for example, for Indian families, since there are over 30 major languages in that country.
2. A move involving no language change but considerable cultural differences. To go from a poor part of an inner city in Britain to a farm in New Zealand would meet this criterion.
3. A move involving a change of culture but with similar language being spoken. This can be so for some families moving from parts of the Commonwealth where a form of English has been developed which retains the name English with its own vocabulary and structure.
4. A move involving changes in both language and culture.

Unfortunately, although it is easy to point out these differences it is less easy to suggest what the effects of migration are on children's development, since there has been little work done on this area. Studies of migration to different cultures have, in Britain at least, focused on what happens to Asian and West Indian children academically and behaviourally. Although the causes for observed patterns are not fully understood, or at least there is no general agreement on them, the patterns themselves appear reasonably stable, with Asian children performing as well as their indigenous peers once they have been in this country for a few years, and West Indian children doing less well. A genetic explanation for this finding is not supported by clear evidence based on children of similar upbringing. On the rare occasions that this has been possible—for example, when both groups were brought up in institutions—the differences have not been apparent. However, it is not always safe, scientifically, to generalise to a whole population from such a sub-sample. There have been some hints that the root cause of the difference might be traced to child-rearing habits which have long-lasting effects. On the other hand, the picture is made more complex by the possibility that Asian groups have maintained an extended family system here, while West Indians have not. This means that the latter have to rely on baby-minding of dubious quality. It has also been suggested that West Indians perceive themselves as being labelled as inferior, and so believe that they are, behaving accordingly. It is relatively easy to see the possibilities, less easy to come to conclusions.

Little, if any, effect of migration within countries has been shown to exist. For example, children migrating from London have similar behaviour patterns to those remaining. It is always possible that there are effects not yet studied or discovered but the evidence is lacking.

For a fuller discussion of many of the studies noted above see **David**

Quinton's chapter on Cultural and Community Influences in Michael Rutter's *Scientific Foundations of Developmental Psychiatry.*

Questions

1. Is it valid to assert that children's behaviour can be ascribed as totally due to family influences?
2. Consider ways in which attitudes towards the relative influences of home and school have varied since 1967.
3. Discuss the possible interaction of biological and environmental factors in the difference between boys' and girls' performances in mathematics.
4. Should the notion of the critical period be jettisoned?
5. Critically consider the statement that all children from one parent families are emotionally disturbed.

Exercise

Assess the academic achievement of any group known to you. Consider the results by birth order, i.e. ask if there is a relationship between attainment and:
   (a) Being the eldest in a family.
   (b) Coming late in a large family.
   (c) Any other birth order phenomenon.

Part 2
Foetal Development and the Neonate

4
Genetics

No one tells a baby what to do when it is in the womb. It starts as a couple of tiny cells and then, if all goes well, in nine months' time it is born, with body, arms, legs, head and sometimes even hair. Inside it has a delicate brain, two sets of teeth and an **in-built programme for later development**.

If no one tells the baby how to develop there must be some organisation within it, which arranges everything so that at certain times certain processes will take place. This is just what does exist: each baby is born with a set of **instructions** for development.

To start at the beginning: life begins with a collision between male and female. The male part is one of millions of sperm cells which are deposited into the female body at a time of sexual intercourse. These cells 'swim' up into the female's uterus where they encounter female cells (ova) that have been released by the ovary shortly before intercourse took place. One sperm buries itself in one ovum and together they travel down the uterus where they lodge in a thick, warm lining and immediately begin to grow. Together these two tiny cells, known as a **zygote**, contain a complete set of instructions for development.

To discover more about these instructions we need to know more about the way these cells are made up. Each has two main parts, a **nucleus** in the centre and a jelly-like substance surrounding it called the **cytoplasm**. Cells grow following the action of the nucleus on the cytoplasm and it is in the nucleus that we can discover more about the programme of instructions. Almost every cell has, in its nucleus, 46 **chromosomes**, in pairs, one from the father and one from the mother. Each pair is numbered from 1 to 22. Why only 22, when it is known that each parent contributes 23? The answer is that the last chromosome is given a letter, either X or Y, rather than a number. These XY chromosomes determine the baby's sex: if the packet has two Xs then the baby will be a girl and if it has XY it will be a boy.

The only cells which do not have 46 chromosomes are the sex cells, which develop at puberty. Since these are designed to join with another cell to start the whole process again they have only 23.

But chromosomes themselves have to be further examined if we are to understand the genetic programme fully. Chromosomes consist basically of a long stretch of **deoxyribonucleic acid** (DNA) with associated molecules.

A **gene** is a segment of the DNA on a chromosome. Genes seem to exert their control over development by regulating the production of proteins, thus affecting the chemical reactions in the body.

Genes then, are the **agents of development**. They are very, very small. It is difficult to imagine just how small they are but it helps to realise that if all the genes concerned in the initial instructions of all the people alive in the world today were added together they would weigh less than a postage stamp.

It sometimes seems odd that no two people in the world are exactly alike. To understand why this is so go back to the genes. If we had only a few genes each then the possible combination of height, weight, shape of nose and colour of skin would be quite small. But we have lots of genes, about 12,000 pairs each. This means that the possible combinations of sperm and ovum total nearly 300 trillion. No wonder we are all different.

There are, of course, occasions when two people are alike, when identical twins are born, although the word 'identical' is misleading since even twins are not exactly the same, having, apart from anything else, slightly different experiences in the womb. But similarities are certainly there, due to the fact that identical twins are formed from a separation of the two original cells, so that both sets contain the same 46 chromosomes. Non-identical twins are simply the result of two ova being fertilised at the same time. The technical terms used for twins are **monozygotic** for identical and **dizygotic** for non-identical.

Two other words frequently encountered in the literature on genetics are **genotype** (the genetic make up of an individual) and **phenotype** (the actual physical or behavioural trait—e.g. height or intelligence—of an individual).

Genetics—the Laws of Inheritance

An early student of the laws of inheritance was a German mathematician called **Maupertuis** who, in 1752, recorded a Berlin family which had some members in each of four generations with extra fingers or toes. Being a mathematician, Maupertuis worked out the odds against this happening by chance and it was this kind of work that was the forerunner of the calculations of the man whose name is still associated with the basic laws of genetics: **Gregor Mendel**. Mendel was a monk who had hoped to be a teacher but who failed his exams because he was said to have lacked 'insight and the requisite clarity of knowledge'. Disappointed, he returned to his monastery and devoted most of the rest of his life to a study of plants.

At this time, rather more than 100 years ago, it was commonly thought that while a boy could inherit his father's hair or his mother's mouth the general pattern of inheritance was a blending of family characteristics. Mendel's contribution to the study of genetics was the formulation of two major laws, the first of which being that **genes do not blend, they separate**. Since genes come in pairs there are two possible courses of action:

1. If both are the same, then the child will be born with that characteristic.

2. If they are different, then one gene will win.

The winning or losing is predetermined because genes are either **dominant** or **recessive**, and the dominant always wins. But the recessive gene stays in the cell and may be passed on to following generations. This explains why a certain characteristic can remain within a family for several generations without coming out.

To take an example: brown eyes are dominant, grey are recessive. So if a brown-eye gene couples with a grey-eye one the child will have brown eyes but the brown-eyed person will carry the grey-eye gene. If he or she mates with another person also carrying a grey-eye gene, then the two recessive genes may meet, in which case their child will have grey eyes. So two brown-eyed people may have a grey-eyed child. See Table 5 for an illustration of this point.

Table 5. Dominant and recessive characteristics.

Dominant	over	Recessive
Round head		Long head
Shortness		Tallness
Brown eyes		Blue or grey eyes
Green eyes		Blue or grey eyes
Astigmatism		Normal sight
Long or short sight		Normal sight
Wavy hair		Straight hair
Long eye lashes		Short eye lashes

Some characteristics are carried on the X chromosomes and are therefore known as **sex-linked**. The most well known are colour blindness and haemophilia (a condition in which bleeding does not stop naturally). Far more males than females are colour blind because females always inherit two X chromosomes and can therefore have the colour blindness gene cancelled out by one from the other chromosome. Since males have only one X chromosome they do not have this chance.

Mendel's second law was that of the ratios of inherited characteristics. Earlier work was devoted to finding out the odds of having extra fingers or toes, so Mendel took this a stage further and put forward a general law. To return to brown and grey eyes: if eight people, each with a brown and a grey gene, produce four children, Mendel's law is that the odds of a child being born with grey eyes are one in four (see Table 6). So only Mr and Mrs B's child has grey eyes, because he or she inherited two recessive genes. It can be seen from this that the dominant gene 'wins' only when both have entered a cell—they both have an equal chance of actually being inherited.

A possible objection to the picture that has just been presented is that some characteristics are observably blends, skin colour being an example. Yet Mendel said that genes do not blend. The explanation for this is that not all characteristics involve only a single gene, some involve two or more. Skin colour is the result of four genes in two pairs. Thus the first generation of a black-white couple will be an intermediate colour. If the family inter-

Table 6. Mendel's second law.

Genes	Mr A	Mrs A	Mr B	Mrs B	Mr C	Mrs C	Mr D	Mrs D
	BROWN	BROWN	BROWN	BROWN	BROWN	BROWN	BROWN	BROWN
	grey	grey	grey	grey	grey	grey	grey	grey
Passed on	BB		gg		Bg		gB	
Child's eye colour	brown		grey		brown		brown	

bred the resulting 16 grandchildren are likely to be: one black, one white, four dark, four light and six in between.

Gene and Life Span Development

It is sometimes naively assumed that the influence of genes stops at birth; in fact only a fraction of the genes in an individual's genotype are active at any one time. Different genes may be active at different times and different sets of genes may be active at the same time in different cells of the body. The understanding of child development is not complete without a realisation that new genes are brought into play with age: certain behavioural characteristics absent in early childhood but present later are not due entirely to environmental origins.

Genes or Environment

In Chapter 1 there was a mention of a fundamental theoretical viewpoint: the interaction between biological factors in an individual and the environment. A study of genetics brings one face to face with this interaction.

Cases of **identical (monozygotic) twins reared apart** provide fascinating reading. A centre for such studies is the University of Minnesota where **Thomas Bouchard** and colleagues have carried out a series of tests on twins, many of whom had not seen each other since infancy. The 'Jim twins', both called Jim, are an extreme example. They were adopted as infants into working-class families. Both liked maths but not spelling, both worked part-time as deputy sheriffs, both drove Chevrolets and went to the same state for holidays, they share smoking and drinking habits, both put on 10 pounds at the same time in their lives, both have a 'mixed headache syndrome' which came on at the age of 18 in both cases—they have headaches with the same frequency and the same degree of discomfort.

The pattern emerging from the Minnesota work is one of much greater similarities between twins that Bouchard himself had expected, psychiatric histories and measured intelligence quotients being strikingly close.

But there have been some differences emerging from the Minnesota pairs, notably smoking habits, so even these data do not support the notion that the environment is of no importance. It must also be borne in mind that the popular press is likely to seize on the remarkable and ignore the humdrum stories of twins who are not alike; who would ever print a story of two brothers who drove different cars and went to different states for their holidays? While the notion of a combined influence of genes and the environment is discussed further in Chapter 14 on intelligence, it is apposite here to quote one of the Minnesota scientists: '... there will be material that will make environmentalists very happy and material that will make hereditarians very happy.'

Racial Groups and Genetics

There are undoubted, obvious to the naked eye, consistent genetic differences between racial groups—one has only to look at skin and hair to see that. It is likely that these immediately obvious differences are the result of biological adaptation to climatic conditions. For example, a fair skin is suited to a climate when there is relatively little sun since this allows a greater uptake of vitamin D from sunlight.

It may seem facile, but it is true, to say further that the observable differences between races are, genetically speaking, often no more than skin deep. The position is this: there is enormous genetic variation *within* any racial group and the uniformity of appearance does not imply uniformity in other genetically influenced characteristics. Recent biochemical research suggests that if two individuals are taken at random from the same racial group they will be almost as different from each other, genetically, as two chosen at random from different racial groups.

Chromosomal Disorders

Chromosomes may break, or join in the wrong order, or an extra one may appear. Minor defects may cause relatively few problems but a major defect can be serious.

One of the best understood examples of a **mental disorder** caused by a major gene defect is **phenylketonuria** (PKU). People with PKU suffer a build-up in the blood stream of toxic chemicals that interfere with the normal development of the nervous system. It is now known that the condition is inherited via a recessive gene—that is, it comes from both parents.

One of the best known examples of **abnormality** caused by an extra chromosome is **Down's syndrome**, sometimes known as mongolism, in which the child has an extra 21 chomosome.

What is less well known is that defects involving chromosomes often have a critical effect *in utero*; in the United States they account, possibly, for about 100,000 miscarriages a year—that is, about one fifth of the total for that country.

Allied to clear-cut conditions like Down's syndrome are a number of disabilities in which heredity seems to play a part but in which our knowledge of the precise means of transmission is incomplete. Some of these are shown in Table 7. The recurrence rate is raised if there is already more than one affected person in the family. For example, if parents have already had two children with spina bifida the risk rises to about 1 in 8. In all cases

Table 7. Genetically related risk factors.

Spina bifida cystica	1 in 20 risk for siblings of affected people
Cleft lip, with or without cleft palate	1 in 30 risk for siblings or for sons or daughters of affected people
Congenital dislocation of the hip	1 in 40 risk for brothers and sons, 1 in 10 risk for sisters and daughters of affected females
Down's syndrome	1 in 100 risk for siblings of affected person irrespective of maternal age
Diabetes (onset under 30 years of age)	1 in 20 risk for siblings of affected people

From *Human Genetics*, July 1972, Department of Health and Social Security.

where there is a chance of a child inheriting a handicapping condition parents should seek genetic advice which takes their own family into account. They should not try to work out the odds themselves from a book.

Close Relatives as Parents

From what has already been noted about recessive genes it may be assumed that any parents who are likely to pass on to their children a 'double dose' of defective genes are, by definition, more likely to produce an abnormal child. This is observably so, in that the closer the parents are related the more probable it is that their children will be defective in some way. The highest risk comes from a brother-sister liaison, a finding which some say is at the root of the incest taboo.

Questions and **exercises** appear at the end of Chapter 5.

5
From Conception To Birth

Prenatal Development

Ways of Gaining Information on Foetal Development

There are four sources of information about life before birth:

1. **Animal studies.** It is possible to watch the development of a chick by treating the membrane of an egg to make it transparent. Other animal studies—for example, on the guinea pig—have stimulated a good deal of further work on humans.

2. **Human studies.** Information can be obtained about human development from the observation of a foetus which has had to be removed from the mother while still alive. The foetus, along with the placenta, can be removed by caesarian-section and placed in a salt solution at blood temperature. Since the normal supply of oxygen is cut off the period of life is short. For ethical reasons this procedure is rarely carried out.

3. **Prematurely born** infants often survive if born during the sixth or seventh month of pregnancy.

4. **Special apparatus** can be attached to the mother's abdomen, enabling observations to be made. For example, one mother studied the intensity, location and frequency of her baby's movements during the fifth and seventh month and found that there was a relationship between her activity and that of the baby.

Embryonic Development

The word **embryo** is used for the developing cells during the first three months of their life.

Early growth, a result of the action of the nucleus on the cytoplasm in each cell, has been discussed in Chapter 4. At first the changes are simple division, the original cells multiply and become a ball-like mass. Next, some cells are forced to the top of this structure and the ball becomes a hollow sphere. The organisms which will be born develop from these upper cells.

By the **second week** development has been rapid and the embryo is linked by means of the umbilical cord, to a spongy mass known as the **placenta**.

About **three weeks** after conception the embryo is approximately 4 mm long and the heart begins to beat.

At the **sixth week** recognisable structures of arms, feet and eyes have

emerged, although the organism is, at this time, motionless.
During the **eighth week** spontaneous movement begins.

Foetal Development

From the beginning of the third month the individual is known as a **foetus**.
Growth continues at a rapid rate, as shown in Tables 8 and 9.

As Fig. 3 indicates, proportionately the foetus is much more 'top heavy'
than a fully grown person—that is, the head is relatively large.

Table 8. Foetal development: functions.

Approximately:

Beginning of the 3rd month	grasp reflexes appear
3rd month	taste buds develop in what is to be the mouth
4th month	many reflexes are present
5th month	some kicking may begin
6th month	movement continues, sucking begins
7th–8th month	an intensification of movement and the beginning of crying

Table 9. Embryonic and foetal development: size and weight.

Age in months	Average length in centimetres	Average weight in grams
ovum	1/93	1/1,700,000
2	2.6	—
3	9.0	19
4	16.7	100
5	24.3	312
6	31.1	667
7	37.1	1151
8	42.4	1754
9	47.0	2396

What Affects Prenatal Development

An old superstition asserts that if a pregnant woman is frightened by a
rabbit she will have a baby with a rabbit-shaped birthmark. This, of course,
is no more than a superstition but like many old beliefs there is a grain
of truth in it if one digs deeply enough.

The grain of truth in this case is the fact that a mother's anxiety can
affect the baby she is carrying. The mechanism is like this: marked changes
take place in one's body when one is under stress. One of the changes brings
certain substances into the blood stream. A pregnant woman who is stressed
will have these substances in her blood and they can be conveyed to the
baby via the umbilical cord. This does not mean that all pregnant women
under stress will have deformed or in any way different babies, it does mean
that a mother who experiences **severe stress** is likely to have a fretful baby.

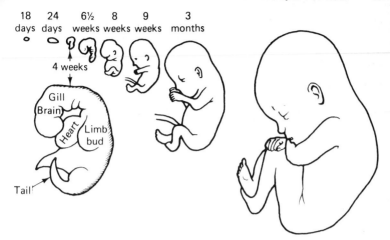

Fig. 3. Prenatal development. Adapted from C. Martin and E. L. Vincent, *Human Development*, Ronald (1960).

Shortages of food can play a part, too, although nature has ensured that the baby has first pick of materials that may be in short supply. So a mother who is undernourished may produce a healthy baby but at her own expense. **Severe undernourishment** can lead to still births or physical impairments.

Toxaemia of pregnancy (poisons in the blood supply), **bleeding** during pregnancy or **anoxia** (an undersupply of oxygen) can all lead to damage in the developing baby. Some investigators have suggested that many of the naughty children one encounters, especially those who are overactive, clumsy and confused, are suffering from a mild form of brain disorder which is a result of prenatal influences. Such theories, if shown to be true, would be of great importance when the treatment of such children is considered. It is, however, generally acknowledged that many factors contribute to behaviour problems, prenatal influences being only a part.

The mother's health can affect the baby, although the placenta filters out most viruses and germs that may be present in the mother's blood stream. A well-known cause of damage is, however, German measles (Rubella) which, if contracted during the first three months of pregnancy, can lead to defective vision, hearing loss or intellectual retardation.

There is an undoubted association between **smoking during pregnancy** and the development of the child. The National Child Development Study demonstrated that when a mother smoked 10 or more cigarettes a day foetal mortality increased by 28 per cent and the average birth weight was reduced by 170 grams compared to babies of non-smokers.

Such associations do not *prove* that smoking causes low birth weight. Perhaps the kind of woman likely to smoke is also the kind of woman likely to have a low-weight baby for reasons other than smoking, but when maternal age, social class and height are allowed for statistically, the relationship between smoking, foetal mortality and lower birth weight remained. Further strength to the argument is given by the observation that women who gave up smoking by their fourth month of pregnancy were no more at risk than those who had never smoked.

A similar picture has emerged from American studies of **drinking during pregnancy**. Alcohol can cross the placenta to the foetus and it is known that heavy drinking can produce the **foetal alcohol syndrome** which leads to significant impairment in children. Now it is thought that even moderate drinking, especially during the first four months of pregnancy, may lead to a greater risk of spontaneous abortion, minor malformation and slower development during the early stages of infancy at least. Not all British doctors accept the American findings and this is undoubtedly an area where further research will be forthcoming.

Birth

The Event

The physical act of birth is still surrounded by much mystery. It is no accident that a slang term for being pregnant is 'in the club' for it is an exclusive club, with shared experiences just as powerful and cutting across far more social barriers than any that bind old students of a school or college. If pregnancy is a club then birth is a further initiation rite.

What **precipitates the birth** of a baby is still not fully understood and there are enormous variations in the extent and the events of labour. For some women the process is simple and enjoyable but for others the experience is nasty, painful and long. The baby may be the wrong way round, or get stuck or just take a long time before being born at all. Anything out of the ordinary carries an element of risk as far as subsequent development is concerned. Although not every breach birth (when the baby is the wrong way round) or forceps delivery, or precipitate birth results in a damaged child there is a link between difficulties at birth and subsequent vulnerability. Controversy surrounding **induction** is an example of awareness of this point. If a baby seems to be slow in coming it is possible to hurry the process along, i.e. to induce the birth. Unfortunately the baby is often not fully developed—the liver may not be working properly, for example—and it may be necessary to use an incubator for the first day or so. As a result of anxieties about this practice it is now not adopted in many hospitals unless there are pressing medical reasons.

Prematurity

The average length of pregnancy is about 40 weeks. The average birth weight in developed countries is between 7 and $7\frac{1}{2}$ lb, about 3.2–3.4 kilograms. Children born as early as 26 weeks have survived, as have those weighing as little as $1\frac{1}{2}$ lb, or 0.7 kilograms.

It was common in the past to lump all kinds of prematurity together, but now a differentiation is made between:

1. **Low birth weight**—that is, less than $5\frac{1}{2}$ lb. or 2.5 kilograms.
2. **A short gestation period**—that is, less than 37 weeks.

3. **Light for dates**—that is, being disproportionately light bearing in mind the gestation period.

About six out of every 100 babies born in Great Britain will be premature. Although the causes of any of the three forms of prematurity are not fully understood it is known that any of them are more likely to occur among first-born children, in lower socioeconomic classes, to small women and in multiple births.

Any premature baby is at risk, especially from brain damage, during the birth process and when there is difficulty in establishing respiration. However, developmental patterns are the same as for those born to full term and although they may lag for the first five or six months there can be a more or less complete catch-up by the age of 24 months, providing there have been no other complications. In general, the lower the birth weight the greater the vulnerability. The 'no other complications' is an important qualification since premature births occur more frequently among the less advantaged; hence the generalisation that prematurity is associated with intellectual retardation among other factors.

Postmaturity

Postmaturity is now far less common than in the past since it is possible to examine the foetus to check its growth rate. The greatest risk to the postmature child is brain damage (see below) and studies of the later development of postmature infants have indicated that there is a greater than average risk of learning and behavioural problems among this group.

Brain Damage

This is an emotive term which many psychologists are, quite properly, wary of using. Nevertheless, it must be admitted that there is a risk of damage to the brain at birth from two main causes. The first is that there may be **undue pressure on the foetal head**. Inevitably there will be some pressure as the head passes down the birth canal, but if extra pressure is exerted—for example, if the baby is postmature and so has a proportionately large head—then damage is possible. The second is from **anoxia**, or lack of oxygen to the brain. Damage may be permanent or temporary depending on the length of time during which the oxygen supply is reduced: 18 seconds is long enough to cause very serious effects.

The effects of brain damage do not reveal themselves in any one pattern of behaviour, a point which makes it all too easy to invoke brain damage to explain many subsequent problems of childhood. There is no doubt, though, that an increased investment of medical care around the time of birth is likely to pay off in terms of healthier children in general and a lower rate of the severely brain damaged in particular. Here, perhaps, is one point at which the cycle of deprivation may be broken.

The Effects of Analgesic Drugs and Anaesthetics given in Childbirth

It is known that up to 95 per cent of women in Britain are given some kind of analgesic drug or anaesthetic during childbirth. It is also known that drugs given to a pregnant woman can pass via the placenta to the baby. Unfortunately our knowledge stops there for we are far from clear in our understanding of the effects on the baby of coming into the world with drugs in the blood stream. Research has been attempted, but with no conclusive results. Possibly sucking is affected, possibly the newborn is less responsive to sound, possibly any effect passes rapidly and is of little long-term consequence.

Postnatal Depression and other Psychological Factors

There is often a sense of anticlimax after any major event and childbirth is no exception to this rule. Women may feel that they never want to have another baby, do not much like the one they have and are no longer attractive. The depression is made worse by the fact that childbirth leaves one physically weak, yet almost immediately one may be responsible for caring for this new creature, who is, as one commentator put it, far from an ideal roommate. If the depression passes within a few weeks, as is often the case, it is unlikely that there will be permanent effects on the rest of the family.

Little has been written about the fears or other emotions of *fathers*: little is known. Some play an active part in all stages of the pregnancy and assist at the birth; others wish to have little part in the whole business. Many men have little love for the newcomer and wonder if there is such a thing as paternal instinct. For that matter many women seem to care little for their baby until they can actually see and hold it.

More is known about the effect of a pregnancy and birth on the **relationship between the parents**. At one extreme is the happily married couple whose emotional, physical and financial state make the child wanted before conception and welcome at birth. At the other extreme is the unstable, unmarried, sickly woman, whose pregnancy brings the departure of her man and a rift with her family.

So far the problems surrounding birth have all been seen in terms either of the adult's or of the child's physical state; there are, however, a good many theories about the **newborn's psychological state** as well. One theory concerns what many psychologists see as a rather far-fetched idea, that of the **birth trauma**. For nine months, it is argued, the baby has grown in an even temperature, nourished with no effort on his part, having no demands made on him, being able to exercise when necessary. Then, suddenly, he is precipitated into a world of confusion, cold and a sudden bombardment of light, sound and touch. No wonder the newborn baby cries out—he is not just filling his lungs with air, he is expressing the anguish he feels at leaving the Garden of Eden. The philosopher Kant described this yell as 'a cry of wrath at the catastrophe of birth'. Observers with rather harder views question whether the baby's neural apparatus is sufficiently well developed for such emotions to be felt and argue that the first movements down the birth canal indicate an actual desire to be out in the world.

Bonding

The establishment of a relationship between the mother and baby marks the point of transition from birth to the world. It is discussed in detail in Chapter 15.

The Newborn Child

How can we describe the world of the newborn child? In the nineteenth century **William James** tried to get inside this world and in so doing produced a phrase that was, if nothing else, memorable. The neonate's world is, he said, one of **booming, buzzing confusion**.

Arthur Jersild took rather longer when he attempted to list what the neonate does: 'He sucks, swallows, excretes, defecates, vomits, salivates, hiccoughs, sneezes, yawns, stretches, kicks, waves arms and legs, trembles, shivers, turns his head, grimaces, moves his eyes, blinks, grunts and sighs.'

Elizabeth Hurlock has taken a rather more prosaic but potentially more fruitful approach in describing the newborn under three main headings: appearance, helplessness and individuality.

Appearance

The average weight of babies has been noted above and bodily proportions are shown in Fig. 3. There it can be seen that the head is about a quarter of the entire body length, compared to the tenth proportion of the average adult. The biggest difference is the cranial region—that is, the area above the eyes. In the infant the ratio between the cranium and the face is 8:1; by adulthood this has changed to 1:2.

White babies typically have blue-grey eyes while non-white babies' eyes are brown. Gradually eye colour changes to whatever it will ultimately be. The eyes are almost mature in size (the extent to which the visual system functions will be discussed below). Hair colour, if there is any to have colour, signifies little for it may be replaced by some of a different colour and texture.

Helplessness

Humans have a longer period of childhood than any other mammal; some say ruefully that in some cases it lasts for twenty years or so. The extreme helplessness of the newborn is evident in five ways:

1. **An inability to maintain homeostasis.** Adults and older children have a well developed regulatory mechanism, rather like the thermostat system of central heating, which enables them to maintain a relatively stable level of temperature and chemical composition within the body. Prenatally the mother maintained homeostasis for the foetus but the newborn's central nervous system (see Chapter 7) is not sufficiently developed to allow the baby to take over at once. An example of variation is the base pulse rate, which in adults is about 70 per minute. The neonate's pulse will swing from 130 to 150 at birth, dropping to just under 120 a few days later.

The most marked example of lack of homeostasis is found in the baby's sleep. The newborn will be awake for only about 8 hours a day but the 16 hours' sleeping will occur in fitful patterns, which may take two or three months to settle into a routine whereby most of the sleep occurs at night.

2. **An inability to control motor activity.** Full control implies voluntary activity—that is, bodily movement occurs only after a conscious wish. Babies move everything in all directions.

But not all movement even at this age is random. Babies vary one from another in both their mass activity (i.e. movement of the whole body in response to a stimulation) and specific activity (for example, hand-mouth contact). There are observable patterns during the day as well, the quietest period generally being about noon.

3. **An inability to communicate.** This is an area of some possible controversy. There is no question of a baby pointing or indicating needs physically but they do cry and to some this is a form of communication. The 'birth cry' is reflexive, a result of air being drawn over the vocal cords. But from the first 24 hours onwards crying will occur at a time when the baby is hungry or appears to be in some discomfort. Mothers soon learn to recognise their own baby and may even interpret what the cries mean.

Another type of sound occurring at this time is often ignored, although it is potentially of the utmost significance. This is the explosive sound: the whimpering, cooing and gurgling which usually come when the baby is contented. Their significance lies in the fact that these sounds strengthen as the baby gets older and become babbles, in turn becoming speech.

4. **An undeveloped state of the sense organs.** Older texts state categorically that the newborn baby cannot see. Recent research has shown not only that this is wrong but also that a baby of even a few weeks old or younger is probably capable of using sensory apparatus to a far greater extent than was hitherto imagined.

The general picture seems to be that all sensory organs are ready to function at birth although some are more highly developed than others.

Vision is the sensory system on which some of the most recent work has been done, notably by **Robert Fantz** in America and **Tom Bower** in Britain. Physiologically the cones in the retina are poorly developed, suggesting that neonates are colour blind. Although the rods are better developed their area is limited, which suggests a restriction of the visual field. The muscles controlling eye movements are undeveloped and so both eyes do not focus on the same object.

But a newborn baby will react to light, turning apparently to search for it; within a few hours of birth babies have been observed to sustain gaze despite poor focusing skills. (The ideal focal distance at this time is about 8 inches, the distance between a baby's face and that of a feeding mother.) Within the first few weeks many babies follow a moving object visually. (See Chapter 10 for a fuller discussion of early visual skills.) There is no doubt that the ability to see and distinguish some visual patterns is very much greater than was imagined twenty or more years ago.

Smell is the least important sense for humans but it is well developed at birth as is demonstrated by head-turning away from unpleasant stimuli.

Taste cells on the tongue are not only well developed at birth but they are also as numerous as they will be later. Supplemented by smell, the sense of taste probably operates from the beginning; the baby presented with an unpleasant tasting stimulus, something bitter or salty, will cry and squirm.

Touch. The sensory system is differentially developed at birth: sensitivity to cold is greater than that to heat; sensitivity to touch and pressure are greater in the region of the face than the trunk, thighs and arms. Sensitivity to pain may be affected by medication given to the mother during labour (see above).

Hearing. Despite some evidence to suggest that the foetus can hear in the later stages of development, hearing is recognised as the least well developed of all the senses at birth. The newborn cannot easily hear partly because the middle ear is stopped with amniotic fluid. Nevertheless, at least one study has suggested that a baby has turned to sound within a few minutes of birth.

Less certain than the assumption that the foetus can hear is whether or not the foetus or the neonate can distinguish tones. It seems likely from observations of babies from birth to 21 days of age that not all do. It has also been observed that low-frequency sounds seems more effective than high in soothing a crying baby.

5. **An inability to learn.** Here again there is no general agreement. Some authorities argue that even the simplest form of conditioning (see Chapter 2) is too complex for the neonate. Others suggest not only that learning of a sort begins from the moment of contact with the mother's skin but also that it is possible to condition a baby *in utero*.

Individuality

Even identical twins show some individuality, as was mentioned in Chapter 4. Despite their relatively restricted behavioural repertoire, all babies have their own ways of movement, of feeding, of crying and of sleeping. The critical point here is that this variation implies that one should be very wary indeed before concluding that a neonate is doing anything unduly abnormal.

Questions (Chapters 4 and 5)

1. How have Mendel's discoveries assisted our ability to predict the likely appearance of a baby?
2. What advice would you give to the newly pregnant woman?
3. Is 'living in a world of booming, buzzing confusion' still an accurate description of the neonate?
4. Explain the terms monozygotic, dizygotic, genotype and phenotype.
5. Explain the differences in the inheritance of colour of eyes and skin.

Exercises

1. Take any two people and check their interests, e.g. where they like to go for holidays, what food they like. Do your results shed any light on the possible interpretation to be placed on the reported preference patterns of twins?
2. Establish the birth weight of any group of people. Then compare this with present weights and height and establish the predictive value of the birth measurements.

Part 3
The Baby becomes a Child:
Physical Growth

6
The Body Develops

Note that while the overall principles of growth can be seen to relate to all children, the figures quoted in the first part of this chapter refer to those who live in the Western world and are derived largely from data available on British children.

Height

Some parents, and some children, seem obsessed by height gain. Every few months the child is placed against a wall and the height is recorded, there being an unspoken message that to be tall is in every way superior to being short. The psychological reasons for this view are not difficult to understand.

There are two reasonably reliable ways of estimating final height. One is to multiply the neonate's birth length by $3\frac{1}{2}$; the other is to double the height reached on the child's third birthday. The existence of these formulae suggests that there is little that an individual can do to affect height —unlike weight which is, to a much greater extent, under personal control. Growth in height is governed by secretions of a growth hormone from the thyroid gland and few people can directly control that mechanism.

Changes in height can be observed from three points of view: overall size, variations in the proportions of the body and changes in height relative to weight.

As can be seen from Fig. 4(a), overall height does not progress in a linear fashion. There is a period of relatively rapid growth for the first three years, then a time of slowing down, followed by a spurt as adolescence approaches.

Proportions vary with age: at birth the head is about a quarter of the body, by the third birthday it is still about a fifth but by adulthood the ratio has diminished to about an eighth. Readers who refer back to Chapter 1 will notice that this gradual change in ratio follows the **cephalocaudal law** mentioned there.

Weight

Generally, as Fig. 4 indicates, there is a consistent relationship between height and weight. In many western countries, though, this balance is not main-

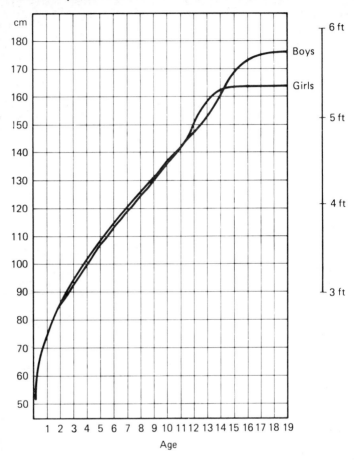

Fig. 4. (*a*) Height chart.
From J. M. Tanner, R. H. Whitehouse and M. Takaishi, *Archives of Disease in Childhood* (1966).

tained and obesity becomes a severe problem in a proportion of children.

As with height, there is a degree of variability in weight gain, with a flattening of the growth curve after the first year or so. It is just as well that this curve does flatten: if one continued to put on weight during the whole of one's childhood at the same rate that one does in the first year of life, a baby born weighing 7 lb. would, at maturity, weigh 562 tonnes!

Types of Body Build

It is possible, following the work of **W. S. Sheldon**, to group humans into three body types:

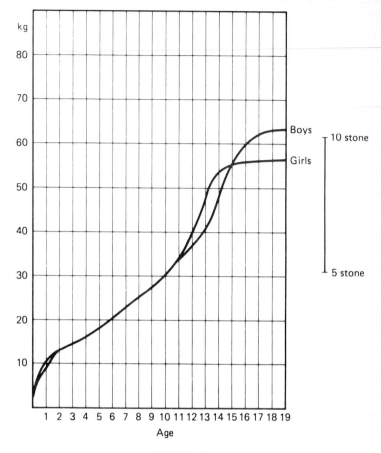

(*b*) Weight chart.

Ectomorphs—long and slender.
Endomorphs—round and fat.
Mesomorphs—heavy, hard and more rectangular in shape.

Few people are totally in one or another of these categories but most can be more or less assigned to one. There has been much speculation on the relationship between body type and personality, an issue discussed in Chapter 18.

Factors Related to Height and Weight Gain

The following are general statements, based mainly on large-scale surveys—individual differences will always be observed:

Ectomorph   Mesomorph   Endomorph

Fig. 5. Types of body build.

Sex differences are clearly observable in any mixed school: boys tending to be taller and heavier than girls. Before puberty there is, however, little difference in body build although as puberty approaches boys move somewhat in the direction of mesomorphy.

Racial differences are again apparent from observation. As well as differences in height there are some variations in body build, negro children in America having relatively shorter trunks, more slender hips and longer limbs than their white counterparts.

Prenatal influences can, to some extent, alter the height and weight of a child that would be predicted on genetic grounds. Mothers who are malnourished, or who smoke heavily during pregnancy, tend to have shorter children (see Chapters 3 and 5).

Breast-fed babies are less likely to become fat, since the composition of breast milk changes throughout the feed, with proportionately more lipids and protein towards the end. This enables a baby to monitor the feed in a way that a bottle-fed baby cannot.

Babies who are heavy at birth tend to grow faster, and have their growth spurt earlier.

Singletons grow faster than twins or other multiple births.

Placid children put on weight at a faster rate than those who are tense.

Persistent emotional tension has been associated with a failure to gain height. The argument is that tension in sufficient quantity causes an overproduction of adrenal steroids which inhibit the production of growth hormone. Emotional factors can play a part in both obesity and severe weight loss (see Chapter 27 for a fuller discussion of both).

Nutrition plays a crucial part in determining whether or not a child reaches the potential height and weight that his genetic endowment offers. Closely related to nutrition are **socioeconomic status** and **intelligence**. The general pattern is that better-off children are both taller and score higher on intelligence tests. They are also usually better fed as well, and one must not fall into the trap of confusing an association with a causal relationship (see Chapter 28 for a further discussion of this last point).

Psychological Consequences of Unusual Height, Weight or Body Build

Every culture has its ideals. In Great Britain and America to be slim is to be beautiful, in contrast to some other countries where to be thin is to be pitied. Most societies value height, for boys if not for girls, but this is not universal: the anthropologist Colin Turnbull is about six feet tall and was viewed by a Pygmy tribe as a freak.

Psychological consequence of any variation from the norm, or from the ideal, can be viewed from two points of view: the **self-image** of the child and the set of **expectations** that are aroused by that child in society.

The child's self-image is derived from the ways he interprets what others feel about him (see Chapter 21 for a fuller discussion on this). Thus a child who is abnormally short may feel that others are constantly and literally looking down on him. How this affects his self-image will depend to a large extent on the way he has perceived his immediate family to see him. **Irving Goffman** has referred to families of unusual children bringing them up in 'a protective capsule', insulating them from the world's slings and arrows for the first, vital few years. If this stage can be accomplished successfully the effects of an unusual appearance can be mitigated.

Adults' expectations of children are governed by many factors, physical size being one of them. The small, thin child may be eight years old but if he looks like a five-year-old he will be treated accordingly.

Weight gain is a result of changes in bone, muscle and fat. At birth muscle fibres are present but undeveloped. They grow in length and thickness in two main spurts, from about five to six years of age and again at puberty. The amount of fat, or adipose tissue, possessed by any individual depends partly on heredity, partly on body build and partly on eating habits. It is possible that there are critical periods when a too rapid development of fat cells can have a greater effect than is apparent at other times. These critical periods have been seen as the first two to three years and the time approximately between 11 and 13 years. Having said that, it must be noted that any overeating in childhood leading to excessive fat is likely to be extremely difficult to counteract in adult life.

Teeth

The last permanent teeth a person has, the so called 'wisdom' teeth, reach their full size in the person's early 20s; until then dentition is continuous.

The first, 'milk' teeth are normally cut from between the sixth and eighth month, but much depends on health, heredity and nutrition. By nine months the average baby has three teeth; by 2½ years most have all 20 baby teeth. Between six and eight years children lose their first teeth and by the age of 10 most can expect to have about 15 permanent teeth.

The **physical and psychological implications of dentition** are often overlooked in studies of child development. The tooth fairy is seen as a pleasing fancy and that is that. Yet the appearance of the first teeth can be associated with many powerful other factors in the young child's life. They come at a period of already heightened emotion (see Chapter 17 for a discussion of the 'terrible twos'). Parents may make allowances for a child who is teething but they may not realise that teeth can hurt at any time and young children, or those who are retarded, are not always good at pointing out that they have toothache.

The shedding of baby teeth is one of the *rites de passage*, a marker that one stage in life is passing. Babyhood is being left behind in all sorts of ways at the age of six or seven, for it is by this age that most children are reading and grappling with number concepts, or at least beginning to do so.

Another marker of change can be the orthodontic brace, a status symbol for some children in some societies. On the other hand, crooked teeth can lead to teasing—the area around the mouth seems to be psychologically vulnerable. If a child is already very tall, thin, short or fat then having unusual teeth as well is likely to exacerbate problems already present.

Finally there is a further example of interdependence: poorly aligned teeth can lead to poor speech. An absence of baby teeth can result in the child lisping and bad habits established at this time can persist. Badly positioned permanent teeth can also affect speech and that in turn can affect the way a person sees himself and so on.

A couple of badly aligned teeth may seem of little importance to someone new to the study of child development; to anyone who has watched children grow it is clear that the apparently insignificant aspects of a child's life often determine far more than one would imagine, and teeth are no exception to this rule.

Questions

1. Discuss changes in bodily proportions in the light of the cephalocaudal law.
2. What factors determine a 10-year-old child's weight?
3. Milk teeth come and go so quickly they are of no psychological significance. Consider this statement.

Exercise

Take any 10 people and measure their height and weight. Plot a graph to gauge the extent to which one is related to the other.

7
The Brain Develops

The Brain's Complexity

Man's most distinctive feature is his brain, an astonishing organ weighing 3–3½ lb. (1350–1600 grams) that even now is only partly understood. Without it, none of the behaviour described in this book could occur. With it we can perceive, think, talk and move in ways so diverse that no other species on earth is so powerful. This diversity of behaviour is the key to man's superiority and it reflects the much greater complexity of the human compared to animal brains. The enormous complexity of the human brain is in the last analysis what should be kept in mind when considering its growth and its function.

The Map of the Brain and the Central Nervous System

Just as explorers of old discovered new countries and drew maps, naming parts, so investigators have mapped the brain, naming parts. The first scholars were accustomed to using classical languages as the accepted media for science—hence the use of Latin or Greek terminology. In this section the nearest English translation will be given in brackets, and the one to start with is the general word **cerebrum** (brain).

Opening the skull. The exposed human brain looks like a large walnut, in two halves, wrinkled, with many folds. The wrinkled outside is the **cortex** (bark), a surface layer of about 3–4 mm, divided into **gyri** (ridges) and **sulci** (valleys).

The forebrain. The cortex is the surface layer of two almost but not quite identical hemispheres, known simply as left and right. They are joined by a thick bundle of fibres, the **corpus collosum** (tough body). The hemispheres are made up of **lobes**, each of which is roughly associated with different functions: for example, the **frontal** and **temporal** lobes seem to deal with speech and memory and the **parietal** lobe appears to contain those parts concerned with the relationship between body and mind.

At the centre of the brain is the **thalamus** (inner chamber) which forms a junction for many fibres sending signals from various sensory systems to the cortex. Below it the **hypothalamus** (*hypo* = below) is seen as the regulator of instinctive behaviour, including thirst and hunger. It is concerned also with emotions and the secretions of the **pituitary gland**.

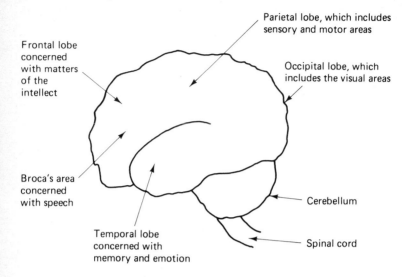

Fig. 6. The lobes of the brain and the left hemisphere.

The midbrain, much smaller than the forebrain, is associated with the control of responses to sight and sound and some control of sleep.

The hindbrain includes the **cerebellum** (little brain), which is involved in the control of movement.

The midbrain and hindbrain are sometimes grouped together and called **the brain stem.**

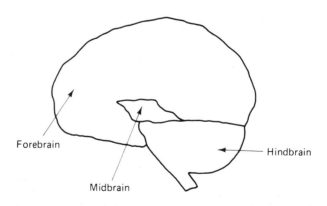

Fig. 7. The forebrain, midbrain and hindbrain.

The Brain and the Body

The brain stem is connected to the rest of the body by the **spinal cord** carrying fibres which connect the brain with muscles or sense organs in all parts of the body. Together the brain, the brain stem and the spinal cord form the **central nervous system** or CNS. The network running through the rest of the body is known as the **peripheral nervous system**, giving messages of, for example, toothache or a pin stuck in a foot.

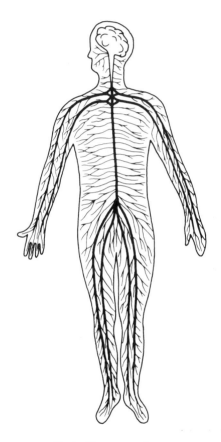

Fig. 8. The nerve pathways.

So far parts of the nervous systems have been described as though they were quite separate. In fact messages are constantly flowing from one part to another and it is misleading to conceptualise the systems as though made up of discrete entities. Labelling is a convenience only.

The Working of the Nervous System

The nervous system is made up of nerve cells of two types. The **neurones** are unlike other cells in the body in that they send out many fibres. The fibres *receiving messages* from other cells are called **dendrites**; others, which *send messages*, are the **axons**. Another nerve cell type, the **glia**, are thought to provide nutritive support to the neurones as well as providing the **myelin sheath** protecting and insulating many nerve fibres.

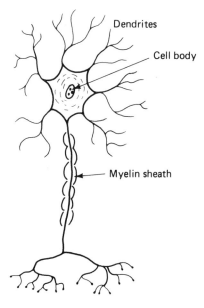

Fig. 9. The nerve cell.

Information transmission along the nervous system is by means of electrical signals which travel along each nerve, the messages passing from one nerve to another at the **synapse** (handclasp). At this point this is a gap between nerves. When the electrical wave reaches the synaptic gap the cell releases a chemical substance which diffuses across the gap to the next cell which then reconverts the chemical message to electricity. The nature of the chemistry concerned is complex. Up to ten years ago it was believed that only two classes of chemicals, known as **neurotransmitters**, were involved. Now it is thought that many more neurotransmitters play a part, each of which may have a different function.

At the beginning of this chapter it was noted that the crucial characteristic of the human brain and nervous system is its complexity. Now that the basic structures have been described it may be possible to attempt to grapple with the complexity by means of some astonishing figures.

The brain itself is thought to be made up of some 10,000,000,000 nerve cells—the figure may be 10 times more or 10 times less. Each nerve

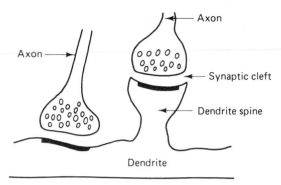

Fig. 10. Synaptic connections between neurones.

cell is in contact with about 1,000 others. At this point counting or multiplication passes most people's comprehension.

Up to now there has been an emphasis on the relationship between the CNS and the rest of the body. In some ways, though, the two are distinct for the so-called 'blood brain barrier' prevents many harmful substances in the blood from reaching the brain. The CNS has its own fluid supply in the **cerebro-spinal fluid** surrounding it and has a blood supply as well. If this blood supply is interrupted for more than a couple of minutes or so cells are starved of oxygen and glucose and die. This is what happens to parts of the brain when one suffers a stroke.

The functions of the brain in memory, movement, emotions and so on are discussed in the chapters that follow. The rest of this chapter will consider development first phylogenetically and then ontogenetically.

The Evolution of the Brain

Developmentally the brain and the hand go together. As Alfred North Whitehead put it: 'It is a moot point whether the human hand created the human brain or the brain created the hand. Certainly the connection is intimate and reciprocal.'

The key characteristic of brain/hand activity is the way they combine to produce an increasingly flexible behavioural repertoire thus enabling man to change his immediate environment more quickly and more effectively than any other species.

Man-apes, living some million years ago, are thought to have had a cranial capacity only half that of modern man, i.e. 450–500 cm³. A crucial aspect of man-ape's life was his use of tools of horn, bone and, later, of stone. As the brain developed so hands became more skilled and so the brain developed further by being able to use the skill.

Cranial capacity as such is no measure of brain power. The cortex has increased massively in the intervening million years; if the size of the head had grown in proportion it would be far too big for our body. The response of the brain has been to become folded in order to fit into the space.

The Development of the Brain

At birth the brain is approximately 25 per cent of its adult size and by 2½ years it has reached about 75 per cent. By four the overall growth is more or less complete. The midbrain is most fully developed at birth but by about six months the cortex begins to take over as the more dominant part.

This aspect of growth is but one. Much more complex and controversial is the development of **interconnections between cells**. Not only is this topic complex: it may have considerable bearing on education and child rearing.

We know that at birth, or very soon after, the human brain has as many cells as it is likely to have as an adult, i.e. about 10,000 million. (The number implies, incidentally, a rate of growth *in utero* of about 250,000 neurones a minute.) But the neonate's brain lacks the complex message-carrying pattern of interconnections that characterises the adult's brain. One of the critical questions of child development is knowing whether these connections develop as a result of a genetic blueprint or whether the organism's experience plays a part. Observations of human behaviour compared to that of animals lower down the evolutionary scale suggests that experience is powerful. With some reservations it can be said that the lower down the scale the less need there seems to learn anything: as **Roger Lewin** has neatly put it, 'bees know what to do with flowers'. But we have to teach our young to do almost everything.

Experiments on animals, especially cats, have suggested two major conclusions in this field: first, experience does appear to be critical, at least in the limited areas studied, and second, there appears to be a sensitive period of the utmost importance.

The two names most often associated with animal experiments are **David Hubel** and **Torsten Wiesel**, two American neurobiologists who have shown that it is possible to isolate certain cells in the visual cortex of the cat which are programmed or 'wired up' to respond to certain visual stimuli. Thus some cells respond to horizontal lines, some to vertical and so on. Other workers have followed Hubel and Wiesel's pioneering studies and have shown how experience affects this wiring up. For example, in one experiment kittens were reared in an environment in which the only visual stimuli they were exposed to were either horizontal *or* vertical. The result was kittens who, when entering a normal world, were apparently blind to stimuli other than those to which they had been exposed. A 'horizontal kitten' could jump onto the seat of a chair but bumped into the legs.

An even more bizarre outcome of this work was another study which brought up kittens in a spotted environment. This gave results showing that such is the **plasticity** or flexibility of the brain that many cells were converted into spot detectors. The critical period for plasticity in the kitten seems to be between three weeks and three months, with the most sensitive time being four to six weeks. (The notion of the critical period has already been discussed in Chapter 3.) If one could establish the nature and extent of the formation of neural interconnections in the human brain there would be obvious advantages when designing the child's environment and educational programme.

The process of **myelination** is a further form of development in the brain, one which continues into adolescence and possibly even to old age. Myelination is the process in which glial cells form a sheath around fibre systems, providing a protective insulation to aid the efficient transmission of impulses. Charting the development of myelination is a way of marking the different regions of the brain mediating certain skills. The auditory pathways of the brain begin to be myelinated in about the fifth month *in utero*; the visual pathways do not begin the process until just after birth, after which it develops rapidly. These two patterns follow from what is known of sensory experience: it seems that the foetus can respond to sound but not to light.

A Second Communication Network: Hormones and the Endocrine System

Instead of the electrical impulses we have encountered in the nervous system, this second network uses chemical messages, called **hormones**, which are carried in the blood stream from the endocrine glands where they are secreted to the receiving organs. The messages are much slower in action since their topics of concern are less urgent, being related to functions such as bodily growth and water balance.

The **endocrine glands**, of which the most important for a student of child development are the pituitary, the thyroid, the adrenals and the gonads, form an interlocking system: disturb one and others are likely to malfunction. The part they play is discussed further in Chapters 17 and 24. They are mentioned here partly because of their message system and partly because they interact with the brain. The nervous system can, for example, affect the production of some hormones, notably those concerned with secondary sexual development, and the nervous system can be affected by hormones influencing emotional arousal and water balance.

Hormones are present in the blood from birth. The precise relationship between them and developmental characteristics is unknown, although there is an established relationship between the secretion of the thyroid gland and physical growth: too little is associated with delayed development of bones, teeth and brain.

One of the pitfalls of psychology is the lure of the simple answer to a complex question. In any study of human behaviour, and child psychology is no exception, every aspect worth studying is multifactorial in origin—that is, there is more than one contributory factor. A close study of neurological development can be seductive, for one is easily misled into imagining that there is a simple, one-to-one relationship between the brain, the endocrine system and behaviour. Walking and growth are examples: we cannot walk at the age of six months because our cortical development is insufficient. We grow, or not, according to the secretions of the thyroid gland. It all sounds convincingly regular. But while early walking is undoubtedly limited by the cortex, subsequent control of the legs and feet are determined in part at least by the opportunities offered the child to practise skills. Growth, and the production of growth hormones, can be determined by emotional factors. No matter how expert we become in understanding message systems we still need to study the origin and the effect of the messages if we are fully to understand what is going on before our eyes.

Localisation, Plasticity and Lateralisation

Already there have been several references to **localisation**: the concept of one or other region of the brain being a mediator of certain functions. Thus the temporal lobe is said to be concerned with memory.

Two main points should be made about localisation. The first is that there is a difference in the **degree of precision** of localisation. In language, for example, the area related to spoken speech is relatively well defined but that mediating the understanding of language, both written and spoken, is more diffuse.

The second is that much of our understanding of localisation and function is based on work with adult brains. The child's brain is possibly much more **plastic**, i.e. if one area is destroyed other wiring systems can come into play to take over that function. (See the reference to cats' brains above.) Indeed, recent work on the brains of hydrocephalic people suggests that even a very thin cortex, much thinner than normal, can function as well as many others. The question of plasticity is still not properly understood and the remarkable findings on hydrocephalic brains point up our ignorance.

Lateralisation refers to the specialisation of each of the two hemispheres for certain functions, with one hemisphere becoming **dominant**. Nearly all right-handed people (98–99 per cent) have left-dominant brains with language functions being located in the left hemisphere and spatial functions in the right. Lateralisation among the left-handed is more complex, 30 per cent having right-dominant brains and the others having either left or less evident dominance.

Some lateralisation of the brain appears to be present at birth, notably that concerned with language (see Chapter 13). However, the process continues and dominance may not be complete until the fourth to sixth year. Children entering school may use both hands equally well but by the time they reach six or seven they have usually settled for one hand or the other.

Work with 'split-brain' patients—those whose neural connections between the hemispheres have been severed—can shed some light on lateralisation, and have produced the **interference hypothesis**. This states that the two hemispheres' modes of processing are antagonistic; when the two modes occur in the same hemisphere they interfere with each other. So if for any reason one hemisphere has to process both language and spatial function neither will achieve top performance. This hypothesis goes some way to support that of Orton who, in 1934, suggested that a lack of cerebral lateral specialisation plays a part in causing stuttering and dyslexia.

Further implications of right–left differences have been drawn in studies not only of right- and left-handers but of different social and cultural groups. Several authorities in America writing in the 1970s suggested that middle-class children may be more likely to use a verbal analytical mode, while their working-class counterparts rely on the spatial-holistic mode. This has led some to what others regard as the fanciful notion that schools should develop programmes to train the less efficient side of the brain.

Further discussions of localisation and lateralisation can be found in Chapter 12.

The Brain: a Computer or a Garden?

Older texts on child development liken the brain to a telephone switchboard, with messages coming and going. A newer analogy is the computer, processing information using a memory store and sending an output as a result of the working of the programme.

One of the world's leading experts on the brain, **Gerald Edelman**, takes issue with the computer approach. Who, he asked in an interview given in 1983, writes the programme? His studies have lead him to stress the unique nature of every human brain; for him diversity and individuality are the crucial characteristics of this organ, a point made in the last century by Darwin.

Edelman's views owe much to Darwin. The brain, he asserts, is essentially a **selective system**, more like evolution itself than computation. The implications of this view are that each individual has a chance for a 'second evolutionary path' during a lifetime. With a combination of chance and necessity and what he calls 'a kind of remembered programme from the successes of the past' each individual adapts in a unique way. As each garden is unique, owing something to the past but adapting to the circumstances of the day, so the brain develops. Edelman quotes Keats's *Ode to Psyche*:

And in the midst of this wild quietness
A rosy sanctuary will I dress
With the wreath'd trellis of a working brain,
With buds, and bells, and starts without a name,
With all the gardener Fancy e'er could feign,
Who, breeding flowers, will never breed the same.

Questions

1. What do you understand by references to the extreme complexity of the human brain?
2. Outline the mechanism of one message system of the human body.
3. What is the relevance to an understanding of behaviour of lateralisation?
4. Explain the following terms: neurone, myelination, synapse, CNS, the plasticity of the brain.

Exercise

Take any group of children and measure:
(a) Their head circumference
(b) Any aspect of academic attainment

Is it possible to conclude that there is a relationship between the two? Discuss your results.

8
Motor Development

Introduction

In its simplest terms motor development refers to movement. It includes the waddling, clumping, ungainly movement of the toddler, the fine skill of the ice skater and the enormously intricate, delicate touch of the glass blower coaxing a vessel from the end of a tube.

It is not one of the more glamorous areas of child development. It lacks the obvious intellectual bite of epistemology, there is little of the controversy that surrounds Freudian theories of personality and, at first glance, it may seem less relevant than topics like memory or perception. Nevertheless, the student of child development who does not have a good grasp of motor skills will function like a car missing on one cylinder.

Some Definitions

Motor development: the development of control over bodily movements through the coordinated activity of the nerve centres, the nerves and the muscles.

Skill: purposive behaviour requiring the coordination of sensory information and muscular responses to attain some specific goal.

Gross motor behaviour involves the large areas of the body used, for example, in walking or swimming.

Fine motor behaviour involves smaller muscles and includes such skills as grasping, catching and writing.

Characteristics of Motor Development

1. There is generally a **consistency in the sequence** in which skills emerge in different parts of the world. This means that a degree of prediction is possible—for example, we may confidently say that a baby who sits early will walk early. (A formula for predicting the age of walking is to multiply the age of sitting by 2.)

A word of warning: motor development is not in itself a good predictor of general intelligence. That is, there is no reason to believe that a child who is advanced in walking will be outstandingly academic in later years, or that a child who is a little slow in walking will necessarily be backward in school.

2. **Stages of development** are observable—in everyday language, one cannot run before one can walk.

3. Gross motor development follows the **cephalocaudal law** mentioned in Chapter 1—that is, development goes from the head downwards.

4. Fine motor development follows another law mentioned in Chapter 1, the **proximodistal law**, that development goes from near to far.

Locomotion: an Example of Gross Motor Development

As an illustration of the cephalocaudal law, the first stage in the sequence leading to locomotion is head movement. Some head turning or raising is expected by about the third week but it is probable that these movements are reflexive rather than purposive. What appears to be a purposive movement is reached around the fourth month when babies begin to lift head and chest from a prone position—that is, when lying on their tummy. This is a critical stage because it immediately allows an increase in the available visual field.

Between four and six months comes the ability to roll from back to tummy and vice versa, followed by sitting without support which is usually achieved by seven or eight months.

Before they stand, babies have almost always adopted some means of getting about: they may **hitch** (shuffle along on their bottom) or **crawl** (pull themselves along by their arms with tummy on the floor) or **creep** (move with both hands and knees on the floor).

Standing alone is preceded by standing with support. The first moment that the child rears up alone, gazes around and thumps down again is memorable, for from then onwards the world opens up.

Fine Motor Skills

The most important point to note about fine motor skills is the crucial part played by the **thumb**. As was noted in Chapter 7, the development of the hand and the brain go together; the development of the role of the thumb is a more refined aspect of the general proposition. One can sub-

Fig. 11. Palmar grip.

stantiate this from everyday observation: watch the part played by the thumb in the next movement you make involving a hand.

The development of the **pincer grip** is a sequence that is given much weight in textbooks and developmental scales, correctly in view of the increased versatility that this grip provides. The first grip that most children employ is **palmar**—that is, an object is swept up by all the fingers into the outside side of the palm. A palmar is shown in Fig. 11. Gradually the grip shifts towards a position in which the thumb is in opposition to the other fingers, culminating in the precise grip illustrated in Fig. 12.

Fig. 12. Adult grip.

Two characteristics of skilled movement, its **purposive nature** and the **coordination of sensory information**, are illustrated in an example originally put forward by **Kevin Connolly**: he analysed the skill involved in eating an egg.

(Before reading further it may be interesting to try to list for yourself the skills that this activity encompasses.)

Connolly pointed out that the child must be able to sit up with head and back erect, must have some idea of what is being aimed at and must be able to pick up a spoon and hold it correctly. Next the whole of the arm must be under control in order to bring the spoon to the egg; too much force and the egg will be spilt. Delicate control is also required to break the egg and to load the spoon. Then a whole new sequence follows to take the loaded spoon to the mouth. A further sequence comes when the egg is put into the mouth and the spoon removed.

Handwriting

A second example of fine motor skills, extending to an older age range, is that of handwriting. **C. Jarman** has observed seven stages of writing which have been linked to approximate age ranges. The teaching of writing is often neglected in schools today; Jarman's conclusions might, therefore, be of considerable practical value.

Up to 5 years	Copying is frequent.
5–6	Children learn to write their own name with large writing and some reversals (for example, *b* for *d*).
6–7	The alphabet can be printed on request but there is still some reversing.
7–8	Most children can now write and most attempt to make their letters smaller. There is some evidence of consciousness of design.
8–9	Some, but not all, letters are joined. This can lead to untidiness and an apparent deterioration in ability, made worse if the child is also mastering skills of punctuation and spelling.
9–11	Writing is now well established with each child's individuality beginning to show. It is essential that teachers allow for individuality; for example, if a child writes naturally without joining letters this should be accepted.
11 +	Individual styles flourish and should be encouraged.

Throughout due allowance should be made for left-handers, who do not always easily adapt to a left-to-right style.

Handedness

There are two criteria for the determination of handedness: which hand is preferred and which is the more skilful. Most people throughout the world are right-handed by both criteria, an approximate figure being 92% for adults. The reasons for this overwhelming preference are not fully understood.

In their early months babies are **ambidextrous**; that is, they use either hand indiscriminately. By eight months most show some slight preference for the right hand but there may be no clear-cut choice even up to the end of the third year. Between four and five there are indications of which hand will be preferred.

It was once common to try to force all children to use the right hand for there are undoubted advantages of following the norms of the majority, especially in countries where reading and writing go from left to right. Now, however, a more liberal attitude pertains, at least in Great Britain. There is, incidentally, no evidence that left-handers have any more than their fair share of reading and spelling problems. Anyone wishing to pursue the topic further should consult **Margaret Clark**'s *Teaching Left-Handed Children* (University of London Press, 1974).

The Origins of Motor Skills

Every healthy baby acquires the ability to sit, stand, walk, run, reach and grasp—whether or not adults offer conscious training. Voluntary actions appear to be built on a **substrate of inherited reflexes** and the traditional explanation for motor development is that it is a **maturational** phenomenon.

Supporting the part played by maturation is evidence that practice plays relatively little part in the development of early gross motor skills. **Arnold**

Gesell and colleagues focussed on this question in twin studies in which one twin was given a great deal of practice in a particular skill. It was found that providing the other twin was given a brief period of practice the two achieved much the same final level of competence. Further examples of the need for only limited practice come from observations of babies carried strapped to the mother's back; for example, the Hopi Indians and Nigerians. These babies develop walking skills at normally appropriate ages. It must be noted, however, that they do not spend all their early lives on someone's back; there is a period each day when they are taken off.

Some evidence *against* the maturational hypothesis comes from observations of babies brought up in institutions. In 1969 **W. Dennis** reported on some children whose opportunities for movement had been severely restricted. They were retarded in walking by up to 12 months and were equally backward in other motor skills. Whether one can legitimately generalise from any deprived children to the normal population is a matter discussed further in Chapter 27.

Ethnic differences may seem to provide a key to the question of maturation versus practice: several researchers have reported that black children are more advanced than others in motor development during the first year of life. **Mary Ainsworth** found this in Uganda and **Nancy Bayley** did the same in America. The maturational theory explains the difference in terms of genetically determined differences in the rate of the development of muscles and the nervous system.

But, as usual, there are alternative explanations. Another Ugandan study reported on a group of children whose parents had adopted Western ways: children were kept in cribs more than others brought up traditionally and were carried less. Compared to more traditional families the children were actually handled less. The children of the more Western-orientated families had motor milestones closer to those of Caucasian children. A similar study carried out in America by **J. R. Williams** and **R. B. Scott** compared black infants from poor backgrounds with those from middle-class backgrounds. The poorer families restricted their babies less but regardless of economic status there was a relationship between the encouragement and the realisation of walking. Finally, from Mexico, a study of another group of children carried on their mothers' back has found them to be more re-retarded in walking. The clue to this group's poor performance may be the fact that they were heavily swaddled, often with their faces covered.

The conclusion, then, seems to be that one should look further than maturation alone if one is fully to comprehend the origins and pattern of motor development. A possible direction in which to look follows in the next section.

The Development of Skills and the Computer: an Analogy

Computer language is a possible aid in coming to a conclusion on the place of maturation in the field of motor development. Computers function with two major variables: **hardware** and **software**. The former is the nuts and bolts of the machinery itself, the latter refers to the program used to direct the machinery. In human terms:

Hardware can be used to refer to the body: the muscles, bones and the nervous system.

Software refers to the person's ability to understand what is required.

Support is given to this approach by a consideration of certain ways in which the computer and human behaviour seem to mirror each other. One example of this is the **subroutine**, a self-contained section of a program used for repeating bits of that program. If it could be shown that human activities used subroutines then it would be worth pursuing the computer analogy further. Return to the child eating an egg. It is possible here to discern several subroutines, grasping an egg being one of them, which are combined in this program.

As Connolly has pointed out, the variety of subroutines is not enormous, but we are enabled to do so much with them because we learn to combine them. There are, after all, only 26 letters in the alphabet but they combine most effectively. If children are to learn to use subroutines in the most efficient combinations they have to practice, but practice in this context does not mean mere repetition; it is the constant search for optimal solutions to appropriate problems. The child may have learned how to use a spoon for an egg, but there remains the need to practise the skill in other contexts.

Two other aspects of computer programs are relevant. The first is the need the program has to build in **feedback**; that is, the sending of information back to the directing centre which will indicate what modifications are needed. The second is **feedforward**, the anticipation of what is going to occur so that the outcome of a certain action can be computed before it happens. A moment's reflection on human skills will reveal how both feedback and feedforward play their part.

The computer analogy should not be pushed too far; humans are not machines and we do not have programs imposed upon us. Nevertheless, to see the body as hardware and cognition as software helps to some extent to resolve the problem we started out with.

The Development of Characteristics of Performance

There are wide individual differences in the development of all motor skills. Opportunity, temperament and motivation partly explain these variations, but only partly, for many children have all three of these and yet fail to become the sportsman, musician or painter that they aspire to. Although it is not possible to explain all differences, some trends across age can be discerned:

Speed of action. The very young both act and react more slowly than older children and adults. Slowness of reaction is of importance when considering motor skills for it implies a slowness in processing information (a central activity if we are to follow the computer analogy). Experimental work using tasks like card-sorting has demonstrated steadily increasing changes in the speed of performance with age from around four years to adulthood.

Strength as such is not required for most everyday activities, although increasing strength clearly widens the range of skills available. More important developmentally is the ability to control force: compare the five-year-old pressing on paper while writing to the dentist delicately probing a tooth.

Accuracy is less clear-cut developmentally. Possibly the increased efficiency of older children is more related to speed of work and to the use of more mature strategies.

Conclusion

The original idea that motor development is an unfolding of skills that depend only on maturation for their appearance can no longer be held. If we are fully to understand motor skills we must pay attention to the nature of purposive behaviour, we must be able to use the analogy of the computer and we must always be aware of the overriding principle of the child working within a system, the system in this case being first the family, then the wider culture.

Questions

1. Consider the notion of sequence in motor development.
2. Explain the following terms: skill, fine motor behaviour, palmar grip.
3. Why is the loss of a thumb of much greater consequence than the loss of any other digit?
4. What is the evidence for and against the statement that motor skills unfold with time?

Exercises

1. Strap both thumbs to the palm of your hand for half a day and monitor the degree of disability experienced.
2. Take any skilled activity (as simple as possible) and describe it in detail.

Part 4
The Baby becomes a Child: Cognition

Cognition is a general term that means knowing or understanding. Included within the umbrella word are judgement, perception, memory and reasoning. To understand cognition it is necessary to appreciate the part played by attention and language.

Because there are so many separate but interlocking topics it is inevitable that there will be some overlapping of subject matter in the following chapters. Perception cannot be understood without memory; memory cannot be grasped without an understanding of attention, and so on. It is suggested that the section be read first as a whole to get some idea of each topic and then read again, not necessarily in the order in which it is presented, taking each chapter in its own right.

9
The Development of Human Understanding

Piaget

Epistemology and Stage Theory

The understanding of understanding was the core of Piaget's work. Known technically as **epistemology**, the study of how children come to understand their world is still dominated by the work of this Swiss giant, whose fundamental approach has been outlined in Chapter 2.

That chapter ended with a reference to **stage theory**, an idea which has just been mentioned in Chapter 8 when reference was made to the fact that children must walk before they can run. That in essence is what stage theory is all about: each step is built on what has gone before. To grasp this is already to appreciate one of Piaget's fundamental ideas.

The widespread acceptance of stage theory in education has had a profound effect on the way schools, particularly primary schools, are run. From this notion developed the concept of **readiness**: the child cannot move to certain skills until the earlier ones that form the basis are mastered.

Stages and Ages

Tables of Piaget's stages often allocate an age to each, implying that this is the age at which the stage should operate. Piaget's intention was to illustrate that stages of cognitive development occur in the same sequence for everyone, but he allowed that the ages at which stages are reached will vary depending on factors related both to maturation and experience. It is essential, therefore, to note that ages are indicated as a rough guide only.

Cognitive Development and Other Behaviour

For Piaget, the stages of cognitive development provide a basis for other behaviour. Thus, for example, he saw **moral development** as a progression of stages that depends on cognitive processes (see Chapter 20).

1. *The Sensory-Motor Period*

This stage goes from birth to about 24 months. The main **general characteristics** are the ability to move and to respond to the environment and to begin to communicate.

The infant is seen as being born with a set of reflexes. By interacting with the environment through movement (hence the term sensory-motor) the infant sets in motion the assimilation/accommodation process, explained in Chapter 2, thus transforming the reflexes into **organised patterns of behaviour** which Piaget labelled **schemas**. Once established, schemas can then be used intentionally. An example of an organised pattern of behaviour being used intentionally during this period is the ability to obtain something out of reach. The infant learns techniques to achieve this.

Less easily observed is the movement from the **egocentric** state of the neonate. By egocentric Piaget did not mean selfish as we mean it; he referred to a state of mind in which there is no distinction between oneself and the rest of the world. By the end of the sensory-motor period children have moved away from totally egocentric thought to an understanding that there are objects permanently independent of themselves.

A way of observing evidence for the attaining of object permanence is to watch a child's reactions when a toy is taken away and hidden. At first, up to about six months, there will be no attempt to recover the toy; after this the probability is that the child will try to pull away the cloth or whatever is hiding it.

Egocentric behaviour does not disappear at the end of the sensory-motor period. Some vestiges of thinking that the world revolves around oneself remain even into adulthood in some cases.

Subdivisions of the sensory-motor period are as follows:

Approximate age in months	Substage	Examples of activity
0–2	Hereditary reflexes	Sucking, grasping.
2–4	Acquired adaptations	Two separate actions are brought together (for example, fist waving and sucking)
4–8	Circular reactions	Constant practice at actions until they can be produced at will.
8–12	Intentional behaviour	Pushing an obstacle aside.
12–18	Directed groping	Varying movements as if to see what will result.
18–24	Symbolic representation	Actions can be represented symbolically without their actual performance. Piaget gave an example of his daughter opening her mouth to symbolise the opening of a box.

2. The Preoperational Period

This goes from about two years to seven. The main **general characteristics** are:

1. Elemenatary forms of **speech** are used in communication.
2. The use of **symbols** is developed.
3. Thinking is marked still by **egocentrism** and **animistic thinking** is evident, i.e. objects are regarded as alive or aware.
4. There is a preparation for **concrete operations** (see below).

The preoperational period can also be subdivided:

The preconceptual stage goes from about two to about four years.

There is a rapid development of **language** but some overgeneralisation occurs as the child makes early attempts at conceptualisation. All men may be 'daddy'.

Thinking remains egocentric, dominated by a sense of magical omnipotence. Children assume that because they have feelings and intentions and are alive all objects must be the same, i.e. thinking is **animistic**. What is more, nothing is seen as accidental: every event has a cause. The combination of all these factors can lead to children smacking a door which has banged back on them, saying 'naughty door'.

The prelogical or intuitive stage goes from about four to about seven years.

Prelogical reasoning is based on perceptual appearances. A frequently quoted experiment to test this is one assessing the concept of **conservation**. Two glass jars are shown, one tall and thin, the other short and squat. Liquid is poured into the shorter of the two and then, in full view of the child, into the taller. The child is asked whether there was more liquid in one glass or the other. At this stage of reasoning children say that the taller glass had more water.

Thinking is also limited by the difficulty the child has in taking into account more than one attribute of an object at a time. Thus a set of blue beads cannot at the same time be perceived as wooden as well as blue.

On the other hand, there is a leap forward in the **manipulation of symbols**. Here is an example of stage theory. The use of symbols begins in the sensory-motor period but by the end of the preoperational period a child is able to manipulate symbols: a child of two can put bricks into a box; a child of seven can imagine doing this action.

The stage is thus set for the next period, that of concrete operations.

A slight detour for definitions

The word **operation** has for Piaget a precise meaning with three aspects:

1. Operations are actions carried out in the mind.
2. They are actions of great generality: combining, recombining, ordering and separating.
3. They do not exist alone, but are formed within an organised system known as a **group**.

The group is a concept fundamental to an understanding of what Piaget was driving at. He saw it as specifying some of the basic structures of human ability. An example of grouping comes in the mathematical process of adding and subtraction:

1. **Composition**   The result of the operation of adding is a third element within the system: $1 + 2 = 3$.
2. **Associativity**   The sequence in which operations take place is irrelevant, it is the *association* which is critical: $2 + 3 + 4$ produces the same result as $4 + 3 + 2$.
3. **Identity**   Among any elements there is always only one which does not alter other elements with which it is combined: $2 + 0 = 2$.
4. **Reversibility**   Every element has an **inverse**. When any element is combined with its inverse the result is the identity element: the inverse of 3 is -3, so $3 - 3 = 0$.

3. *The Period of Concrete Operations*

This goes from seven to about 12 years. The main **general characteristic** is the development of reasoning about size, weight and number.

At this stage the child begins to think logically about things he has experienced. **Conservation** is mastered, as is the concept of **class** inclusion—that is, the child realises that the number of objects in a set remains constant even if the pattern is changed. The child can also think backwards and forwards in time—that is, has begun to master **reversibility**. In mathematical thinking this is evident when it is realised that if $2 + 2 = 4$ then $4 - 2$ must equal 2.

Underlying the development of operational thought is an increase in **flexibility**, seen by Piaget as being closely related to the ability to **decentre**. Decentration is the opposite of egocentric thinking; it means that one is able to see things from someone else's point of view.

4. *The Period of Formal Operations*

This goes from about 12 years to adulthood and the **main characteristic** is the ability to formulate general laws, principles and hypotheses.

The thinking of this period is, in essence, the sophisticated, flexible, symbolic thought of the adult. Children become able to reason about abstract propositions, objects or properties that they have never themselves experienced. Examples come from mathematics, chemistry or history. An example of Piaget's way of assessing thought at this period is the following:

Edith is fairer than Susan; Edith is darker than Lily. Who is the darkest?

Before reaching the period of formal operations children need the aid of dolls to work that one out.

Not everyone reaches this stage, even in adulthood.

Piagetian Theory: Some Miscellaneous Points

1. **Action.** Intelligence, for Piaget, rests solely on activity. Understanding is

constructed by each individual, it is not given like a computer program, nor is it copied from what is seen.

2. **Maturation** does no more than open or limit possibilities. Depending only on maturation is, for Piaget, waiting in vain.

3. **Language** is one manifestation of *general symbolic function*. It is not the creator of intelligent thought but its result.

4. **Equilibration and learning.** Piaget distinguishes between *development* and *learning*. The former is the basis of his theory: *the growth of thought through action*. Learning is an acquisition of knowledge from an extended source. This distinction has exerted a powerful influence on educational thought, particularly in the infant school, for from it has come the notion of children needing to do things for themselves rather than to receive, and to understand rather than to repeat lessons parrot-fashion.

Piaget's Critics

In the past few years a group of psychologists have questioned much of Piaget's experimental work. It is important to note that the questions have not been directed at the whole corpus; what has been most under fire are his methods of testing his hypotheses and his conclusion about stages. Several tests have been reworked.

An example of a reworking of a test is the use of a teddy bear in a conservation task. A test thus considered was one in which children are shown first two aligned sticks of equal length; one is then moved so that they are no longer in alignment. Under the age of seven children commonly fail to say that the two are still the same once they are presented differently. Piaget took this as a failure to decentre. Piaget's critics noted that the examiner always drew the child's attention to the movement of the sticks; in other words, the child might have *expected* a change because of the adult's action. **James McGarrigle** devised an ingenious way of overcoming this by having a 'naughty teddy' come and mix the sticks up. In other words, there was no reason for the child to expect a change in length because the second presentation was teddy's work. McGarrigle found that many children between the ages of four and six maintained that the sticks were the same all along when this second presentation was used.

Margaret Donaldson, in her book *Children's Minds* (Fontana, 1978), has provided an excellent summary of Piaget's work and many examples of research which has questioned it. Much of this section has used her account. She concludes at one point that a main result of Piaget Questioning has been to argue that at least from the age of four the gap in reasoning power between children and adults is much less than Piaget and his followers imagine. What is more, children are not necessarily as egocentric in their thought as Piaget imagined.

A colloquial way of describing the attack on Piagetian findings is 'Piaget bashing'. While it would be foolish to accept every item of Piaget's work as for ever true, there is such richness there that the conceptual framework is likely to withstand bashing for some time to come.

Other Theories of Understanding

The amount of space given to Piaget in most texts is an indication of the weight of his contribution to developmental psychology. Readers might be forgiven for imagining that no other theory exists.

In fact there have been several other approaches, some of which owe much to Piaget and some of which rework his examples within a different framework. **Learning theorists**, for example, argue that it is possible to explain Piaget's observations in terms of stimulus and response. **Heinz Werner** sees understanding as a process leading towards a steady increase in the way people can differentiate and organise their world. There are clear similarities with Gibson's theory of perception (see Chapter 10). **Jerome Bruner** is concerned especially with the *process* of knowing rather than knowledge itself. Readers interested in following up these theories are advised to start with Johanna Turner's *Cognitive Development* (Methuen Essential Psychology Series, 1975).

Conceptual Development

The Nature of the Concept

The bricks and mortar of epistemology can be found in children's concepts. A dictionary definition of conceptual thought is: 'That type or level of cognitive process which is characterised by the thinking of qualities, aspects and relations of objects.'

The essence of this definition is to do with the *relations* of objects: it is the *linking together* of certain qualities or aspects which leads to the formation of a concept. The two crucial points to note, then, about concepts are that they involve **complexity** and a **hierarchical structure**. An example is given in Fig. 13.

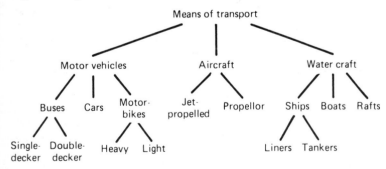

Fig. 13. The hierarchy of a concept.

Other characteristics of concepts are:

1. They are individual: although many people's concepts are closely alike no two people have exactly the same set.

2. They may relate to people, to objects or to abstract ideas.

3. They may be definite (5 cm of wood) or indefinite (some wood).

4. They may have emotional weighting; the closer they are to the self the more emotionally weighted they will be (concepts of religion and politics are examples).

5. Once developed they are frequently resistant to change.

The Development of the Concept

1. Concepts change: from the undefined to the specific;
   from the specific to the general;
   from the simple to the complex.

From this it is clear that general and undefined do not mean the same. Undefined means vague: the child responds to the mass or whole rather than putting the parts together to form a whole.

2. Some concepts depend on others; that is, they cannot be formed unless the earlier are present. An example is humour: one definition of the humorous situation or remark is that it depends on an element of the unexpected. So before one can appreciate that slipping on a banana skin is funny one has to have developed the idea that most people walk upright most of the time.

3. The development of a concept goes hand in hand with an understanding of underlying meanings; children do not at first comprehend 'as if' sentences. So if one says to a young child 'take that with a pinch of salt' that child may not assume a questioning attitude—rather there may be a query about where the salt should be placed.

Some Specific Concepts

Life

As was noted above in the section on preoperational thought, a child in this stage will think animistically—that is, will ascribe life to all and any object, be it a stone, a cushion, a cloud or the moon. Piaget suggested that there are four successive stages in animistic thinking:

Stage One (approximately four to six years): everything that moves in any way is seen as being conscious.

Stage Two (six to seven years): consciousness is ascribed to anything that moves—so the sun is alive, a stone is not.

Stage Three (eight to 10 years) sees a distinction between movement due to the object itself and movement due to an outside agent. The sun and clouds are conscious, bicycles are not.

Stage Four (11 years and upwards): consciousness is restricted to plants and animals or to animals alone.

Death

The concept of death is much more complex than that of life and its development is less well understood. By three most children can say something or other is dead but they may expect it to come to life again. It has been argued that there are nine or ten components to the concept, among which are universality, irreversibility and causality. Studies in Britain, America and India tend to point to the full concept being developed round about the age of eight but there is much individual variation.

The concept of death is one which becomes more emotionally laden with age and experience. For many adults death is so frightening that it has taken the place of sex as a taboo subject. Because of this fear adults tend to shy away from talking to children about the topic and may assume a greater knowledge in children than actually exists.

Causality

Many young children come to believe not only that their parents know everything and can do everything but also that they cause everything. Children who are exposed to fairy stories will come to look for magical causes.

In general, notions of physical causality come before psychological: a child will understand why clothes move on a washing line before comprehending what makes people angry or frightened. This is probably due to the fact that an adult is likely to explain the properties of wind but will not think of discussing emotions.

Space

Young children's concepts of space tend all to be distorted: they see close objects as larger than they really are and distant objects as smaller. As they handle objects they come first to be able to judge short distances accurately but longer distances remain difficult to judge. Accurate judgements over long distances may not be made until adolescence.

Some detailed aspects of space concepts are:

1. **Geometric form:** Many six-month-olds can distinguish between circles, triangles and squares. By two years they can often put shapes into the correct hole and by three they may be able to match by shape.

2. **Relative size** is judged with reasonable accuracy by three or four years— that is, a child of this age can usually point to the biggest or the smallest object. The judgment of the middle position comes much later, often not being achieved in some situations until eight or nine.

3. **Right and left** is for some children a bug-bear—some never learn to respond accurately without reflection to the order 'turn to your left'. Complete understanding of the concept, including the ability to point to someone else's right or left hand, may not be achieved before the age of 10 and is rare before seven.

Weight

Judgements of weight come much later than those of size and for some time many children are misled by a small heavy object which they think must be light because of its size. Gradually experience teaches them that some objects are heavy, others light, irrespective of size, as they learn to pay attention to the material rather than the form.

Number

An ability to count to 10 is not the same as an ability to cope with the concepts of number, a point that many parents do not always grasp. Once children start school number concepts proper develop quickly. Simultaneously with the development of the concept of number as such comes the ability to use number-related words: more, less, four, several, and so on.

Time

Time concepts are developed more or less uniformly, at least in Western cultures. At first comes the ability to locate one event in terms of another: breakfast comes before dinner. Other concepts are developed as follows:

	Approximate age
Morning or afternoon	4
The day of the week	5
The approximate time	7
The month	7
The year	8
The day of the month	8
The time to go to bed	5
When to get up	6
When to go to school	6
The child's age	3
When their next birthday is	4
How old they will be at their next birthday	5

Telling the time also follows a reasonably consistent pattern: at first children tell time by the hour, then by the half hour and then quarters. Telling the time with reasonable accuracy is usually developed by the age of six or seven.

The duration of time is a very different matter from the parroting of 'I am four' in reply to a question about age, and asking any child under the age of seven or eight to think in such terms is usually asking too much. Many children, and some adults, never develop a full concept of historical time: 'the olden days' are all one amorphous mass.

Social Concepts

One of the earliest examples of conceptual development comes at about a month when babies seem able to differentiate the human voice from other sounds. A month or so later they are able to differentiate the familiar from the strange and by eight months they seem sufficiently advanced to comprehend the meaning of facial expression.

A subset of social concepts is notions of age. At first children, understandably, relate age to size: an adult is judged older than a child. Examples of uncertainty in this area can be seen when a child meets a very small adult: the latter may be invited to play. By the age of nine age judgements are rather more firmly developed for at this stage their playmates' ages become a matter of some preoccupation. Even throughout early adolescence, though, judgements of adults' ages are often hazy, as parents sometimes discover to their embarrassment.

For a discussion of social development see Chapter 16 and for an account of the development of the self-concept see Chapter 21.

Questions

1. A little girl was found wandering at night. 'It's all right,' she said, 'I'm going for a walk with the moon'. Discuss this statement in terms of Piaget's developmental stages.
2. How might a physical disability retard cognitive development?
3. Explain animistic thinking.

Exercises

1. Observe a child between the ages of two and nine and decide whereabouts, in Piagetian stage terms, to place him or her.
2. Give three everyday examples of animistic thinking, including at least one to be found commonly in adults.

10
Perceptual Development

Perceiving something means making sense of it. We may have perfect hearing and vision and an exquisite sense of touch but if we cannot use these senses to interpret the world around us we are nothing.

The Process of Perception

The process of perception is the means by which we use our senses to gain **immediate awareness** of what is happening outside ourselves. By immediate awareness is meant an ability to **recognise** and **classify** the essential characteristics of what we see, hear, smell, touch or taste.

While it is a relatively simple task to sum up the process in this way, studying it in detail is far more complex. To understand its place in child development one must consider not only the five senses but also the part played by memory, by attention, by learning and by language.

Perception occurs in **two stages**. First comes the **organisation stage**. Initially what we hear, see, smell or touch is organised into **figure** and **ground**—in everyday language, something is distinguished from its surroundings. An example is a teacher's voice recognised against a background of classroom noise. Next, still part of the first stage, comes the recognition of the **characteristics** of whatever we have heard, seen, etc. By characteristics one means the invariant features which distinguish the object, or sound, or smell, from all others.

Once the invariant features have been recognised the **second stage** takes place; that is, fitting the stimuli into a mental pattern. To continue the teacher's voice example: the **first** stage is the recognition that the teacher is talking, the **second** is the registering that what she is saying is a command, or praise, or a warning or just burble. In technical language, any perceptual search begins with uncertainty. When the perceiver becomes certain that the object concerned can be related to the memory store, so that part of the process stops. Diagrammatically the process is illustrated in Fig. 14.

The Development of Perception

Notions of the development of perception have changed radically in the last twenty years or so. As was noted in Chapter 5, the former belief was

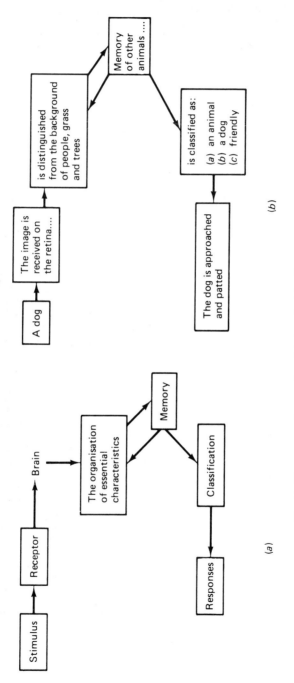

Fig. 14. The process of perception: (*a*) the principle; (*b*) an example.

that the newborn baby lived, in the words of the philosopher William James, in **booming, buzzing confusion**. It was self-evident that a baby comes into the world with no previous experience, no powers of discrimination and therefore no perceptual ability. All had to be learned and the length of the period of relative helplessness, greater in humans than in any other creature, was such because there is so much to learn.

However, it is also known that in every species so far studied there is *a direct relationship between competence as a newborn and competence as an adult*. Research on real, live human babies, rather than armchair speculation, has indicated that they are far more able, in all sorts of ways, than was once thought. Not only do they have a functioning sensory system, albeit not fully functioning, they appear to possess some *pre-programmed powers of discrimination and preference*. There is even some evidence of a degree of coordination between the senses in the neonate.

This is not to say that **learning** plays no part in perceptual development—far from it. There is early learning that the nipple or bottle brings pleasurable sensations. There is learning that the mother's face and voice are associated with this pleasure. Thus babies experience their first lesson in the recognition of form. Here is an early example of the part played by other factors. If the baby is to learn that the mother's face means pleasure that face has to be *attended to*. **Motivation** comes into play through the most powerful need for food and **memory** is of obvious importance. Very soon after this lesson in perception comes learning to smile as a recognition of a significant adult. This illustrates another fundamental principle of the **reciprocal relationship**: the more the baby shows joyful excitement the more attention is given by the adult concerned and perceptual learning is reinforced.

Theories of Perception and of Perceptual Development

There are a number of theories of perception. One example is in **Gestalt psychology**, which argues that mental processes cannot be analysed into separate parts since wholeness and organisation are features present from the start.

A more developmentally inclined theory is that of **Eleanor Gibson**, who sees perceptual development as a process by which one learns to make *increasingly fine and complex discriminations*. She quotes Plato: 'Right opinion implies knowledge of differences'. So at first one perceives only gross differences—for example, the difference between sound or silence. With experience one learns to discriminate between musical sounds and others. With more experience one discriminates between one note and another and the more one's auditory perception develops in this field the finer one's discrimination becomes.

Other theories can be found linked to more general psychology—for example, the followers of learning theory put forward a stimulus-response explanation. An excellent account of theoretical standpoints, and indeed of many other aspects of perception covered in this chapter, can be found in M. Vernon's *The Psychology of Perception* (Penguin, 1962) and *Perception Through Experience* (Methuen, 1972).

Visual Perception

By far the greatest amount of work on perception has been carried out in this area, and the discussion in this chapter reflects this point.

Development of the Visual System

The **visual equipment** of the neonate has already been mentioned in Chapter 5. From birth there ensues a rapid development in the power of the infant's visual apparatus:

0–2 months	**Accommodation** develops—that is, the eyes become capable of adapting to the distance of an object in order to bring it into focus.
0–4	Development of the **fovea**, that part of the retina yielding the area of clearest vision.
4–6	**Convergence** develops—that is, the two eyes are used together.
0–12	The **myelination of the optic nerve** takes place (see Chapter 7 for an explanation of myelination).

Along with all this goes a steadily increasing repertoire of skills:

Form perception and figure ground discrimination. This was one of the earliest areas of study to cast doubt on the 'booming, buzzing confusion' hypothesis. In the late 1950s and early 1960s the American psychologist **R. L. Fantz** produced evidence from observations of babies of only two to three months of age, suggesting that there is a far greater power of discrimination than was hitherto thought. Subsequent work has investigated babies as young as one day old. There seems to be a regular sequence of preference for visual stimuli:

Fig. 15. Letter-like forms (after E. J. Gibson *et al., Comp. J. Physiol. Psychol.*, 1962).

At first the infant fixates on patterned rather than plain stimuli.

Then increased numbers of contours are preferred—that is, finer and finer checks are looked at.

Vertical stripes seem next to be favoured, followed by bull's-eye patterns.

From the beginning *the face* seems to have some special significance, for infants prefer diagramatically correct faces to scrambled pictures which include all the features of a human face.

Pattern discrimination seems to precede the **recognition of shapes**, the latter skill requiring some memory. It is not until the fourth or fifth year that shape identification is well established. Teachers should note that there is some evidence that children who can handle shapes remember them better than those who simply look at them.

By the age of eight or nine years most children can discriminate accurately the shapes shown in Fig. 15. This is not surprising, since these shapes are called 'letter-like forms' and by the age of eight most children have learned to discriminate letters reasonably well.

The ability to **copy shapes** comes later than the ability to recognise them. The sequence of copying is:

about 3 years	circle
5	square
7	diamond

For possible explanations for the late emergence of the diamond, see the section on the diagonal below.

Visual Illusions

An example of a visual illusion is shown in Fig. 16. In this pattern the horizontal lines are consistently perceived as being of different lengths. The

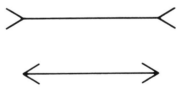

Fig. 16. The Muller-Lyer illusion.

point of this is that it illustrates the way we learn to see **parts in interaction with a whole** pattern. Our brain is fooled by its own previous learning. Another example of a visual illusion is shown in Fig. 17.

Age and the Perception of Illusions

Although many studies have addressed themselves to age and the development of the ability to perceive an illusion, no uniform pattern has emerged. There is a tendency for the effect to be greater in children over the age of five than in adults and they are often lost in children under five.

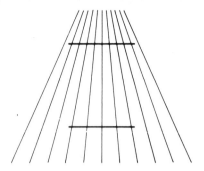

Fig. 17. The Ponzo illusion: are the two horizontal lines of equal length?

Constancies

We recognise a plate as a circular object whether we are above, below or alongside it, yet the actual retinal image varies according to the angle at which the plate is in relation to the eye. Our recognition of the plate as circular irrespective of the exact retinal image is an example of **shape constancy**, when the brain overrides the simple message that is sent. Some notion of constancy seems to develop early. **Tom Bower** found that babies as young as two months appear to be able to respond to some shapes shown in different orientations from those in which they were originally presented.

Depth Perception

Bower has evidence on this area as well; babies of even a few days old seem to have some sense of depth perception, although the inability to use both eyes at once at birth calls into question the idea that such a skill is fully developed.

One of the most dramatic experiments in this field is the *Visual Cliff*, devised by **R. D. Walk** and **E. J. Gibson**. Babies were placed on a flat surface of glass, so designed that half appeared to be a chequered board, the other half a gaping hole (see Fig. 18). Although the entire surface was quite safe, babies of about six months approached what seemed to be the edge apprehensively and most refused to venture over it, even when called by their mother. They had, it is argued, a well developed sense of depth preception. This does not mean that babies can safely be left to look after themselves: some did crawl over the 'deep' side and others were so clumsy that they would have fallen had the cliff been real.

The Perception of Colour

Children as young as 15 days can differentiate one colour from another. This has been demonstrated in an experiment in which they followed a moving coloured light shown against a background of a different colour. By three months infants have been observed to gaze longer at a brightly coloured piece of paper than at an equally grey piece. From six to 14 months

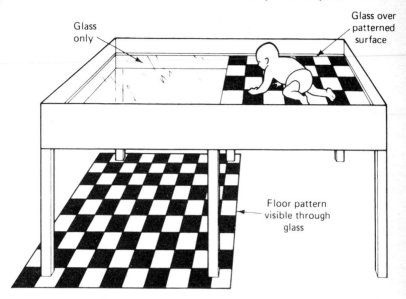

Fig. 18. The visual cliff.
Adapted from R. D. Walk and E. J. Gibson, *Psychological Monographs* No. 519 (1961).

colour preferences are shown, red being the first favourite followed by yellow.

Simple matching of colours precedes naming, but it is probable that accurate colour perception is not fully developed until naming is grasped. Generally the naming of colours comes after the naming of familiar objects and once again red is usually the first to be named correctly. For some children colours remain fixed to objects for several years: the sky is always blue, trees are always brown and so on, so that there is no concept of general blueness, only of a blue something.

The Perception of Sound

The stage of the greatest auditory acuity is reached around the age of five when the human ear can respond to tones ranging in frequency from 15 to 20,000 Hz (cycles per second).

A type of auditory perception required by school age is the ability to discriminate between similar sounds—for example, *pen* and *pin*. A child with poorly developed auditory perception who cannot distinguish between such sounds is likely to find learning to read more difficult than would otherwise be the case, although there is no certainty that this applies to all children.

By adolescence there is some danger for some people through frequent listening to loud music, which can lead to a deterioration in hearing and thus in auditory perception. Some pop groups have registered 120 decibels and 110 decibels is enough to produce temporary hearing defects in some individuals. The Environmental Protection Agency of America estimated in 1980 that the prevalence of noise in that country will double by the year 2000.

Factors Associated with the Perceptual Process

In the opening section to this chapter it was noted that several developmental factors are associated with the perceptual process. The part played by **memory** and **attention** has already been touched on: we must attend to a stimulus before the whole process can begin and the 'making sense' of what we encounter comes only when we can use our memory to enable us to fit the sensation into a pattern of previous experience. To round off this point one can consider an example when memory plays a trick on us.

Many people read the notice in Fig. 19 as 'Please keep off the grass' because this is what they expect. Their memory has led to a slackening of attention to detail. This anticipation of what is to be read explains also

Fig. 19. An everyday error of perception.

why proof-reading is so difficult for the experienced reader. (For further discussion of attention see Chapter 12.)

Language greatly facilitates both the discrimination and classification of stimuli and as it develops so perceptual ability increases. Children learn that what they see or hear has a name, although their early over-inclusive generalisations are often inaccurate and sometimes amusing. Calling all men daddy has already been mentioned; **M. D. Vernon** cites a girl who used the word 'hot' for everything she was not allowed to touch.

Language is seen as so important a part of the process by the Russian psychologist **Luria** that he referred to it as a **second signalling system**. One of his experiments illustrates the point: children aged three to four years could not discriminate between tones played to them. They were then told a story in which each tone was associated with a character, in this case the three bears. When retested on the discrimination task the children were much more successful, presumably calling them in their minds the daddy sound, the mummy sound and the baby sound.

B. L. Whorf was among the first to point to the use of language in everyday perception, asserting that 'we dissect nature along lines laid down by our native language'. The most familiar example of this process is not so much in discrimination but description: Eskimos and skiers make much finer distinctions between types of snow and have correspondingly richer vocabularies than those who see snow as only hard, soft or slushy.

The Diagonal: a Problem of Differential Perception

Many of the points already made in this chapter are exemplified in the problem of the diagonal. It has already been noted that children learn to copy a diamond—four diagonal lines—well after they have mastered a square—also four lines but in different orientations. The difficulty that the five- to six-year-old encounters in attempting to copy a diamond is intriguing to adults and frustrating to children.

An examination of the part played by language helps in our understanding. As **David Olson** has pointed out, the language of the diagonal is much poorer than that of the vertical or horizontal. To test out Olson's theory, try this exercise:

(*a*) Draw a vertical line of 3 cm. Then ask someone to 'draw a vertical line of about 3 cm'.

(*b*) Draw a diagonal of 3 cm. Then ask someone to 'draw a diagonal line of about 3 cm'.

Compare the other drawings with your own. It is likely that the verticals will be similar when the pages are held side by side, but the diagonals will almost certainly be at different angles. Indeed, we have no single word to described the line shown in Fig. 20; we have to resort to clumsy phrases such as 'up and to the right'.

A study of language supports the place of the diagonal in the hierarchy of perception but it does not explain it. Some further clues are obtained from a study of cats' brains. In Chapter 7 work on cats' neural apparatus was mentioned; one of the results of such studies has been the finding that

Fig. 20

their brains are better equipped to deal with the vertical and horizontal than with the diagonal. Perhaps there is a biological reason which leads to our needing to learn about one orientation before another. David Olson, in *Cognitive Development* (Academic Press, 1970), argues that in moving about the world we must be able to discriminate between up and down and, although of less importance, between right and left. Fine shades of the diagonal are of little practical importance. Perhaps our neural structures, our language, our learning and our perceptions can all be explained in terms of primitive needs.

Questions

1. Is perception without memory possible?
2. Analyse the process that occurs when a child playing a game hears the sound of a whistle.
3. What can be learned from the visual cliff experiment?
4. What advice would you give to a new mother on the best way to provide visual stimuli for a very young child?

Exercises

1. Ask children aged four to nine to copy a circle, a square and a diamond and plot the results by the age of the children.
2. Ask someone to trace through a maze, then given the same task to the person using the reflection of the maze in a mirror. Explain the difference in performance.

11
Memory

'We live by memory; we live in memory'—*Hjalmar Bergman*

Components of Memory

Alan Baddeley, a British psychologist, uses the analogy of the library to help understand memory. The human memory is, he says, basically a system for storing and subsequently retrieving information. This information must be stored systematically if retrieval is to be at its most efficient. Forgetting is like losing a book or losing track of whereabouts in the library the books are. They are still there but the information in them is not accessible.

Short-term and Long-term Memory

If someone is given a telephone number to dial it can usually be remembered for a few seconds but will probably have been forgotten half an hour later. Yet most people can remember numerical information dating from their childhood. The difference between the brief memory of the phone number to be dialled there and then and the memory that has been maintained over years illustrates two components of memory: short and long term. It is assumed that short-term memory, what Baddeley and his colleagues call **working memory**, functions over a short period to allow a person to manipulate whatever is in the store at the time.

Baddeley has further subdivided the working memory into **three subsystems**. In an article published in 1982 he elaborates on his approach using reading to illustrate his points. The core of the system is the **central executive**; the two other subsystems are the **articulatory loop** and the **visuo-spatial scratch pad**.

The articulatory loop is responsible for many of the speech-like characteristics of memory: for example, when remembering a number we tend to say it over and over subvocally. The visuo-spatial scratch pad is the visual equivalent of the articulatory loop; most people recognise that they are better at remembering what they see rather than what they hear, or vice versa.

When a child is learning to read all three subsystems come into play. *First* it is necessary to take in a series of letters to be decoded (that is, analysed into sound components) which are *then* stored in a temporary system, the articulatory loop, while the central executive is freed to blend the contents of this store to produce a word. If the articulatory blend does not work efficiently the process will break down. An example of a possible breakdown is the child who has difficulty with the effect of the final *e* on a word. This child has to take the letters into the scratch pad and then, having encoded the first letters into the articulatory loop, has to backtrack and change them because the final *e* has altered the sound of the vowel. It is suggested that children who are learning to read should be taught to scan words for a final *e* of this sort so that they can be prepared for the extra load on their short-term memory system.

Recall and **recognition** are also to be differentiated. Asked to recall the names of children who were at school with us when we were 10 we might be able to manage some but probably not all. But given a list of names which includes all those who were in our class we are likely to be able to recognise almost all if not the complete list.

Memory and the Brain

There are two main contributions that an understanding of brain functioning make to our knowledge of memory. The first is related to **memory areas** in the brain; the second to the **neural process** underlying memory.

In Chapter 7 it was noted that certain regions appear to be associated with memory. Evidence on this point comes largely from studies of adults who have suffered known brain damage. For example, patients who have suffered bilateral hippocampal damage (that is, two-sided damage to the hippocampus which is found inside the temporal lobe) can recall events that happened before the damage was incurred but not after it. One patient moved house after sustaining such damage: he could remember his old address and how to get there but constantly forgot how to get home to the new house. His scores on an intelligence test did not indicate that he was subnormal. An intriguing finding from this patient was that he could learn new visuo-motor skills (maze-tracing in a mirror was the task given). It seems, then, that the acquisition of visuo-motor skills may be independent of the hippocampal area.

An early worker in this field was the Canadian brain surgeon **Wilder Penfield**. Applying a mild electrical probe to the brain stimulates neuronal firing in the surrounding area (see Chapter 7 for a discussion of the central nervous system). Applying the probe differentially to the cortex produces involuntary speech, or what Penfield's patient described as a feeling of reliving past experiences. From this work has stemmed the speculation that somewhere in the brain is a **complete store of all our memories**, a speculation that has been treated with scepticism by some other authorities. One reason for the scepticism is the difficulty experienced by others who have attempted to repeat Penfield's work. It is now thought by many who have studied this topic that localisation of memory in the brain remains an open question.

The **neural processes** underlying memory are still largely a matter for speculation. One theory is that the **synapse** is the key area (see Chapter 7 for a description of synaptic transmission). If work on the sea slug is shown to have parallels in human memory it is possible that the neurotransmitters operating at the synapse hold the key, with both short- and long-term memories taking place in the same brain areas.

A further theory is also related to the synapse but this one, based on work on the hippocampus of the rat, suggests that the result of just half a second's stimulation of the brain leads, within ten minutes, to the production of new synapses. It has been known for some time that the cerebral cortex and the hippocampus can build new connections; what is remarkable is the extent of the new growth after such brief activity. As the proponents of this work admit themselves, too ready an extrapolation to humans can lead to realms close to science fiction.

Memory and Meaning

Explanations of why someone may have a good, or bad, memory usually divide into three broad categories: **input** (or the encoding of information) **storage** and **retrieval**. The library analogy on page 123 may be helpful here.

Much weight should be put on the way material is **processed during learning**. For example, if the word *dog* is to be remembered and only the shape of the letters is processed, memory will be poor. If some meaning is extracted and it is noted that the word rhymes with *log* memory will be better. Best still is when meaning involving a wider network of connections is invoked, e.g. noting that the word refers to a four-legged domestic animal. (See also Chapter 10 on language and perception.)

Another example of meaning and processing can be tried as an everyday exercise. Ask someone to look at and remember these numbers for 10 seconds:

1606185411491399

Then ask for their recall. If they are not recalled perfectly give another 10 seconds and so on until recall is correct. Now, using another person to avoid the effect of practice, give these numbers:

1066148519141939

It is highly likely that the second set will be remembered after only one exposure, since it can be clustered into meaningful groups of dates.

The Development of Memory

Evidence of memory in the neonate comes from observations of **habituation**. Habituation is a technical term for getting used to something; if we expose a certain stimulus to people they are likely to attend to it for some time but then, if memory is operating at all, boredom sets in. Habituation has been noted in babies as young as two months old.

The **earliest memory** claimed by some people is being born. Others are hazy about anything before their fifth or sixth birthday. One study found that 4 per cent of college students claimed to remember something of their first year of life, 19 per cent something of the second and 37 per cent of the third; 38 per cent could not go earlier than the fourth year but only 2 per cent claimed to have no memories before the fifth year.

The **ability to recall** increases with age. By three most children can give

Table 10. Latency periods.

Approximate age	Approximate latency period
2nd year	2–3 weeks
3rd year	2–3 months
4–6 years	12 months

at least a sketchy account of what they have done during the day and latency periods (the time elapsing between an event and its recall) clearly increase with age, as Table 10 shows.

Developmental Factors Limiting Early Memory Function

The younger the child the more likely it is that memory will be limited to **concrete events** or specific places. A consideration of Piagetian notions of cognitive development is of obvious relevance here (see Chapter 9).

A further constraint on the younger child's memory is the fact that although events with an emotional content are more commonly recalled than those without, younger children find it hard to remember the emotional *component* of an event.

Language also plays its part, as it does in the process of perception (see Chapter 10). Language provides an inner speech, enhancing the manipulation of memories. One argument explaining the failure to remember very much before the age of two is that we had little language then to assist memory.

Memory and Intelligence

An ability to remember numbers, pictures or sentences is an assumed component of intelligence. Certainly there is an age-related sequence in the ability to remember strings of digits, as Table 11 shows. What is not clear is whether

Table 11. Recall of digits by age.

Approximate age	Number of digits recalled
3	3
4½	4
7	5
10	6
adult	8–9

there is a separate factor of memory or whether an ability to use memory is a function of general intelligence. A possible resolution of apparently contradictory experimental results is the conclusion that general intelligence is heavily involved in the recall of meaningful material but less so when other material is tapped (see Chapter 14 for further discussion on the concept of general intelligence).

Learning to Remember

An overall pattern of development is one of increasing activity. Throughout this book there is a recurring theme of the child as a being interacting with the environment. In this case the child learns to act upon what has to be remembered. A prominent worker in this field is **J. W. Hagan**, who published a review article in 1971 in which several aspects of memory were considered developmentally.

Techniques of Memory

1. **Verbal mediation**, or talking to oneself during the remembering phase, helps one to remember. It is generally used spontaneously by the age of 10 and rarely occurs in five-year-olds although they can learn the technique (see discussion above on the articulatory loop).

2. **Rehearsal** means going over what has to be remembered. One can observe adults doing this if they have to remember a telephone number for a short period. This technique is, again, used spontaneously by 10-year-olds but, like verbal mediation, it develops over 4–5 years.

3. **Selective attention.** Younger children pay attention haphazardly; the older ones from about nine upwards spend more time on items they find difficult to grasp immediately.

4. **'Chunking' items.** This refers to grouping items together to form subsets. So a child learning *table, cat, lamp, fish, chair, dog* may reproduce them *table—lamp—chairs, cat—fish—dog*, having ordered them into two groups.

Very few children under the age of five or six will chunk spontaneously; by seven or eight more do, and far more have achieved the skill by 10. Within these age groups there are different preferences for associations. Thus the 2–3-year-old prefers to group phonemically (by sound): *sun* and *fun* go together. From about three to about five the taxonomic (or classification) grouping appears—*peach* and *apple*—and by five plus a syntactical relationship emerges as dominant—*dog* and *bark* being an example.

Questions

1. Explain the association between memory and language.
2. 'If we understood neurology we would understand memory.' Is this a valid statement?
3. Glance through a newspaper. Put it aside for 15 minutes and then try to think which headlines you have remembered. Analyse why these stood out.

Exercise

Ask a group of people their earliest memory and see if it is possible to come to any conclusions on what is produced.

12
Attention

Introduction: Definitions

Teacher: He really seems quite bright, if only he would concentrate.
Parent: Why don't you listen when I talk to you?
Child: That's funny, I didn't notice that.

In a study of nine- to 13-year-olds on the Isle of Wight published by **Michael Rutter** and colleagues in 1970 about 30% of the children were perceived as having poor concentration. The remarks quoted above are typical of those made thousands of times a day; attention, or lack of it, ranks as one of the most commonly cited causes of educational failure. Yet this chapter is one of the shortest in the book, for our understanding both of what constitutes attention and how it develops is slight. Some books on child development include no mention of the topic at all.

A dictionary definition of attention is easy to come by: *analysing and responding adequately to signals* is one. But, as **Eric Taylor** has pointed out in a review article published in 1980, when we say that a child is distractible we may mean one of many things: the child may not be interested in the task to hand, or may tire easily, or may find the task too difficult, or may respond in a way different from that usually followed by the observer. Taylor also points out that attention can be directed, switched, captured, distributed, divided, narrowed, sustained, or withheld. When discussing what adults loosely call 'concentration' it is better to be precise about which of these eight processes is being considered.

The Development of Attention

A generalisation about the development of attention is that it consists of an increasing ability to attend closely to details while ignoring irrelevant stimuli. Observations of neonates, noted in Chapter 5, suggest that there may be an innate element in attentional behaviour at this age, unless it is assumed that the baby has learned during the first few weeks of life to attend, for example, differentially according to what can be heard. Initially it seems that babies' attention is *caught*—that is, certain stimulus properties are more powerful than others in attracting gaze (see Chapters 5 and 10 for further discussion). Note that one says 'it seems' this and that; in this field, as in others to do with behaviour in the neonate, we make inferences from what we observe.

A major change comes at about **two months**. Babies seem to be more free in their attentional skills, whole figures are scanned more and a moderate degree of novelty is likely to enhance attraction. This suggests that the simple physical properties of the stimulus are no longer the sole centre of attention; the influence of novelty indicates that the infant's learning is beginning to to play a part. At the same time there are a number of neurological changes taking place, changes which can be measured in heart rate and EEG (electroencephalogram) counts. There is an argument which says that we should look at the development of the brain if we are to understand the development of attention.

But neurological maturation is only one of many factors. An example of another, occurring also in the first few months, is the social process that takes place between mother and child. Think of an infant and mother: she approaches, perhaps making cooing noises; he gazes at her and smiles; she smiles back; he wriggles, his gaze still on her. Both are rewarded.

From these early months attention develops in a number of ways:

1. It becomes **more systematic**. Children learn, for example, to look from top to bottom, or if presented with something to touch they will feel it in an increasingly more organised way as they get older.

2. It becomes **more flexible**. Young children presented with an object may attend only to one attribute, perhaps shape. Later they learn to examine texture or colour as well.

3. It is **no longer determined by novelty** once a child has reached about four years. Nevertheless, novelty remains a powerful gainer of attention, as any teacher is aware when presenting old material in a new guise.

Children learn to attend to **more than one stimulus** at a time. It is known that this follows an age-related sequence: eight-year-olds are better at it than four-year-olds, for example. On the other hand, it is also known that if input becomes too complex a person will switch rapidly from one item to another and back again.

Children learn **selective attention**—that is, they learn to attend to one of many stimuli presented to them. This is of great importance to the teacher for the ability to direct attention without being distracted by what else is going on around one in a busy class is of critical importance to the primary school-age child. It should be noted also that too heavily directed attention can be dangerous: imagine what would happen to someone so deeply immersed in a book that a fire alarm was ignored.

Related to selective attention is **sustained attention**, what most people mean when they talk of concentration. This, too, seems to develop with age but relatively little is known of the process.

Different types of attentional skills seem to develop differentially within any one child. It might be expected that a child who is good at a task involving pressing a button when a light goes on will also be good at one in which all the examples of the letter O on an alphabet sheet have to be crossed out in a given amount of time. This is not necessarily so.

Theories of Attention

Jerome Kagan has invoked the **discrepancy principle**. In this children are seen as having a set of expectations about the world. Any stimulus that can be related to one or more of these expectations in a way that generates hypotheses will receive attention—the more hypotheses the more attention. The number of hypotheses is related to the discrepancy between what is observed and what is expected. Everyday life gives an example of discrepancy: when on a familiar walk we pay little or no attention to the path or the road, but we do look, more or less closely, at a fallen tree or a newly painted front door. Many film makers are expert in their use of the discrepancy principle.

Eleanor Gibson, on the other hand, sees expectations as an end rather than a beginning. She argues that we proceed through four main stages to reach them:

1. **From capture to activity.** At first we are 'captured' by what we perceive. When referred to above this phenomenon was described as attention being caught. Later we act more voluntarily.
2. **From the unsystematic to the systematic.** This point was also made above.
3. **From the broad to the selective.**
4. **From distractibility** to ignoring irrelevant information.

Interactions with Other Psychological Factors

Taylor's point, noted in the introduction to this chapter, is relevant here: a description of a child as distractible may mean many things, and may go some way to explaining the development of attentional skills. Motivation is one factor only too clear to those observing children in and out of school. The child castigated by a teacher as one who just cannot concentrate may be absorbed at home by a model or a magazine of choice.

Intelligence is another associated factor: low scores on an intelligence test have been seen to go with low scores on tests of attention. It has been argued that a crucial skill lacking in the less intelligent is that of attending to the relevant dimension of a task.

Stages of Attention Control

The following stages give some idea of the development of attention control that can be expected from children. Adults working with the young should be aware of the stage reached since responding to attention control needs will make life much easier for everyone.

At first children are more or less totally **distractible**; they will respond to whatever impinges.

Next comes **rigid control**. The child attends to what is being done and tends to block out other directions. So if the child is playing with a set of bricks spoken instructions to do something will be ignored.

By two to three years the child learns to **shift from task to instructions** but the adult must refocus control back to the original.

During the fourth year **single-channel control** is available—that is, the child can switch back and forth but cannot easily attend to what is said while playing with something seen.

Finally **multi-channel control** is achieved, when the child can switch from task to instructions and back, using both what is seen and what is heard.

Conclusion

The part played by attention has already been mentioned in Chapter 10 on perception and Chapter 11 on memory. Perhaps it is, for the student of child development, a better strategy to look at the processes involved in the context of another activity rather than for its own sake. Given our present low level of understanding in this field such an approach is likely to be more fruitful.

Questions

1. 'Attention is the hidden component to every skill.' Discuss with reference to the child in school.

2. Trace the development of attention in the child.

3. What are the main stages in attention control?

4. What is meant, in the context of children's behaviour, by the term distractible?

13
Language

Introduction

'It is by language that we trace with the greatest certainty the progress of the human mind.'—*Lord Monboddo*

'Language is never the rather static skill which many definitions make it appear; rather it is a dynamic, active, social process affecting almost all man's behaviour.'—*Patricia Howlin*

A study of the development of language exemplifies much of the difficulty inherent in the study of child development as a whole. Superficially, one simply describes certain stage-related skills. This purely descriptive exercise, although a valuable starting point, is no more than that. The next step is the attempt to link language with other aspects of a child's functioning—thought, for example. When one does this theoretical hurdles are raised and one moves into an area approaching speculation rather than observable fact. When the highest-order question is raised—how children learn to use language—the hurdle becomes insurmountable, given our present knowledge.

Some Basic Definitions

Language: A system of symbols with commonly recognised meanings (N.B. mathematics is a language).

    Expressive language: The executive skill used in speaking.

    Comprehension: The ability to understand language.

    Speech: Utterances.

    True speech: Communication using a conventional sound pattern and the anticipation of a response appropriate to the word(s) uttered.

    Linguistic competence: The person's underlying knowledge of his language which must be available to him before speech can be produced or before words can be understood. It is this aspect that is the prime concern of the psychologist.

    Grammar: That which deals with a language's inflexions or other means of showing the relation between words as used in speech or writing and its phonetic system.

Phonetics: Representation of vocal sounds by symbols.
Phonology: The study of vocal sounds or systems of sounds in a language.
Semantics: The study of the evolution of the meaning of words.
Syntax: Rules for the combination of words to form phrases and sentences.

Morphemes: The minimum units of meaning.
Phonemes: Speech sounds.
Holophrases: Whole phrases expressed in a single word, e.g. 'milk' may stand for 'I would like some milk now, please'.
Open words: Content words, usually nouns, with no fixed position, e.g. arm, baby.
Pivot words: Functional words—e.g. big, see, go, off, more, my—appearing in a fixed position in an utterance, e.g. 'my arm', 'my baby'.
Cooing and babbling: Phonetically diversified sounds produced by a manipulation of tongue and lips along with throat and voice, often including a high proportion of consonants leading to consonant/vowel combinations: ba, ba, ba.

Echolalia: The reiteration of sounds, words or phrases.
Expressive jargon: Babbling with the sound of adult speech.
Inflections: Grammatical markers, e.g. -s for plurals.
Iteration: Self-imitating pseudo-talking.
Lalling: The continuous repetition of a single sound.
Patterned speech: Vocalisation when sounds can be distinguished but not reproduced.
Reflexive vocalisation: Non-differentiated crying caused by reflexive inhalation and exhalation of air. Normally past by the end of the second or third week of life.

Aphasia: A disorder of speech function resulting from cortical damage.
Dysphasia: Any impairment of language function due to cortical damage.

A language is governed by **rules** and is related to **events**. The speaker must understand the rules (the grammar) to generate language and to comprehend it, or to use more technical jargon, to decode the signals. A spoken language is composed of sounds, words and sentences.

For the rest of this chapter language will be taken to refer to **spoken language**.

Language and the Brain

Take two apparently normal, right-handed men in their early twenties. Assume that they both have an accident, one to the left hemisphere of the brain, the other to the right. The chances are that the one whose left hemisphere is damaged will suffer from some degree of dysphasia while the other will not.

From such evidence, and from work with children, it has been argued that the **left hemisphere** is predominant in governing the development of **spoken language**, including, that is, both the comprehension and production of language. Certain specific areas have been identified as having particular importance, e.g. **Broca's area**, the left inferior frontal gyrus. While there is good experimental evidence to back this notion of the part played by the left hemisphere, for most left-handed people as well as the right-handed, there is probably also some truth in the view that at birth either hemisphere has the *potential* for language acquisition and damage to either in the early years of a child's life does not in itself prevent the development of normal language functioning.

However, during the period of rapid language growth, roughly from the end of the first year to the eighth, the left side of the brain plays an increasingly important part while the right diminishes in power. It is still uncertain, though, that the decrease in one is in direct proportion to the increase in the other. Once the ninth or tenth year has been reached the power of the right side to take over langue function is so diminished that it is unlikely that a person suffering from permanent left side damage will fully recover powers of speech and comprehension although some recovery may take place.

Such is the scientific view of the 1980s, based largely on knowledge of functioning after known damage. In 1874 **Hughlings Jackson** warned against confusing the location of functions with the location of the damage that causes the impairment and it is possible that future work will stand the present conclusion on its head. For the moment we can assert at least that most people seem to need a fully working left hemisphere to acquire and use spoken language.

The Development of Language: A Description

The Prelinguistic Phase

One can trace the beginning of language as we know it to the first communicating sounds made by a baby: **the cry**. It remains open to doubt whether or not the cry of the newborn is a communication of anguish at having left the comfortable womb; what is not in doubt is that there are some differences between one baby's cry and another's. Mothers can recognise their own baby from tape recordings and can, sometimes, judge what the cry indicates.

Reflexive vocalisation is a precursor to expressive language, developing during the first couple of weeks or so, to be followed by **cooing** at about one month. Like all stage-related activities there is wide variation in the ages at which they are reached. By about six months most babies have started to **babble**. Sometimes they seem fascinated by one syllable and echo themselves, hence the use of the word **echolalia**, producing a 'babababababab' sound. Some parents detect the child's first word at this time; the word is more likely than not a form of babbling which is mistaken for a word. There is, however, an element of speech in **lalling** and **imperfect imitation** which can appear during the first eight to nine months, when the child imitates the intonation of speech and may seem to talk to himself.

Two general points about babbling: the first is that it is almost certainly not the result of imitation of adults, for most children born deaf babble for the first nine months, although they do not develop speech inflections. And all children are likely to produce sounds not present in their native language. Secondly, there is no general agreement on the relationship between babbling and subsequent language development, although it seems likely that babbling is a necessary preliminary to the gaining of full articulatory control of the organs of speech. From the very beginning, even during the first few hours of life, there is evidence that language involves a **two-way process** of communication. At less than 24 hours of age a baby may show some degree of **synchronisation of movement** with an adult voice and when, a few months later, they begin to have prelinguistic conversations with an adult each takes it in turn to utter. As one writer has put it, babies teach their mother to talk.

Words

A distinction is made between **comprehension** and **expressive speech**. Common sense says that comprehension precedes expression, but some studies have argued the opposite and the precise relationship between the two is uncertain. However, the comprehension of single words is often attributed to children well below the age of 12 months. It is probable that at this age they are responding more to intonation than to the actual word or phrase used. By the end of the first year one can expect the emergence of **true speech**, with words or sounds being used consistently and intentionally to refer to objects, people or events. This speech may consist of words that no adult has uttered; the criteria are consistency and the use of the sound as a reference. Thus the nine-month-old daughter of the linguist Werner Leopold said 'dididi' as a word of disapproval.

These first words are often **holophrases**, intelligible only when one is aware of the context. It is essential that anyone attempting to observe early language development bear this in mind.

Once the first word has appeared there often follows something of a plateau and the next few months may pass with little or no addition to the vocabulary. This does not mean that language acquisition is at a standstill, for the development of comprehension continues but in a less noticeable way. When the first nine or ten words have been achieved there follows a rapidly increasing expansion in vocabulary. It has been estimated that between years one and six an average of five to eight words are added daily.

This rapid growth is not haphazard. Nouns come early, followed by verbs. Prepositions, adjectives and adverbs do not generally appear until the end of the second year, followed by pronouns and conjunctions. The British linguist **David Crystal** has made an extensive study of the pattern of language emergence; an outline of his work is given in the book he wrote with **Jean Cooper**, *Studies in Language Disability and Remediation* (Edward Arnold, 1979).

The First Sentence

At about 18 months a child is likely to reach what is for both parents and linguists alike the most fascinating stage: the production of a sentence. Although some children produce complex sentences immediately, for most the earliest consist only of two words—for example, 'mummy gone', to be contrasted with 'all gone' which is properly regarded as a one-word utter-

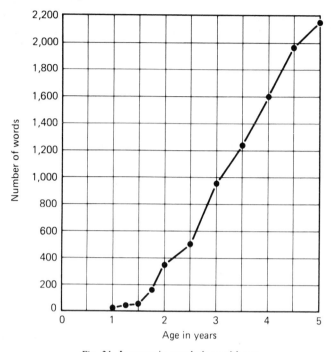

Fig. 21. Increase in vocabulary with age.
Adapted from L. P. Lipsitt, 'Learning Processes of Human Newborns', *Merrill-Palmer Quarterly* (1966).

ance. One 22-month-old produced three utterances when left in a hotel room alone:

'Mummy gone, daddy gone, all gone, bye bye.'

The fact that these early sentences usually contain only nouns, verbs and adjectives gives speech a telegraphic quality. The child commonly uses a combination of **pivot** and **open** words—that is, a functional word like 'mŏre' plus a content word. The use of this rudimentary sentence construction can be seen in the way a child will shorten in imitating. He may hear 'I am going to the shops', but is likely to repeat 'Go shops'. Observations on the **pivot/open combination** led some authorities in the 1960s to postulate that this was a **linguistic universal**, i.e. that all children had this combination as their first grammatical rule. More recent research has shown that not only does the rule not hold for children speaking different languages, but it is not totally applicable to those speaking English.

The Acquisition of Rules

After the first sentences, with their primitive, usually two-word constructions, comes the development of **length**, **complexity** and **precision**. **Roger Brown**'s work is particularly pertinent here, for he has traced a fairly regular pattern in the acquisition of rules.

Children elaborate and clarify their utterances by using additional 'functor' words—prepositions, adjectives, articles and pronouns—and also by the use of **morphemes** or inflections to nouns and verbs. The general sequence is as follows:

1. The inflection -*ing* to make *running*, *jumping*, etc.
2. Prepositions, *in* and *on*.
3. Plural *s*: *cats* and *dogs*.
4. Irregular past: *saw*, *was*.
5. S possessive: *mummy's* or *daddy's*.
6. The articles: *a* and *the*.
7. Regular past: *jumped*, *played*.
8. Third person present endings: *jumps*, *plays*.

The **stages of acquisition** have been seen thus:

1. Little or no use of inflections.
2. Occasional use but with many omissions.
3. Correct use but with overgeneralisation: 'I danced and I eated a cake.'
4. Fully correct use, which may not emerge until the sixth year.

It must be remembered that the acquisition of these rules does not proceed in a straightforward fashion. Some children will learn a rule and then fail to use it as their vocabulary increases and not all children obey the sequence noted above.

Transformational rules come next. An elementary transformation consists of adding to, taking from or reordering a sentence in order to alter its underlying structure. As an example, take the sentence

I can write in French.

A **negative transformation** is: I cannot write in French.
An **interrogative transformation** is: Can I write in French?

Children acquire many transformational rules well before they go to school.

It is now thought that the acquisition of other language rules continues further beyond the age of five or six than was once imagined. **Passive transformations** are not fully used and understood until after the age of six and one study carried out in 1975 found that certain rules governing word endings may not be established until the age of 17. Some adults, of course, never achieve a mastery of the rules in full.

One further warning: Many of the data on which the above have been based have been derived from small samples of middle-class children. Large-scale surveys of a more representative nature are needed to test the generalisability of what has been so far suggested.

Individual Differences in Language Acquisition

If all other relevant factors were held constant there would still be enormous individual differences in the rate of language acquisition. It is customary to expect the first word at about 12 months but a delay of a further four or five months is common. Even if a child has reached the age of

18 months without true speech there are no grounds for assuming automatically that backwardness is indicated. If the child appears not to understand what is said and is not walking either then there may be cause for
concern. A difficulty arises here, though, since it is very easy to be misled
into imagining that a child understands speech when a correct response
is made not actually to the words but to a gesture or to the tone of voice
used. And judgements on individual children must always take other
relevant factors into account:

Sex differences are often cited, girls being perceived as more able than
boys. It is true that they talk earlier and have a larger vocabulary than
boys up to the age of about three years, after which the differences largely
disappear until adolescence when girls again show superiority in some verbal
tasks. Girls, too, tend to speak more clearly than boys, more of the latter
being referred to speech therapists.

Family structure is related to the rate of language acquisition, the larger
the family the greater being the delay. This finding holds up across all social
classes, although its effect is less among more affluent families. A possible
explanation is that when there are many children around the general level
of language is lower than when much of the talking is from adults (see
also Chapter 3).

Adult contact with children outside the family is another contributory
factor, findings on which have lent support to the view on families noted
above. Barbara Tizard's work on children in residential nurseries looked
at this topic and found a significant relationship between the children's
language and the way that adults spoke to them. Adults who used informative
language and who took time to answer questions contributed most to more
rapid language growth.

Social class differences have been the subject of much debate. One student is
alleged to have misinterpreted the findings to such an extent that he
wrote in an essay: 'Professor X has stated that the working classes communicate in grunts.' The professor to whom he was referring was probably
Basil Bernstein, who suggested, in the early 1960s, that middle-class
parents encourage language development in general and the use of abstract
concepts in particular. This leads to the middle-class child using a more
elaborated code, while the working-class child uses only a **restricted code**.
Such a restriction has been seen as putting working-class children at a disadvantage when they enter school, linguistically a middle-class institution.

The early, rigid interpretation of Bernstein's original thesis has been
modified. Bernstein himself has noted that working-class children have
access to elaborated codes but do not use them as readily as their middle-
class peers. The current view, exemplified in the work of **P. S. Dale** in
America, is that middle-class children have a richer vocabulary than those
from poorer homes but that there are far smaller differences in language
complexity or the development of grammar than was hitherto thought.

Bilingual children are generally delayed in the development of both
languages but the delay is relatively brief. There is some suggestion from
recent work that having access to two languages increases the ability to
process material verbally but this work has so far been based only on a
small sample.

Language and Thought

Roger Brown sees the rate of development of language structures as related to their semantic and syntactic complexity: that is, the more complex the structure the greater the cognitive powers that are required to master it. Studying bilingual children one can observe that they will tend to choose to express themselves, when there is a choice, in the simpler structure.

Piaget's notion of stages lends itself to an examination of the stages of language development within his framework and research has broadly supported his view. Thus words (which are symbols) do not appear until the child has reached the sensory-motor stage when children have a capacity for mental representation (see Chapter 2). But Piaget's ideas on language extended further than a simple tying to stages. To him thinking arises from action. In turn, language arises as a symbolic aid to thought. Thus, while *one can have thought without language one cannot have language without thought*. There is some experimental support for this view. Work with deaf children, for example, shows that thought can occur without language and one has only to consider music or painting to see and hear examples of thought without what we conventionally refer to as language. Piaget's view that language is an aid to thought is borne out again in studies of the deaf when it is evident that with impoverished language skills concept formation is both less efficient and less flexible.

However, the Russian psychologist **L. S. Vygotskii** disagreed with Piaget. He saw thought and language as having two different genetic origins. Although he agreed that action comes first, he placed great emphasis on our learning to categorise. Language, which has its own, separate origination, then comes to represent categorisation and so *thought becomes dependent on language*, rather than the other way round.

The American psychologist **Jerome Bruner** moves away from the cause and effect argument. He asserts that language is no different from any other symbolic activity in that they all involve categorisation and the use of hierarchies, i.e. some words are more important than others. Children use these principles first in language but it is likely that thought and language have common origins. Language is, for Bruner, a part of the process of cognition and it is futile to chase after causes or effects.

Roger Brown concluded a summary of the evidence on this topic in 1973 thus: 'Unfortunately we know next to nothing about what language has done for thought and we cannot even be sure that language has importantly affected the power of thought.'

Innate Structure or a Learned Skill?

The debate on the relationship between thought and language may seem sufficiently esoteric to remain happily between the pages of textbooks. The debate on whether language is learned or the result of the maturation of innate structures has spilled over into a vastly greater area. Despite a welter of papers and much intellectual heat there is, though, still no agreement on all sides on the origins of language.

For **B. F. Skinner** and the **early behaviourists** the solution was simple.

Children utter and hear a range of sounds. Some sounds they utter are selectively reinforced—that is, they are rewarded by parents. 'What a clever girl, did she say dada then, say it again, go on, dadada...'Language to the behaviourist is no more than a set of **sequential units held together by associations**. The word 'more' comes to be associated with a second spoonful of food, or another exciting bounce in an adult's arms; 'car' is associated with those things on wheels, at first all things on wheels and later with a specific range of objects. And so the Chinese child learns Chinese sounds and the English child English sounds because these are what they are exposed to.

There are, however, arguments against this rather simple view. One, indeed, is that it is too simple, for it rests on the premise that every word is learned separately, for every word has to be heard or read before it can become associated with anything else. **George Miller** has calculated that it would taken an English speaking person more than 100,000,000,000 centuries to listen to *all* the possible sentences of more than 20 words in his language. The opponents of the Skinnerian view assert that what governs language is not a set of associations but a **generative grammar**, i.e. a **set of rules** which enable one to generate all the acceptable combinations of a language without necessarily having heard them all.

A further argument against the Skinnerian view is that it rests on the concept of language as a **surface structure**—that is, it is conceived of entirely in terms of units which are written or spoken. At first this may not seem to be an objection: of course language is either written or spoken. The point of the objection is that surface structure assumptions are not enough to explain some of the phenomena of language. One phenomenon that it cannot explain is the way that one set of words can convey two meanings. What, for example, does the following sentence mean?

> They are cooking apples.

Are people doing something to fruit or is a person describing apples as sour rather than sweet?

A similar attack based on the limitations of surface structure comes with the observation that the order of words is not enough to account for grammatical relations. It is possible to write two sentences, each with the same word as a subject, but in one at the beginning of the sentence and in another at the end:

> Frank gave the book to Elizabeth.
> Elizabeth was given the book by Frank.

The shortcomings of surface-only features led the linguist **Noam Chomsky** to put forward the idea of a **deep structure** to explain some of the phenomena that earlier theorists could not. If one follows Chomsky's ideas a person producing a sentence *begins* from hypothesised deep structures which are transformed into the **surface strings** that we read or hear. Understanding depends on the conversion of a surface string to a deep structure. To make sense of what we hear or read we go from an ambiguous set of words to the underlying representation in order to decide which of several representations is the most appropriate.

A frequently quoted example of the way that two sentences can have an identical surface structure but different deep structures is found in:

> John is eager to please
> John is easy to please

Both have the same surface structure yet in one John is the subject and in the other he is the object.

Equally, two sentences can have different surface structures but identical deep structures:

> Mary ate the apple.
> The apple was eaten by Mary.

Chomsky argues that **all languages have the same deep structure**. Differences between one language and another are the differences in rules for transforming the deep to the surface. What is more, we are innately equipped with a knowledge of what language is all about. We have from birth a special sensitivity to those features of language which are universal, i.e. which are common to all cultures. To support this view, Chomsky cites the way that children formulate rules themselves rather than slavishly imitating adults. The child who says 'I bringed the ball' is not imitating an adult model: he is using his capacity to generate grammar.

In more detail, Chomsky's view is that we are born with a **language acquisition device**, or LAD for short. The LAD can be likened to a box: sends sounds into it and it is so programmed that it will pick out key features and extract the rules of grammar. He did not, incidentally, assume that the LAD will work on its own, whether the child has experience of language or not. What the experience of language does is to set going the process which in essence is innate.

By the early 1970s Chomsky's ideas were under fire. There is, after all, a fundamental circularity in arguing that we learn a language because we are wired up to learn language. What is more, the LAD implies that the child is passive: in goes a set of sounds and out comes grammar automatically. Such a view of passivity is no more acceptable to theorists who perceive children as essentially active than was the associationist approach of Skinner. Theorists writing recently see children as seeking to *extract* meaning from their environment, attempting actively to make sense of what goes on around them. So followers of writers like **Bruner**, **Goodnow** and **Austin** see children as using language acquisition strategies—that is, they acquire language through a process that is a form of problem-solving.

But the idea of language as problem-solving is in itself of limited value. It may be a powerful notion of what is *necessary* for language acquisition, it is not a description of what is *sufficient*. In other words, it offers nothing new to the basic question of the essential nature of how language is acquired. As **Richard Cromer**, writing in 1980, put it, '. . . we must admit that language acquisition . . . remains a mysterious process'.

For an age-by-age overview of language development see Chapter 28.

A Footnote on Animals

Much effort has been expended on trying to teach chimpanzees to demonstrate an understanding of language. Washoe, Nim, Sarah, Austin and Sherman have all entered the literature. Many of the early hopes have been dashed for some of the essential skills have not been learned. Nim, a chimp at Columbia University, failed to grasp the importance of word order. Although no chimp has yet communicated innermost feelings it could be argued that the failure is not theirs but ours: if only we were better at teaching they would learn. The onus of proof, though, is on the animal teachers.

Questions

1. What is meant by hemispherical functioning in the context of language development?
2. Why is the production of sentences of such interest to the linguist?
3. Critically discuss the concept of the LAD.
4. Why is an understanding of the place of language in cognitive development so important for a teacher?

Exercise

Analyse and compare the sentence structure of a popular and a serious newspaper.

14
Intelligence

Introduction

The study of intelligence is beset with pitfalls. There is no accepted definition of what we are supposed to be studying; there are vitriolic arguments about its origins; bias and prejudice seem to form the basis of many people's thoughts and a political pall hangs over all scientific argument. A strong intellectual stomach is required, as is a cool head.

The Measurement of Intelligence

Intelligence testing has come under much fire in the last twenty years or so, with some of the criticism being justified. In order to appreciate just what is meant when one talks of the results of intelligence tests one must understand the way in which they are developed.

First a series of tests is devised. They may be verbally based or non-verbal, an example of the latter being a task in which an incomplete pattern has to be finished. Once the tests have been tried out to ensure that the instructions are clear and the order of difficulty is established they are then given to a representative group of the population. This process is known as **standardisation** and is crucial since it provides the comparison against which individual results are measured.

The unit of measurement most commonly used is the **intelligence quotient** or **IQ**. An IQ of 100 is average and 68 per cent of the population will score within the average range—that is, between 85 and 115. Only about 2½ per cent will score above 130, with the same figure pertaining for a score of less than 70.

One **pitfall in the interpretation of an IQ** has already been hinted at: it may be unrealistic to compare a child from country A with a standardisation sample from country B. And even if the child comes from the same country the standardisation may be out of date or inadequate in the first place.

Other pitfalls include the point that test scores vary over time: a change of plus or minus 7 in IQ over a period of six months is quite normal. Tests given to babies under two years of age are generally poor predictors of later ability. And some children are unlikely to produce their best if they are not at ease with the examiner—especially when he or she comes from a culture markedly different from that of the child.

On the other hand, if the test has been well standardised, is applied appropriately and interpreted with caution, the IQ remains a very useful piece of information to add to other facts in coming to a conclusion about a child.

Definitions of Intelligence

We all use the concept of intelligence and almost from the time we understand language we are aware of its importance in the eyes of others. Think of the times adults coo 'What a clever girl' to a baby whose cleverness may be no more than the production of a dry nappy. Yet we are hazy about its precise meaning.

According to **Cyril Burt** the word can be traced to Aristotle who distinguished *orexis*, the emotional and moral functions, from *dianoia*, the cognitive and intellectual functions. Cicero translated *dianoia* as *intelligentia* (*inter* meaning 'within' and *legere* meaning to 'bring together to choose, to discriminate').

In the nineteenth century the mind was conceived of as being a **series of faculties**: reasoning, memory, imagination, etc.—all separate. By the early twentieth century some writers saw intelligence as what **Charles Spearman** called **a superpower of the mind** that determined all human abilities. In 1904 Spearman postulated the two-factor theory, which stated that there is one factor, labelled *g*, common to all abilities, with specific factors, labelled *s*, being involved in particular abilities.

In 1921 fourteen psychologists contributed to a symposium published in an educational journal and they gave fourteen views on the nature of intelligence, although to be fair it must be added that there was considerable overlap (see the *Journal of Educational Psychology* for 1921). One example of a definition to emerge from this group of writing was that of **L. M. Terman**, who offered **the ability to carry on abstract thinking**.

In 1958 **David Wechsler**, one of the most influential figures in the current intelligence-testing movement, defined his subject as **the aggregate or global capacity of the individual to act purposefully, to think rationally and to deal effectively with his environment**.

In a powerfully argued book, the *Mismeasure of Man* (Norton, 1981), **Stephen Jay Gould** has attacked the idea of intelligence as a single, measurable entity. He points out that the measured IQ is made up of an amalgam of scores and he goes on to accuse many authorities of reification— that is, the conversion of an abstract idea into a reality. He refers to intelligence as 'this wondrously complex and multifaceted set of human capabilities to which reification gives a dubious status as a unitary thing'.

Philip Vernon's book, *Intelligence, Heredity and Environment* (W. H. Freeman, 1979), is one of the best on this whole topic. Vernon took as a starting point the work of Donald Hebb, who had distinguished between two types of intelligence, called A and B, and added a third. The three are:

Intelligence A refers to the genotype form, that which is genetic. It can never be directly measured.

Intelligence B refers to the phenotypic form—that is, observed behaviour, representing the processes that develop as a result of the interaction between genetic and environmental factors.

Intelligence C refers to the results of an intelligence test.

Vernon points out: 'Far too many writers talk about intelligence without making it clear whether they mean scores on a particular test or tests, the more general construct B or the hypothetical genetic basis A.' The ABC distinction is likely to be helpful in considering many controversial issues.

Theories of Intelligence

As one studies theories of intelligence it becomes increasingly clear why there is such difficulty in defining it. Following Ryle we can say that attempts at describing it involve a 'ghost in the machine'—there is always an observer observing the observer and so on. All we can do, asserts P. E. Vernon, is observe that some actions, words or thoughts are more intelligent, clever, complex or efficient than others. Just as there has been no accepted definition of the phenomenon, just as even describing it is difficult, so there is no one generally accepted theory of its development.

Biological Aspects

A cat's brain is smaller than a human's. A cat is less intelligent than a human. Therefore the development of intelligence must be related to the size of the organism's brain. This is one of those self-evident facts that do not bear close examination, since *within species* there is no direct relationship between the size of the brain and observable intelligence.

If brain size has no bearing on the development of intelligence perhaps one should take a much broader biologically based perspective. **D. Stenhouse** has done this and has argued that there has been a gradual development over time (millions of years that is) of *four attributes* necessary for intelligence in humans:

The *first* was an increase in the variety and capacity of sensory and motor equipment. A great enhancement of human potential came when man stood upright for this enabled him to develop both distance vision and the use of the hand.

The *second* was an improvement in memory and the coding of experience.

Third was the capacity for perceiving relations, implying the ability to generalise and abstract from experience.

Finally came the capacity to delay immediate gratification and the ability to modify previous learning.

Biological aspects of intelligence cannot properly be considered alone, tempting though it may be to examine just a brain and come to conclusions only from the pattern of neural networks that one sees. To take an example: the more complex the neural network, the greater the capability of that person is likely to be. So if the brains of two five-year-olds are examined and one is found to have a richer neuronal structure than the other, it might be assumed that one was born with a biologically determined better brain. But it is known that a stimulating upbringing can foster neuronal growth. Psychological theories are never far away.

Psychological Theories

One of the earliest psychological theories was that of **Charles Spearman** for whom *g* (or general intelligence) was innate, while specific factors were built up by experience. This approach was attacked as too simple, and a more sophisticated theory emerged in the 1930s based on the notion of the schema or **plan**. Plans were seen as the underlying mechanism of thought and response. Reflexes and instincts were inherited plans; new plans were added as a result of experience.

More recently **R. B. Catell** proposed that intelligence consists of two components: *Gf* or **fluid** intelligence and *Gc* or **crystallised**. The former is biologically determined, the latter are the skills and concepts that have been acquired since birth. It is important to note that *Gf* is not purely genetic in origin, it is **constitutional**—that is, what the child is born with. Thus the baby damaged *in utero* may have inherited a quite different *Gf* from that with which he was born.

Summarising recent work, P. E. Vernon in his 1979 book concluded that intelligence 'comprises a collection of very varied skills rather than a clear-cut entity'. It is essential that this be borne in mind when many of the points raised in the rest of this chapter are considered. How, for example, should one regard the child who is unable to cope with physics or history yet shows great academic expertise in music? What do we conclude about the intelligence of the university graduate who makes a mess of anything to do with personal finances?

Related to this last point is the **difference between intelligence and achievement**. To some people, taking an intelligence test is exactly the same as taking an examination in maths or English. Others take the rather simple view that the intelligence test shows a person's potential for achievement and the academic examination shows how far the potential has been reached. A more sophisticated conclusion is to see intelligence as referring to generalised skills and strategies of thought which may have much to do with experience but may not necessarily be related to experience in school. Academic achievement, on the other hand, is more directly related to the experience the child has had at school, experience which will have been determined partly by the standard of teaching and the child's motivation to learn. Although there is a consistent and positive correlation between IQ and achievement in school (anything from 0.5 to 0.8) one cannot say that a high IQ is the total cause of success any more than one can say that the total cause of failure is a low IQ.

If this view be accepted one might argue that genetic factors affect school attainment to a lesser extent than they do intelligence. But this leads on to a consideration of the thorniest point of all: the relative power of heredity and environment. If it is accepted that inherited factors are of overwhelming importance in determining the development of intelligence there will be little point in bothering about the forces of the environment. If genetic factors are seen as irrelevant anyone can become anything. These last two sentences are both gross overstatements but this is, unfortunately, a field in which some writers are much given to the wild assertion.

Heredity and Environment

The Case for Heredity

No one denies that skin colour, or body shape or the characteristics of hair are inherited. The mechanism has been understood for some time and is discussed in Chapter 4. Those who look to genetic factors as explaining most of the observable variation in intelligence between humans base their argument on the finding that all physical attributes have a genetic origin. This finding must apply to the structure of the brain and so there are grounds for assuming that the fundamental basis of intelligence owes its origin to genes inherited from parents.

The argument is further boosted by animal studies. One can breed a strain of rats that is more intelligent than others (with intelligence judged by the time taken to learn to run a maze) and some writers have extrapolated from such work to assert that we could, if ethics allowed, breed a strain of super-intelligent humans.

But ethical constraints have prevented any manipulation of breeding patterns in humans and so all tests of the hypotheses arising from the statements made above have been based on observations.

Close inbreeding provides one such group: there is a general pattern that parents who are themselves related to each other are more likely to produce children with some form of impairment. An example of a study confirming this was work carried out in Japan in the 1960s which reported on almost a thousand children of cousin marriages and found that there was a drop in average IQ of 8 points when the children were compared to controls.

Twins have been a frequently studied example of a natural experiment allowing some hypothesis testing. Identical twins (monozygotes) have identical genes and so should have more similar patterns of intelligence than non-identical twins (dizygotes). (See Chapter 4 for a fuller discussion of zygosity.) As far as intelligence is concerned, the influence of inheritance is measured by a **heritability coefficient**. If genes account for everything there is a heritability coefficient of 1.0 for the monozygotes and 0.5 for the dizygotes. A further prediction which has to be borne in mind when considering the results of observations is that the correlations between children's intelligence and the average of their parents' scores should be the square root of 0.5, i.e. 0.71. Finally, it should be noted that if the 'genes are everything' theory were correct the correlation between unrelated children, or between adopted children and their parents, should average out at 0.0.

In 1963 **L. F. Jarrick** and **L. Erlenmeyer-Kimling** published the results of a collection of 52 twin studies. The median correlation between the IQs of monzygotic twins was 0.87 while that for dizygotic twins was 0.54. A more recent piece of evidence comes from the Louisville Twin Study of 1977. Over 400 pairs of twins took part and the results from serial testing are shown in Table 12. It can be seen from the 1977 results that the concordance

Table 12. Twin resemblance in mental development.

Ages	Correlations between IQ scores	
	Monozygotes	*Dizygotes*
3–12 months	0.88	0.79
6–24 months	0.84	0.73
18–36 months	0.90	0.72
3–5 years	0.93	0.74
4–6 years	0.90	0.76

From R. S. Wilson (1977), 'Mental development in Twins', in *Genetics, Environment and Intelligence*, A. Oliverio (ed.), North Holland Publishing Co.

between dizygotic twins lessened with age, while that of the monozygotic pairs remained constant. The author of the paper concluded: 'The most powerful determinant of mental development was the genetic blueprint supplied to each twin by the parents.'

Identical twins reared apart are seen by some as the acid test, for such a natural experiment overcomes the objection that parents treat monozygotic twins differently from the dizygotic counterparts. Cases of twins reared apart are rare and can offer support to both sides of the argument, as was illustrated in Chapter 4. In recent years four studies have been published, the results of three being given in Table 13. A fourth, by Cyril Burt, has been omitted because of the serious doubt cast on its validity (see L. S. Hearnshaw's book *Cyril Burt, Psychologist*, Hodder and Stoughton, 1979).

Table 13. Intraclass correlations between twins reared apart.

Study	Number of cases	Correlation
Newman, Freeman and Holzinger	19	0.67
Shields	38	0.78
Juel Nielsen	12	0.68

From P. E. Vernon, *Intelligence, Heredity and Environment*, W. H. Freeman & Co., 1979.

Foster child studies. There have been half a dozen major studies of foster children published in the last fifty years. An early example is that of **B. B. Burks** in which 214 children were studied, all adopted at less than one year of age. They were compared with 105 children reared by their own parents matched for social factors. The adopted group were 8 points lower in IQ. Five other studies have examined similar samples, and overall the six together yield a median coefficient of 0.30 between child and true parent and less than 0.20 between child and foster parent (see also Chapter 3).

Children brought up in the same environment should, if the environment is all important, have very similar scores on intelligence tests. In fact they show a wide range of scores.

It will by now be apparent that the data reported above do not support the notion that genetics explains *all* variation in IQ; there have been no reported coefficients of 1.0. But even the most ardent supporters of the genetic explanation do not claim that genes underlie all intelligence, they assert rather that *most* can be so explained.

The Case for Environment

One argument against the genetic explanation, and so by definition in support of environmental factors, is that many of the studies supporting genetic explanations are flawed. The work of Burt has, as was noted above, been discredited with Burt having been accused by some of cheating. Other accusations have been more on grounds of method rather than honesty. **L. J. Kamin** has pointed out that separated twins are never assigned at random to the whole range of possible environments; there is always a tendency to try to place a twin with a family similar to that of origin. Kamin's other criticisms are discussed in his book *The Science and Politics of IQ* (Lawrence Erlbaum Associates, 1974).

Children whose environments have been changed provide some evidence for the environmentalists' case. If environment counted for nothing the IQs of children moved from one to another should remain constant—in fact, they change more or less in the direction predicted. Work by **H. M. Skeels** and **H. B. Dye** in 1939 and by Skeels alone in 1966 has shown that children removed from an orphanage to a more stimulating environment changed from the mentally retarded to the normal category. A well-known piece of work in Britain by **Jack Tizard**, published in 1964, looked at the effects of bringing up subnormal patients in family units rather than the conventional hospital setting and found marked improvements in verbal IQ as a result of the change.

The most striking support for the effect of changing the environment in a community rather than an institutional population came from the work of **R. Heber** and **H. Garber**. They observed poor black children in Milwaukee and noted that although they tested normally on pre-school examination their IQ scores fell to about 65 by the age of 14. Twenty children were selected at birth for an enrichment programme carried out on a massive scale, including improved nutrition and a programme for mothers. By the age of eight to nine the experimental group had IQs averaging 104 while the controls and the experimental group's siblings were about 80. However, as so often happens in studies of this kind, there have been criticisms of the work and the findings should not be taken at their face value.

Resolution of the Opposing Views

The array of evidence and the sheaves of criticisms of both sides' methods leaves some commentators with an impulse to argue that perhaps they are both right. One way of resolving the contradictions is to look at the concept of the **threshold**: it may be that environmental factors are predominant among the well below average group and that the closer one approaches the mean so genetic factors come more into play.

A more common resolution is to accept both sides and argue for an **interaction** between the two factors. A child needs the right environment to bring out the ability that has been inherited; some children are born with mental equipment which is so inferior that even the best environment will not bring performance up to an average level; some children are never allowed to reach the heights they would otherwise have done because of their surroundings. P. E. Vernon concluded his discussion: '... there is no clear cut verdict in either direction. Genetics and environmental factors are always both involved, and their relative variance cannot, as yet, be qᵘantified.'

In similar vein **A. H. Halsey** said that science will serve individualism better when both geneticism and environmentalism are dead, and in a 1983 review of the literature **Dennis Stott** concluded not only that neither side has won the war but that neither ever will and in any case the war is not worth fighting. It would be better to spend time and money studying early human development.

The Intelligence of Children of Different Racial Groups

Between Group and within Group Differences

There is one fundamental concept that must be understood before anyone attempts to come to conclusions on the basis of research data. The concept is that of the difference between 'within group' comparisons and 'between group' comparisons:

A **within group comparison** is one in which all children concerned share certain crucial characteristics. Thus if all come from the same social class and go to the same type of school in the same country it might be possible to make within group comparisons. It might be argued, for example, that it would be valid to investigate career aspirations among such children, comparing boys with girls.

A **between group comparison** is one in which groups who differ along one or more dimension are compared. One example of this would be to compare the career aspirations of middle-class with working-class girls.

The implication from this distinction is that one cannot argue from a within group finding to a conclusion that will necessarily hold generally. So it is possible to say that British children living in the country are less intelligent than those living in towns, if we base our conclusion on test results. We can say that black children are less intelligent than white. But we are on very shaky ground scientifically if we assume that living in a town or being white makes children brighter because the urban/rural and the black/white comparisons are both between groups and certain key variables are not necessarily held in common.

Research Studies

With this warning about the possible invalidity of drawing conclusions from between group studies of intelligence it is possible at least to examine what has recently been found.

Work in America, summarised in **A. M. Shuey's** *The Testing of Negro Intelligence* (Social Science Press, 1966), and in Great Britain, for example, the study of 1,000 children in the Midlands by **Sandra Scarr** and colleagues, published in 1983, has suggested that Heber's observations in Milwaukee referred to above are generally correct: there is little difference between black and white scores at pre-school levels but a gap is observed as the children get older. Scarr compared West Indian with Asian children and found that the scores of the former declined with age, parallelling American findings, but the Asian children increased in IQ over the same period.

Scarr sees no reason to ascribe these differences to racial factors, a point that is supported in earlier American work which reported that black children in Northern states have a higher IQ than those in the South.

Comparisons have also been made between American and Japanese children, the latter tending to register higher scores on the same tests, with some figures suggesting—and so far it is only a suggestion—that the gap is widening. Given that the test used was devised in America it is hard to invoke the influence of cultural factors on the test construction to explain the differences found.

The Stability of the IQ

Several references have already been made to changes in IQ over time: some children show an increase, others the reverse, some remain constant. Two general points can be made.

The first is that the younger the child the less likely one will be to predict later scores from an early test. Up to the age of about six it is most unwise to make predictions. After the age of six test scores do become rather more stable. **William Yule** looked at a group of children tested when aged five and retested them when they were 16. He found a correlation of 0.85 between the two sets of scores. Even so, these figures should be regarded carefully: with a correlation of 0.9 two fifths of the group could have shown changes of 12 IQ points.

The second point is that prediction is more certain when children register either a very low score or a very high one. The baby of 12 months who is still unable to sit and is not babbling or responding to words is likely to be retarded at 12 years.

Questions

1. What do you understand by intelligent behaviour?
2. Is there sufficient evidence to assert that all variation in intelligence is due to constitutional factors?
3. Should one talk of intelligences rather than intelligence?
4. Explain the following: IQ, 'fluid intelligence', the heritability coefficient.
5. Discuss the value of examining twins in the study of intelligence.

Exercise

Ask 20 people to define intelligence and comment on their responses.

Part 5
The Baby becomes a Child:
Personal Growth

15
Bonding and Attachment

Bonding: Myth or Reality?

In the 1970s two Americans, **Marshall Klaus** and **John Kennell**, dropped a bombshell by writing one of those rare psychology research reports whose results reverberate around the world, or at least around certain parts of the world. The bombshell was the assertion that to separate a mother from her baby in the first day of the baby's life is to court disaster. The mother and baby, they argued, must use this time to form a bond. The process is greatly enhanced if there can be skin contact between the two. If no bonding takes place a wide psychological distance can exist between mother and child which, in extreme forms, can lead not only to the two not getting on very well but to excesses of child abuse. This notion of bonding was not new—it was discussed by **Donald Winnicott** in the late 1950s—but Klaus and Kennell brought drama to developmental psychology.

Support for the Concept of Bonding

Some support for the idea comes from animal studies, particularly those dealing with imprinting (see Chapter 3). These studies point to a biological need for a bond between the very young and a protector, for they suggest that the need for a bond is so great that if the real mother is not available a substitute will be cast in the same role.

Further theoretical underpinning to the biological basis is also available from work on perceptual skills. As was discussed in Chapter 3, it is now realised that the neonate is far more capable of making sense of the world than was once thought. Babies seek human contact; the human face is immediately attractive. Perhaps this very early skill is a marker to a deeply ingrained need to establish a link with a friendly adult.

Some Counter Arguments

In 1981 **Martin Richards** pointed to the possibility that the idea of a bond formed as outlined above was more of a myth than a reality. Animal studies are, he asserted, misleading. There are good biological reasons for animals (or birds) which are immediately mobile to form a bond with the mother since without it they might wander off. But humans are anything but mobile for months and months.

What is more, attempts at repeating the original research with more careful controlling of crucial variables has produced negative results. When observers were 'blind' to which group the mothers were in, when mothers themselves were surrounded by others who were being treated in the same way and so did not feel themselves special, there seemed to be no difference in relationships between the extra contact group and others who had only brief contact at delivery and 30 minutes with the baby at feeding time.

If the bonding theory is correct there should be some support for it from the natural experiment of **pre-term or sick babies** who have to be separated from their mother. So far studies of such babies have produced mixed and in some cases negative results.

Richards also argues that there are *theoretical grounds* for opposing the early bonding hypothesis. The main theory on which he rests his case is that in humans the organism is 'buffered'—that is to say, the baby is so constructed that it is protected from derangement from an outside source unless the derangement is totally overwhelming. One factor alone is most unlikely to have a long-term effect. Richards prefers to look to the mother's perception of the separation as the critical variable: if she is happy then less harm will ensue.

Implications for Practice

It might be argued that theoretical discussions and the manipulation of variables in research designs are really unimportant when one considers that hospital routines are now far more flexible than they were. Surely no harm can come from encouraging mothers to be with their babies?

No harm in that perhaps, but there are some ways in which the myth of bonding might be damaging. It might become a **self-fulfilling prophecy**: mothers who are separated may be convinced that something will go wrong with their relationship. And if the conviction is strong enough then it might work to prove itself correct. It may also be too easy to assume that if mother and baby have contact nothing more needs to be done. This course can lead to certain emotional needs of the parent being missed, if such is the concentration on the parent–child bond.

None of this argues, of course, for more separation than is necessary nor does it minimise the importance of good mother–child relations during the first few weeks of life. Above all it does not undermine the concepts of attachment discussed in the rest of this chapter.

Attachment

A definition: An affectionate reciprocal relationship that is formed between an infant and another individual.

A quotation: 'It will be apparent to any thinking person that if you take a sick child away from its mother or nurse you will break its heart at once.'

The definition is from a twentieth-century book on child development; the quotation was the comment of an eighteenth-century physician opposing the building of a children's hospital. He was voicing what had then been common knowledge for centuries: by the end of their first year children have become so attached to one person, usually a parent, that to break the link by separation leads to manifest distress. Although the observation had been made for so long it was not until the early 1950s with the work of **John Bowlby** in London that serious scientific attention was paid to the phenomenon of the mother–infant relationship and its effect on later development. In part this effect is said to be seen in the way the child's later personality is determined (see Chapter 18) and in part it is related to social development, hence its inclusion at this point.

At first attention was focused on the effects of separation from the mother, with particular reference to the distress experienced by children in hospital. Later came an extension to look at the development of attachment and bonding in its own right.

Theories of Attachment

The **psychoanalytic view** (see Chapter 2) is that attachment is a manifestation of drives that are present throughout psychosexual development. The mother is the first external object towards which psychosexual energy is directed and so becomes the prime attachment object. (Object here is used in a technical sense; it is not intended that mothers should be dehumanised.)

The **ethological view** is that on which Bowlby drew in his writing. It argues that in the distant past any being which was not protected while very young would be eaten by a predator. Hence there is a good biological basis in the young forming a close attachment to an adult who will act as a protector.

At the same time, young children have to learn to explore their environment and so a behaviour pattern has developed which allows toddlers to toddle, and to explore, while anchoring them to the security of their attachment figure.

Mother–Infant Interactions

Attachment is a prime example of the interactive nature of child development. Not only does the infant recognise the mother's face and voice, but he, by his crying, smiling, wriggling and kicking, exerts a powerful influence on the mother. One of the critical elements in this early interaction is **turn-taking**: first I do something, then you do; first I look, then you do; first I suck, then you jiggle me about a bit until I start to suck again.

Two crucially important bits of behaviour at this stage, i.e. in the first few months, are **gazing** and **smiling**. Some mothers say that when they were first aware of their baby returning a gaze, or a smile, they really felt that this was 'their' baby. To examine the importance of gaze and smile we can consider, as **Salma Fraiberg** did, the behaviour of blind babies and their mothers. Blind babies do not smile as early as the sighted do and they cannot, of course, return a social smile or gaze. When their mother comes into a room they do not respond by smiling and waving everything about, like sighted children; instead they 'still'—that is, they stop moving and listen. Mothers tend to interpret this stilling, which is usually coupled with a passive facial expression, as depression. Eight of the ten mothers Fraiberg studied had to be taught to read their baby's signals. As Fraiberg herself concluded: 'What we miss in the blind baby, apart from the eyes that do not see, is the vocabulary of signs and signals that provides the most elementary and vital sense of discourse long before words have meanings.'

It is this discourse, this utilisation of the bricks of attachment, which forms the earliest social behaviour of child and mother.

The Development of Attachments

Up to the age of about 7 months the baby is likely to show indiscriminate attachment; that is, he will be quietened by anyone picking him up, he will discriminate his mother but his behaviour is governed by an immediate reciprocal interchange with whoever is with him. **After about 7 months**, and the reported age has varied from 3 to 15 months, there is evidence of specific attachment; that is, the baby will seek out one person, usually the mother, will show fear of strangers even if they are friendly in manner and will begin the 'I want my mummy' phase. This phenomenon is common to a wide range of species including birds, dogs and sheep. The characteristic behaviour of the young creature is the seeking of proximity to the mother or mother figure, and this need for physical closeness gives rise to the term 'attachment'.

Recognising Attachment

A necessary part of attachment behaviour, as was mentioned above, is **differential responsiveness**—that is, one person is singled out as a haven of safety, and greetings, smiles and other forms of communication are no longer indiscriminate. But while differential responsiveness is necessary it is not sufficient in itself to describe attachment. Infants as well as neonates are interested in novelty and differential interest may not indicate attachment to a person. They may even spend more time playing with strangers than their own parents. The features of behaviour allowing a recognition of attachment are:

1. **The effects of anxiety.** If a child is made anxious play is inhibited, and attachment is intensified. Children will often choose to play with a peer but will go to a parent for comfort when distressed. It is important to remember that this cannot be explained simply as learned behaviour. **H. F. Harlow** and colleagues have shown that infant monkeys will cling to a cloth figure when made anxious and both monkey and human infants have been observed to turn for shelter to their mother even if that mother has frequently abused them physically.

2. **A secure base** is provided by an attachment figure. Once children have attached they are more easily able to explore in the secure knowledge that they can return to their secure base for safety. This leads to the apparently paradoxical finding that children will move about more freely in the presence of their mother than when she is not with them. This secure base effect is also seen with inanimate objects such as a blanket, sometimes known as transitional objects. As with the Harlows' cloth mother it appears that the presence of the object is enough.

3. **Reduction of anxiety** is a third characteristic feature, closely overlapping the second outlined above. A frequently repeated observation is the reduction of distress shown by children in hospital when a parent is able

to stay with them. This was recognised by the Ministry of Health in the **Platt Report** of 1959; sadly there are still some hospitals in Britain where visiting children is restricted.

4. Finally, and once again linked with the previous features, is **separation-protest**. **James Robertson** and **John Bowlby** have described a sequence of behaviour seen in children admitted to hospital alone. At first the chldren protest, they are angry and tearful, then they despair, being apathetic and miserable, and finally they become detached, seeming to have settled down. This detachment can easily be misconstrued to indicate that the child is now happy. From the point of view of the student of attachment it is interesting to note that this behaviour pattern is rarely seen in children under the age of six or seven months.

One Attachment or Several?

So far reference has been made to the mother, the mother substitute or the caregiver—all in the singular. In everyday discourse the phrase 'I want my mummy' triggers off a range of thoughts and emotions in a way that 'I want my daddy' does not. One study of 58 children showed that 55 of them developed an initial attachment to their mothers. But by the time they had reached 18 months three quarters of them had also developed an attachment to their fathers and in about one third of the group the most intense relationship was with someone other than the mother. What is more, about one third had also become attached to an inanimate object, a blanket or a cuddly toy, the attachment generally developing during the second year. One interpretation of multiple attachments might be that the child is searching around because the original mother bond is insufficiently strong. In fact, the opposite seems to be the case: a firm initial attachment facilitates further firm relationships. It is worth noting in this context that institutionalised children seem rarely to become attached to a cuddly toy.

Bowlby argues that there is a qualitative difference between the first and subsequent relationships. There is, he asserts, an innate bias towards attachment to one figure. Subsequent attachments are different in kind and figures/objects are not interchangeable. Research evidence supports Bowlby only in part. There are good grounds for seeing attachments as hierarchical, i.e. children will go to one in preference to others. But the specific features of attachment noted above can be applied to siblings, to fathers and to inanimate objects. That is to say, multiple attachments are not necessarily different in kind.

Reciprocity and the Effects of Attachment

Nurturing mother, abusing mother, father or teddy bear, all can become attachment figures but not all provide for the child in the same way. Monkeys may turn to a cloth mother in the absence of a real one but this attachment does not lead to normal parent–child or peer relationships subsequently in the way that an attachment to a real mother monkey does.

An analysis of data from animal experiments and human observation leads to the conclusion that a feature crucial in the determination of the outcome of attachment, just as it is to its establishment in the first place, is the **reciprocal** nature of the behaviour: if the mother (or father) responds positively the attachment is likely to be productive. Experience on Israeli kibbutzim is relevant here: children form much stronger attachments with parents who interact intensively for a couple of hours a day than they do with the nursery nurse who looks after them during the rest of the day.

Determinants of Attachment

(*a*) **Within the child.** The effect of visual handicap on attachment has already been mentioned. Blind babies, incidentally, can relate to their mothers but attachment behaviour may be delayed. Some infants, 'non-cuddlers', resist early physical contact but once again their attachments tend to be delayed rather than avoided altogether.

(*b*) **Time and situational factors** are immediately apparent to anyone who has observed young children. They become more clinging when they are tired, hungry, unwell, anxious, uncomfortable or in pain.

(*c*) **Within the attachment person or object.** Softness and movement seem to be the two common features within attachment figures. As was noted above, providing food is not.

(*d*) **Fear of strangers** may develop at about the same time as an attachment but the two are probably not related. In individual children the two phenomena do not always appear simultaneously and fear of strangers is not the same as separation anxiety: a child may show fear even when with the mother.

Bonding, Attachment and Later Social Relationships

There is report after report on the development of attachments in early infancy but much less information on the influence of early relationships on those occurring later. Some writers have suggested that bonding provides a basis on which subsequent social relationships are built and others have asserted that such a proposition is 'disastrously wrong'. In fact hard data on this topic are not available and much argument is based on speculation. The following points can, however, be made at least about attachment with some confidence:

1. Children tolerate separations more readily as they grow older; by $6\frac{1}{2}$ or 7 few are distressed by a short separation per se. The ties may not be any weaker; it may be that children become better at understanding what is happening and can predict a reunion.

2. Children reared in institutions are less likely to form deep relationships as they grow older and even by the age of eight will be more attention-seeking, restless and disobedient than their peers. The picture is not the same among foster children born in similarly disadvantaged circumstances, an argument for the value of an early attachment (see below on sensitive periods).

Sensitive Periods

The notion of the sensitive period is discussed in Chapter 3. An extreme view is that there is a critical period (i.e. one that is all or nothing and limited in time) lasting only a few hours after the child's birth. If attachments are not made then disaster may loom. A more relaxed assertion is that attachments can be formed only in infancy.

Evidence on this topic is found in the work of **Barbara Tizard** and **Jill Hodges**. They looked at the outcome for children who were adopted or fostered from an institution and found that most children and adoptive parents formed an attachment even if the adoption took place when the child was up to eight years old.

Attachments in Adulthood

Much attention is paid to attachments in infancy and some to those formed in early childhood. Less immediately obvious is their importance in adulthood. The death of a parent or spouse is a significant precipitant of depression or suicide; the lack of a close attachment figure seems to increase vulnerability to depression in women at least (depression in men has been less frequently studied). The loss of a parent in childhood provides a predisposition to depression in adulthood, suggesting some continuity from childhood on. Evidence is not currently available to enable one to make firm pronouncements on the direct link between children's attachments and those formed or maintained in adulthood. So much is likely to have happened to a child deprived of all infant attachments that it would be difficult to disentangle multiple causes of subsequent behaviour. The possibility of a link remains.

Questions

1. The notion of bonding is valuable but erroneous. Discuss this statement.
2. Consider some of the arguments for and against parents being in hospital with their children.
3. Should mothers of young children be forbidden to go out to work?
4. What would you look for if you were examining attachment between a young child and a parent?
5. What can be learned about attachment signals from a blind baby?

16
Social Development

The Human Being: a Social Animal

One of the quickest ways to produce symptoms of insanity is to isolate a person as totally as possible. In Britain there is a phrase 'to send someone to Coventry' meaning to refuse to associate with that person. The origin of the phrase is uncertain but appears to be traceable to the Civil War when certain prisoners were sent to the city of that name.

A more drastic isolation is observable in the so-called stimulus deprivation experiments when people are isolated not only from human contact but from all other contact as well. They are placed in a bath of water which is kept at blood heat, in a darkened room with background noise so balanced that there is no detectable change. At first most people experience a sense of peace but within a very short time they begin to hallucinate.

Both the laboratory experiment and the practice of sending to Coventry point up the fact that humans are social beings—that is, we are almost as dependent on contact with others as we are on food and drink.

Characteristics of Social Development

A definition of social development is **the acquisition of the ability to behave in accordance with social expectations**. A less formal definition might be 'learning the rules of the game'.

The process by which one learns the rules is called **socialisation**, a process which includes three components:

1. **Learning how to behave.** This involves first of all coming to understand what the rules are and then learning to obey them.

2. **Playing approved social roles.** Every group has its own defined roles that people are expected to play: parents are not supposed to behave like children; medical students are indulged but once they qualify they are expected to behave like doctors.

3. **Developing social attitudes.** Children realise the value of group membership and feel a need to join.

Variations on the Theme of the Social Person

Social people fit into the three processes of socialisation noted above. They are, as a result, accepted into the group with which they identify.

Gregarious people crave company, the nature of the contact being less important than its existence.

Nonsocial people do not fit into the three processes noted above.

Unsocial people are not sensitive to group expectations and so do not behave in an acceptable way.

Antisocial people do not behave in an acceptable way, not because of a lack of awareness of group expectations but because they wish to flout norms of behaviour.

Identification, Modelling and Role Playing: the Process of Social Learning

Identification is the process by which an individual behaves, or imagines himself behaving, as if he were another person. At a **superficial** level one identifies with a character in a novel, film or play and imagines oneself behaving like that character. At a **deeper** level, one imitates a person to whom one is closely tied emotionally.

Modelling one's behaviour on another is a form of imitation. Some children in play model themselves on their parents, probably unconsciously, and on their teachers much more consciously.

Role playing is a more elaborate form of imitation, in which a person takes on a more total aspect of someone else's behaviour. An example of early role playing is found in games like 'mothers and fathers' when children adopt the roles of adults, as far, that is, as constraints of age and the situation allow.

Examples of the power of role playing as a socialisation process can be seen in the way we give labels to other people. These labels may be based on some incident or on a series of incidents. So one child may call another a 'crybaby' or a 'nosy parker'. A teacher may call a child stupid or clever. According to role theory these labels then become **self-fulfilling prophecies**— that is, the children's behaviour is influenced by the way they think they have been labelled. As so often is the case everyday language bears out psychological theory: 'give a dog a bad name' is a phrase that sums up this point admirably. (See also Chapter 21 on the development of self-concepts.)

Socialisation and the Stability of the Group

One of the major purposes of socialisation is the promotion of **social stability** —that is, ensuring that the group stays together as a cohesive whole. Groups that feel secure can tolerate a much wider range of behaviour; groups that are vulnerable demand a higher degree of conformity. Consider as examples of this the toleration extended towards the upper-class British eccentric and, on the other hand, the strict rules of conformity surrounding members of an ethnic or religious minority, especially one that is persecuted.

Group in this context has an elastic definition; it can refer to a subculture. Any society can have a number of subcultures within it. Children may belong to several groups or subcultures at any one time: one at home, one at school, one in the street.

Expectations felt by an individual vary according to **sex**. Roles open to

Table 14. Developmental tasks for childhood.

Birth to 6 years

Learning to walk
Learning to take solid foods
Learning to talk
Learning to control the elimination of body wastes
Learning sex differences and sexual modesty
Achieving physiological stability
Forming simple concepts of social and physical reality
Learning to relate oneself emotionally to parents, siblings and other people
Learning to distinguish right and wrong and developing a conscience

6 to 12 years

Learning physical skills necessary for ordinary games
Building wholesome attitudes towards oneself as a growing organism
Learning to get along with age mates
Learning an appropriate masculine or feminine sex role
Developing fundamental skills in reading, writing and calculating
Developing concepts necessary for everyday living
Developing conscience, morality and a scale of values
Achieving personal independence
Developing attitudes towards social groups and institutions

From R. J. Havinghurst, *Developmental Tasks and Education*, McKay, 1972.

girls are, in most Western societies, more variable than those available to boys. For example, it is acceptable for an eight-year-old girl to wear jeans and join in boys' games; heaven help the boy who wears a skirt and pushes a toy pram. (See also chapter 19.)

Expectations also vary by **age**. **R. J. Havinghurst** has drawn up a list of **developmental tasks** which have to be achieved at certain ages if children are to be accepted in their group (see Table 14). It must be remembered that this list applies to Western societies; it may not be valid in other cultures.

Development Patterns of Socialisation

The shape of the developmental pattern is one of increasing width: there is a steadily increasing range of people exerting an influence, from the members of the immediate family to the community as a whole.

The Early Years

Neonates behave in an **autistic** fashion: they seem non-gregarious, interested only in their own bodily comforts. (This is not to say, of course, that they are autistic in the pathological sense.)

By about **three weeks** they are beginning to show some awareness of others, by waving and kicking in response to mother's arrival, by ceasing to cry when picked up and above all by smiling.

Smiling is one of the first signs of feeling to be looked for by parents. They may find themselves looking within the first few days of the child's life, for smiles of a sort may be evident then—smiles, than is, which are little more than a turning up of the corners of the mouth. They often occur during sleep and seem not to be related to activity or state and therefore cannot be construed as 'true' smiles.

A gentle touch or jiggling of the baby may produce a mouth-only smile at one to two weeks and within a couple more weeks this smile has broadened to include the eyes as well as the mouth. During this period a human voice or vigorous physical activity can be added as smile producers.

From five to eight weeks voices become less and faces more important, especially after the smile links up with eye contact and becomes a piece of social behaviour rather than just a response to a stimulus. This is the time that what some regard as a 'true' smile emerges; without it the child's social relationships are gravely hampered.

Laughter shows much individual variation but usually appears around the fourth month as a response to vigorous stimulation. Its course follows that of the smile in that by seven to nine months there enters a cognitive component, i.e. babies laugh in response to something they appear to perceive as being funny, such as a peculiar walk or a deliberately funny face pulled by a parent. The physiological correlates of laughter and tears are, incidentally, identical: first there is a deceleration of heart rate followed by a quickening, suggesting that both are tension reducers. In this context it is interesting to reflect on the way that some people laugh when they are very nervous.

Laughter is contagious; that is, babies laugh more when with others than when alone—an observation that is true of most adults as well. As they get older children learn to laugh, or display joyous feelings in some other way, in a manner that is acceptable to their group, which frequently means that they are expected to exercise control over the more raucous behaviour of earlier years.

Affectionate behaviour covers a wider spectrum than smiling and laughing although there is much in common between the two. Affection has been defined by **Elizabeth Hurlock** as warm regard, friendliness, sympathy or helpfulness. It must be reciprocated if it is to flourish; as Hurlock points out, 'Love seems to be a two-way affair and grows best when it is both given and received.'

It may be objected that it is glaringly obvious that love is two-way. Much less easy to make any sweeping generalisation about is the amount of affection that should be given to a child. At this point there will be some who say that statement is meaningless—one cannot give too much. On the other hand, what to one person is the giving of affection is spoiling to another: there is a case to be made for a child needing the security of being controlled. Affection which manifests itself only as indulgence is likely to lead to as distorted an outcome as a withdrawal of love.

The earliest expressions of affection from a baby are essentially outgoing and physical. The gaze is fixed on the other's face and there is a rapid, 'all systems go', movement of arms and legs, within a few months developing into an active cuddling back in response to an adult's embrace. After the first year hugging and stroking become the favoured way for a child to show affection, to pets, toys and humans and many pets become properly wary of the loving grip of a toddler. Once school is reached the overt physical expresssion of affection often diminishes, although it does not necessarily go altogether and there is wide individual variation in the amount that children will show of their feelings physically.

Reactions to other babies are usually first noted around the fourth or fifth month when there is some social smiling from one to the other. By the sixth or seventh month babies may stretch out to one another and by 12 months there may even be some rudimentary cooperative play.

The Pregang Age

For the first two or three years **the family** remains the paramount influence but from then on there is competition from **peer groups** and from significant adults outside the family. Attending a nursery school or preschool playgroup can provide a good preparation for later encounters with peers. It has been found that those children who had satisfactory relations in the preschool period found it easier to make friends once they were at school.

This period is most often studied through play. At first children play in parallel, happy to be with each other but interacting little. By three or four they will have begun to talk to each other while playing, will have the habit of selecting playmates and will have begun also to watch each other while playing (see also Chapter 22).

The first day at **school** is a major event in childhood and the child's first teacher is a key figure in subsequent development. The influence of schools generally has been mentioned in Chapter 3. Of particular influence in the context of this chapter is the prevailing atmosphere of the classroom, which depends in turn on the personality of the teacher. A frequently quoted study examining this field is that published in 1939 by **K. Lewin**, **R. Lippitt** and **R. K. White**. Ten-year-old children took part in recreational activities led by instructors who adopted an authoritarian, a democratic or a permissive style of leadership. The authoritarian style produced children who were hostile to each other, the permissive style produced boredom and, in some children, hostility as well, and the democratic style yielded more productivity and less hostility. This work is by no means the last word on the subject; others have found that the most successful leader of all is the warm authoritarian. It is quoted here to indicate that leadership style can have a powerful influence on groups, and that this is an area open to experimental investigation.

Later Childhood and the Gang

This, from about six years to adolescence, is the age when the **more or less formal group**, created by children themselves and sometimes referred to as a gang, becomes increasingly important. It offers a relief from adult supervision and meets needs not adequately catered for in an adult-orientated society. It has much in common with the formal group like brownies or scouts but is not identical with them.

A **typical gang** is centred around play: the primary purpose is enjoyment. (Play here has a wide definition—see also Chapter 22.) Gangs develop at about the same age that sexes voluntarily segregate themselves and a marked characteristic of a gang is **sexual exclusivity**. Indeed, in later childhood gangs are far more common among boys than girls. Other characteristics are:

The presence of a **leader** who is a member, rather than one imposed from without. This is one of the ways in which a gang differs from say, a scout group.

An identifying **name**.

The use of **secret signs** or passwords.

Identifying **insignia**: a badge or an item of clothing.

An **initiation ceremony**, mirroring the initiation rite common in many cultures at puberty.

Gangs can vary in size and in activity. Some devote themselves almost entirely to antisocial behaviour; others are entirely benign. What they all do is offer members an opportunity to measure themselves against others and to learn cooperation between peers.

The Development of Prejudice

Prejudice develops from **social discrimination**, in itself an essential component of social learning. Social discrimination refers to the tendency to make a distinction among people according to certain cues; without a measure of this skill one would not be able to behave sensitively to individuals with different social needs. It would be crass, for example, to behave in an identical fashion to a shy four-year-old foreign child as it would be to a self-confident 10-year-old.

Gang membership fosters social discrimination, not always to the good since it encourages notions of the **ingroup** and the **outgroup**, the latter being, by definition, inferior. The key phrase here is 'by definition' for prejudice is *the tendency to judge others not by their personal characteristics but by the characteristics ascribed to them by virtue of their membership of a group*, whether the group be a race, a sex, or a religious belief. Three key elements in prejudice are:

1. Beliefs in the **inferiority** of those against whom prejudice is directed, based on stereotypes rather than experience.

2. An **emotional accompaniment** of beliefs ranging from cold indifference to outright hostility.

3. An accepted **form of treatment** of the despised group which may be a desire to have nothing to do with them or to persecute them.

Awareness of social differences is rare before the age of three but may grow rapidly after that. Prejudice is usually fostered by significant others, parents or peers, and can easily be fostered by prevailing moods in society especially in time of war when a government may deliberately whip it up. More rarely it is based on actual experience which becomes generalised to all others who share similar beliefs or racial characteristics or whatever is salient.

Prejudice is not only negative: it can fulfil a function in providing what **Gordon Allport** has called a 'psychological crutch'—that is, it gives a sense of importance and superiority to the person who is in need of such a boost.

There is a deeper explanation in that groups against which one feels prejudice are usually composed of people whose behaviour or beliefs are mysterious, unknown or little understood. The fear of the unknown is common and may have what evolutionists call survival value—that is, it is a characteristic that has been of value in protecting the tribe in the far distant past and still fulfils the same function. The opposite of fearing the unknown is foolhardiness.

Some Predictions from Social Learning Theory

One way of gauging the value of a theory is to see the extent to which it enables one to make predictions. This approach can be applied to any theory: political, scientific or social. Within the context of this chapter two topics can be studied to test the validity of assertions already make about the importance of socialisation and the power of the role model.

Social Deprivation

Some references have already been made to humans' apparent need for others in the mention of sending people to Coventry and the experiments on stimulus deprivation. These are examples of extreme deprivation; if there is anything in the theory of the importance of social learning it should be possible to set up others.

Animal studies have suggested that there are critical periods during which social behaviour develops. The Harlows in America, working with monkeys, have reported that animals reared in isolation seemed almost incapable of play. A number of studies on rats have shown that those who were systematically handled while young responded better to stress and learned faster. (See also Chapter 3 for a discussion of the critical period and humans.)

The **effects of institutionalisation** provide a natural experiment for humans. A classical study is that of **Rene Spitz**, published in 1945. Children reared in a foundling home were compared with those brought up in a residential nursery attached to a prison for women. The second group received much attention from their mothers and were far more often out of their cots. The differences in outcome at the age of two were dramatic.

Social disadvantage can also be shown to lead to impaired social and intellectual functioning. Malnutrition has many effects, not the least of which is apathy among children. An apathetic child is unlikely to elicit or reinforce social stimulation from adults and so a vicious circle of further deprivation is set up.

A striking confirmation of the importance of social disadvantage comes from developmental work at the other end of the continuum from childhood —namely, the elderly. Studies of cognitive deficits in people over the age of 65 show that they occur more frequently among those who live alone.

The Model of the Television Programme

If what has been said about the power of significant others in one's life is true then there should be some evidence that the style and content of what is watched on television should have an influence on behaviour: viewers should model themselves on what they see.

An example of a study to examine this is the work of **David Laye**, **Roderic Gorney** and **Gary Steele** who, in 1978, published the results of their investigation of the effects of the viewing habits of nearly 200 American men. For a week some men watched tough detective-type films, others only programmes where people were kind to each other. A third group watched neutral programmes and a fourth were left to look at any thing they wished. The men's behaviour, rated by wives who were not told what their husbands had been watching, appeared to reflect the nature of the programme.

An example of a study of the effects of television viewing on children is that carried out by **M. S. Rabinovitch** and colleagues in 1972, contributing to the American Surgeon General's Commission, the Committee on Television and Social Behaviour. Children were shown either a violent or a neutral episode and then compared in a test for awareness of violence. There was some evidence to suggest that the children who saw the violent story were less aware of violence when they were tested—in other words, they were less sensitive to it, and therefore were, possibly, more likely to be violent themselves without being aware of the true nature of their behaviour.

There is much to criticise in these and similar experiments. It can be argued that television reflects rather than creates a social mood, or that anyone affected by a programme will have a predisposition to act in that way anyway. Nevertheless, some support for social learning is provided.

Questions

1. How can an understanding of social learning theory be applied in a nursery or school?
2. Consider the place of identification in socialisation.
3. Why is so much attention paid to the development of the smile?
4. Explain the following: identification, modelling, peer groups.

Exercises

1. Consider any social group of which you are or have been a member. What were the rules of that group and how were transgressors treated?
2. Do we still have initiation ceremonies? Describe any you are familiar with.

17
Emotional Development

Components of Emotions

Emotion, like intelligence, is one of those words that most people can use but few can define. It involves **three components**:

1. The first is a feeling state: happiness, fear or whatever.
2. The second involves changes in the internal functioning of the body.
3. The third is related to external changes in the body, in particular to posture, movement or facial expression.

Taking these in reverse order it is readily apparent that **bodily posture, movement and facial expression** are related to emotional states. We are familiar with the stiffening body of someone who is afraid or the relaxed smile of someone at ease. While this component is familiar there is no universal agreement on the messages that they convey. It is true that a laugh or a smile is a laugh or a smile wherever one is but hand gestures are easily misinterpreted. A cheery wave to one person may be seen as a threatening movement to another.

The second component can be illustrated with an example. Someone walks into a house and hears a noise that could be made by a burglar. Immediately there is a **physical response**: increased heart rate probably, sweating and a dry mouth possibly. The mechanism underlying these physical changes is located in the body's **central and autonomic nervous systems**.

The central and peripheral nervous systems have already been described in Chapter 7. The **autonomic nervous system** controls smooth muscles and glands, and its functioning is closely related to that of the central nervous system. When something stressful is perceived the CNS (central nervous system) goes into action and initiates activity which leads to a release of the hormone ACTH (adrenocorticotropic hormone) stimulating the adrenal glands, situated just above the kidneys. It is the adrenal glands which secrete adrenalin and noradrenalin, leading to physical arousal, and it is this physical arousal that manifests itself in a pounding heart and a dry mouth.

The first component referred to above is that which most people immediately think of when they hear the word emotion—it is that related to **feelings**.

Studying the feelings of an infant is almost entirely a matter of conjecture for no baby can tell the observer anything of the feeling behind the expression of emotion. It is not totally guesswork though, for one can make an educated guess from the nature of the circumstances pertaining at the time.

Pleasure and Fear

Pleasure is first evinced by smiling and laughter. As was noted in Chapter 16, the smile and other signs of affectionate behaviour are among the first manifestations of emotion looked for by parents.

Fear is more age-specific than any other emotion; that is, certain fears are typically found at certain ages. This is not to say that there are two-year-old fears and four-year-old fears and so on; they shade into one another more than that. But it is possible to predict that there will be a gradual shift from the specific to the general—that is, in early childhood fears are centred around specific objects of events while by adulthood more general themes are paramount.

In early childhood the most common fear-producing stimuli are **loud noises, animals, high places, sudden movement, the dark, pain and strange people, places and objects**.

Not all these appear in full force. Fig. 22 shows the development of the fear of strangers, for example. As the graph shows, a fear of strangers develops between seven and nine months; it is sometimes called 'the eight-month anxiety'. What the graph does not show is that at the same time some children develop an interest in strangers; some babies even show interest and fear within a few moments of each other. Putting together what has already been noted on attachment (see Chapter 15) it is possible to predict that a baby will show less fear when at home, in the mother's

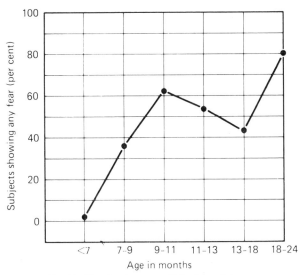

Fig. 22. The development of the fear of strangers.

Adapted from S. Scarr and P. Salapatek, 'Patterns of fear development during infancy', *Merrill-Palmer Quarterly* (1970).

presence, when the stranger is a child rather than an adult and female rather than male and when the stranger moves slowly. (See also the section on shyness, below.)

The **peak period for specific fears** is roughly from two to six years. During this time children are mature enough to recognise that something may be dangerous (whereas the younger ones may not do this) but they are not yet capable of realising that there may not be a personal threat involved.

Older children move towards fearing *ideas* rather than objects: the supernatural, characters from television series, ghosts, witches and so on. They, too, retain a heightened fear of stimuli which occur suddenly and unexpectedly, as horror film makers are only too aware. The abrupt movement that terrifies the baby is mirrored in the sudden appearance of the villain's face on the screen.

Variation in fear is not related only to the situation in which the stimuli appear. Precocious young children tend to have more fears than their age mates, perhaps because they are more aware of possible dangers. It is more socially acceptable for girls to show fear and to have more fears than boys; girls in some circles are taught to fear mice or spiders. Fatigue and hunger are likely to predispose towards fear, as is being with others who are afraid: fear, like laughter and crying, can be catching.

Fear-related Emotions

Shyness is defined as a shrinking from contact with strange people, rather than objects or situations. During the first year of life a fear of strangers is more often observed than not, the theory behind this phenomenon being that at this time babies are aware that the other person is strange but have not yet learned that strange people are not necessarily a threat. Most children pass through to a stage where they may be properly wary of strangers but not shy once a friendly relationship has been offered. Others remain shy and since this state is overcome only through experience and since they are too shy to gain the experience of making a relationship with strangers, the condition persists, sometimes into adulthood. A common factor at all ages seems to be an uncertainty about others' reactions—a fear in older children, for example, that they will be ridiculed.

Embarrassment overlaps with shyness in that it is evoked by people and relates to an inability to predict how others will behave. It differs from shyness in that it is not aroused directly by strangers but is more narrowly related to fear of how others will judge one. Because it demands a certain sophistication of thought it is rarely observed before five or six years of age although, as with all emotions, there is considerable individual variation.

Embarrassment is one emotion that is likely to get worse with age, for older children are haunted by memories of times when everything went wrong and everyone laughed. This leads to a vicious circle: embarrassed children have memories of their embarrassment, which leads to a poor self-image which leads to a greater chance of embarrassment the next time round. One further difference between the shy and the embarrassed is that the former are likely to say very little, the latter may say too much.

Worry is seen by some as an 'imaginary fear'. Unlike 'real' fear it is not a direct result of an external stimulus but is the product of the child's own thinking.

The first point to note is that there should be no automatic assumption that worry is bad or abnormal, any more than fear is abnormal in itself. What causes concern is an amount of fear, worry or whatever that causes undue distress to the child or those around him. A life without fear of any kind would be a relatively short one, for the world is a dangerous place with much properly to be afraid of.

Childhood is sometimes construed by adults as a period without worries: the carefree child trips through life, with food and shelter and love all provided, how can there be worry? Such a view is quite wrong. From the age that they are able to imagine something not immediately present children have the capability for worrying and they often use it. But they do not always fix on adult subjects. One girl of six heard that in the class she was about to move to there was a strange subject called 'geography'. She had no idea what this meant and for the whole summer holiday she worried that a teacher would order her to 'do geography' and she would not know what to do.

Generalising about the topics of worries is not possible since much depends on the culture in which the child lives and the social, political and economic conditions of the family. Typical worries in some societies are that parents will divorce, in others that a father will lose his job. With puberty, worries begin to centre more directly around the body and its functions and appearance (see Chapters 24 and 25).

The **expression of worry** is much harder to be aware of than is the expression of many other emotions. Some children look worried, some manage to hide their feelings but communicate that something is wrong by being very quiet. Others may develop abdominal pains or some other somatic expression.

Anxiety develops from fear and worry. It is an uneasy state concerning impending or anticipated ill, a characteristic being a sense that the individual cannot escape. It is different from worry in that it is concerned with general rather than specific topics and it comes essentially from subjective rather than objective origins. It often develops after a period of intense worry that seems to undermine the child's self-confidence so that there is a predisposition to anxiety. Like other emotions, the presence of others who also manifest it can make it worse: an anxious mother is likely to transmit anxiety to a child.

Because it is both a product of the mind and because of its subjective nature, anxiety is much harder than most emotions for a child to deal with. Worries can be talked over because there is, by definition, something to discuss, but this is not so with anxiety. The result is that many children try to mask their feelings, by showing off, by withdrawing into a fantasy world, by excessive television watching, by constantly denigrating others. (It is not only children who use these devices for masking anxiety.) Anxious children may also overeat, or sleep a great deal, or feign boredom. In many cases the behaviour listed above is unconscious and all the harder to deal with.

Depression in adults in characterised by a sense of despair, coupled with disturbed sleeping patterns and possibly loss of appetite. It is argued by some that prepubertal children never experience a full, adult-type depression, but whether they do or not there is circumstantial evidence of despair in young children; for example, the baby left alone in hospital or orphanage often shows behaviour including listlessness which certainly looks like depression. The study of 10-year-olds on the Isle of Wight already mentioned suggested that about 12 per cent showed signs of misery.

Anger is experienced when wishes or activities are blocked, either by someone or something else or by one's own incompetence or weakness. One of the best sources of data on temper outbursts is the work of **Florence Goodenough**, who asked parents to make daily reports of their children's behaviour. Although this work was carried out in the 1930s it remains a valuable piece of evidence.

Babies respond to minor physical discomfort with outbursts of anger and they may respond similarly if they are unable to make themselves understood. The peak of outbursts is around the age of two years—not for nothing is this period referred to as the **terrible twos**—when children are beginning to assert their individuality, when they can do so much more than they could earlier, but are aware of how much they cannot do. During the first three years over half the conflicts noted in Goodenough's sample were with parents but during the fourth and fifth years peers became more involved. After the second or third year outbursts became shorter, with a corresponding increase in sulking.

Older children still have conflicts with their parents (see Chapter 25) but the causes are more complex than mere restrictions of physical activity. One example of the complexity of the older child's anger is the fact that some will insist on setting themselves unrealisable goals. When these are not reached the child becomes angry and casts around for someone to blame.

Jealousy is a response to actual, supposed or threatened loss of affection. Once again, it is in itself a normal emotion but it can cripple. It is an outgrowth of anger and fear, the jealous person feeling insecure in his relationship with a loved one. Two major sources of jealousy are:

1. **The sibling**: the new baby is an obvious source of jealousy but some younger children express the emotion in the face of perceived continued favouritism shown to an older sibling. A sick child invariably receives a great deal of attention from the parents and can also be a source of jealousy in others. This can even take the form of the well child feigning the same symptoms as the one who is sick.

2. **Social situations**: for children these are usually centred around school. A child who is insecure at home may set much store by the favours of a teacher or another child and then may have feelings of jealousy about that person.

Envy should be distinguished from jealousy: it is a state of anger directed at a person who possesses something coveted. The most obvious example is envy of material goods but the more imaginative child can be envious of the emotional support given to others but not to them.

Emotional Deprivation

Emotional deprivation is one of those vague phrases than can be used glibly, providing an oversimplified explanation for a complex situation. In fact, total deprivation of emotions is impossible: what is usually meant is a severe **imbalance in emotional experience**, leading to a **lack of affection**. In turn this gives rise to few opportunities for joy, healthy curiosity or happiness.

There are several **causes** for a deprivation of affection. A child may be in the kind of institution where little personal attention is given. A parent may reject the child for any number of reasons. Later in life the child may reject parents, perhaps because upward mobility has led to a shift in social class for the child.

The **effects** of deprivation of affection are much harder to describe. It is easy to fall into the trap of concluding that there is a simple equation: deprivation of affection = outcome. Actually, the outcome is likely to be determined by many factors, with deprivation of affection being only one.

An example of suggested outcome is failure to thrive: a delay in normal growth and development. **L. I. Gardner** used the word deprivation to describe a case of a male twin who was rejected emotionally by his mother while his sister was cared for normally. At 13 months the female twin was of almost normal height while the boy was the size of a seven-month-old. As was mentioned above, there is a relationship between perceptions and the functioning of the nervous system and it is assumed in cases such as this twin that a depressed state leads to the inhibition of secretions of the pituitary hormones, including the growth hormones. It is deceptively easy to stop at this point. In fact of course there is always the possibility that children deprived of affection are also deprived of food or at least of food of the more nourishing kind. Deprivation of affection can also lead to loss of appetite and apathy so there may be a two-way process involved.

Other reported outcomes of deprivation include slow motor development, delayed speech, poor concentration, hostility to others and selfishness. The same warning about the dangers of oversimplification should be kept in mind.

The **long-term effects** of deprivation of affection are now seen as less serious and less clear-cut than was the case a few years ago. Formerly it was believed that such experiences automatically resulted in an adult with an 'affectionless' personality. Now it is recognised that later good experiences can go some way to offsetting the bad; the deprivation of early years is a contributory but not a sole factor.

Too much affection can be as potentially damaging as too little. Parents who are oversolicitous teach their children to be the centre of the universe, as anyone who has had anything to do with a classically spoilt child realises very quickly. These children are summed up in the demand 'I want, I want, I want and I want it now'. Unless their perspective shifts, and it often does when they go to school, such children demonstrate little interest in others and find themselves isolated from their peers and disliked by adults.

Theories of Emotions

One theory of emotions and their origin is concerned with the functioning of **the brain and the autonomic nervous system**, as outlined above. Since such theories are not strictly speaking developmental, except insofar as the nervous system develops, they should not concern us here, but for the sake of completeness one example of experimental work can be given. In the 1930s there was much interest in the hippocampus as an important area in mediating emotional behaviour. Two workers ablated the temporal lobes, including the hippocampus and amygdala, in monkeys, rendering the animals 'emotionally unreactive, docile and fearless'.

Learning theory (see Chapter 2) is properly a developmental approach and there are some readily believable examples of learning certain emotional responses. Many children learn to be afraid of dogs, for example. Learning can be by imitation; a parent who is afraid of mice is likely to find children following the example. And children learn the socially acceptable ways of behaving when they feel emotions: in most cultures boys are taught not to cry. While learning theory is attractive in this context, it does not explain all aspects that have been discussed in this chapter; notably it does not explain totally the age changes in the types of fears that are experienced throughout childhood.

Cognitive theories focus on the child's *understanding* of what is happening, and again are useful in explaining some of the phenomena. For example, the fear of strangers is summed up as 'an unassimilated discrepant event producing uncertainty'. In everyday language we might say 'we are not sure what to make of this person and so we are at a loss as to what to do'.

Attachment theory (see Chapter 15) has obvious relevance for some emotional behaviour, especially that related to loss and abandonment. But it, too, fails to explain all aspects of emotions. It has little to say on sex differences and again more is needed if one is to understand all changes with age.

Perhaps the search for a single explanatory theory of emotional behaviour is, given our present knowledge, futile. An understanding of many different approaches can result in an almost complete picture, analogous to a jigsaw. If we are at a jigsaw stage in explaining emotions we are not admitting defeat in our search.

Questions

1. Distinguish between feelings and function as they are related to an understanding of emotions.

2. Explain behaviour towards strangers within a developmental context.

3. What would you look for to confirm the view that a child is emotionally deprived? Is the term valid anyway?

4. Is it invariably harmful to be worried?

5. Compare and contrast jealousy and envy.

18
The Development of Personality

Introduction

A definition: Personality is the organisation of the physical, mental, moral and social qualities of the individual as that manifests itself to other people in the give and take of social life.

This definition, taken from the *Penguin Dictionary of Psychology*, points up several key aspects to personality. It is an **organisation**—that is, there is some form of system involved; it is a system that is reached by **observations from others**; it is **related to social experience**.

The derivation of the word personality illustrates one of its key components: it comes from the Latin word *persona* meaning mask. Classical actors wore elaborate masks, one function of which was to identify the person being portrayed.

If one studies half a dozen writers on personality one could be forgiven for thinking that each inhabits a world different from the others. One will talk in terms of inherited temperaments, another will see the earliest relationships with a mother figure as the crucial determinant, while a third will invoke statistically derived factors. Concluding a chapter on the philosophy of personality study, **Joseph Rychlak** noted that philosophers of all ages have wondered about human nature while today we speak of personality: 'We are studying ourselves, wondering why we do what we do and how it is that not everyone does precisely the same thing.... What we should hope to do is, rather than finding agreement on a single personality theory, agree upon the diversity in assumptions which we make and ... pursue a multiplicity of approaches.... In the long run this will prove most beneficial to the understanding of human behaviour.'

The Personality System

One way of pinning personality down is to consider two fundamental aspects: the self-concept and the pattern of traits.

The **self-concept**, or the notion that one has of the essence of oneself, is developed largely if not entirely from the picture one has of others' views of oneself. It can itself be subdivided into 'self as I am psychologically' and 'self as I am physically' although, as will be discussed below, one's body image interacts with one's psychological image. It can also be extended into 'ideal self', or self as I would like to be.

Traits are individual characteristics of thought, feeling or acts, such as aggression of defensive behaviour in the face of threat. Some can be seen as distinct; more often they combine into clusters of related behaviours.

Personality and Body Build

'Let me have men about me who are fat', wrote Shakespeare. There has long been an assumption that body build and personality go together, an assumption that was given a scientific boost by the work of **W. H. Sheldon**, who measured body build and put forward a classification based on three main types, each associated with a personality type:

Endomorphs (round and fat) are seen as aggressive and assertive.
Ectomorphs (long and slender) are thoughtful and introverted.
Mesomorphs (heavy, hard and rectangular) are active, self-confident and quarrelsome.

Neither Sheldon nor his followers argue that everyone fits into one of these three types completely; most people have a tendency in one direction.

There is a slight degree of support for the notion of associated personality characteristics although it would be unwise to treat this aspect as more than a rough generalisation. It is possible that society has certain expectations of personality characteristics associated with certain body types. It is possible also that certain hormonal changes which influence physique influence personality as well. For example, the ectomorph is likely to have a late growth spurt and will grow more slowly over a longer period than the endomorph. This suggests that the former has less male hormone at the beginning of puberty and there is some evidence that male hormones are associated with dominance and aggression.

The Development of Personality

There are two broad approaches to be taken when attempting to explain personality development. One is to look discretely at areas of influence: family, peers, teachers, cultural inheritance and so on. The other is to subsume all of these areas into one inclusive theory. The second approach is adopted there to avoid repetition.

Psychoanalytic Theories

Sigmund Freud, although not calling himself a developmental psychologist, has had a profound influence on child psychology. (See Chapter 2 for a general introduction to his work.) He drew heavily on the notion of stages, seeing the sexual instinct being directed towards various different objects in a fixed sequence. Sexual energy or libido (again, see Chapter 2 for an explanation of these terms) is invested in a single part of the body at each stage.

During each stage there are inevitable **conflicts** between the child's instinctual needs and the constraints exercised within the child's circumstances. According to Freudian theory later personality is determined by the way that these conflicts are resolved. Changes from one stage to the next come as a result of shifts in bodily sensitivity: at one time one part of the body is of paramount sensitivity, at another a different part takes over. If the conflicts surrounding one part are not resolved by the time the shift comes the chld will be **fixated** at that stage, continuing to act as though the shift had not occurred.

Freud's main stages were:

Birth to about one year: **the oral stage**. The mouth is the area of the greatest sensitivity and the most important person is the one who regularly provides oral gratification, this usually being the mother. If conflict is not resolved by the end of this stage the result will be an **oral personality**, fixated at the nursing-sucking stage. A **passive-oral** person is dependent and optimistic; the **sadistic** version is pessimistic, feeling the world owes him a living. Such a person, if not overtly sadistic in behaviour, is likely to be caustic in conversation.

One to three years: **the anal stage**. Pleasure is gained from bowel movements and the sense of relief from discomfort. There is also indirect satisfaction from parental approval once one is toilet trained. Failure to resolve conflict leads to the **anal personality**, the characteristics of which are all seen as being related to retention or keeping things. The typical anal person is obsessively tidy, a mean hoarder of objects and a collector.

Three to five years: **the phallic stage**. Pleasure comes from genital stimulation. During this stage **oedipal conflicts** arise, a boy perceiving his mother as a sexual object and his father as a rival. The boy resolves this conflict by identifying with his father; imitation of dad's ways at this age is very common indeed. Freud, incidentally, is less clear on girls' views of their mother as a rival although it is apparent that they too have to identify with their mother if subsequent sexual development is to be satisfactory. The **phallic personality**—one who has not resolved conflicts around this area—is narcissistic (that is, highly self-regarding), excessively ambitious, an exhibitionist and a braggart.

Five to 12 years: **latency** is the calm after the phallic storm, when children tend to seek same sex friends.

Twelve to 18+ years: **the genital stage**, when sexual objects for most people are those of the opposite sex, first perhaps adults (the teenage 'crush') and then peers.

It is tempting to look at one's friends and acquaintances and try to fit them into one of these personality types. But they are no more mutually exclusive than are Sheldon's body types. Freudian theory allows for this by asserting that most people are a mixture of several.

Erik Erikson, born of Danish parents in Germany and now living in America, trained as a psychoanalyst and was an acquaintance of Freud. (He is also one of the few men to have received a certificate of competence from the Maria Montessori School.) He describes Freud's work as the rock on which he built his own theory.

Although there are obvious origins in classical psychoanalysis, Erikson's contribution to personality theory marks a shift from an emphasis on the id to one on the ego. He accepts the place of unconscious motivation but replaces Freud's mother–father–child triangle with a wider concept of the child in a family which is itself part of society which itself exists within a historical heritage. In essence, Erikson's main contribution has been his stress upon the **historical reality** in which the child grows up.

While Freud drew conclusions largely from analytic work with adults, Erikson focuses on **children's play** as a vital means of obtaining information. (He was not for nothing Montessori-trained.)

The core of human functioning is based on the **quality of interpersonal relationships**: a healthy personality is one combining individual happiness with responsible citizenship, the foundation being laid in the first two years of life. **Development** is made up of 'a series of childhoods, which call for a variety of subenvironments, depending on the stage which the child has reached and also depending on the environment experienced during previous stages'.

Erikson delineates eight stages, consisting of perpetual motion: an individual never 'has' a personality; he is constantly developing. In each stage there is **a central problem** to be resolved. The central problem is universal; its manifestation is culturally determined. Stages are interrelated, every early acquisition lives on and later experience provides new answers to old problems. *Above all, the individual strives to attain a sense of competence.*

Erikson's first five stages deal with the child and the adolescent:

1. **Acquiring a sense of basic trust** (from birth to 18 months). This is the foundation of all later development, enabling new experience to be accepted willingly. The infant and caregiver need to experience frustration jointly.

2. **Acquiring a sense of autonomy** (roughly 18 months to four years), when the ego needs to see what can and cannot be done, when boundaries are established between self and the parents. Toilet training exemplifies the 'holding on—letting go' dichotomy central at this time. Play is a safe island in which to develop autonomy and parental handling of potential anarchy in the child is a powerful determinant of later, adult political attitudes.

3. **Acquiring a sense of initiative and overcoming a sense of guilt** (5–11 years). Mobility is the key to this stage, the child taking first steps away from parental control. The superego consists not just of what parents say but also what they stand for in terms of their cultural heritage. This is the time of the development of sexual identity and of oedipal conflicts which can be resolved only when autonomy has been achieved.

4. **Acquiring a sense of industry and fending off a sense of inferiority** (5–11 years). This is the stage of the young school child when energy is devoted to mastering social problems. Play becomes less important and adults other than parents become key figures. Later attitudes to work are traced to the way this stage is managed.

5. **Acquiring a sense of identity** (11–18 years). This comes with a mastery of the problems of childhood and a readiness to face the world. The adolescent is seen as declaring: 'I ain't what I ought to be, I ain't what I'm going to be but I ain't what I was.'

Learning Theories

Learning theory looks primarily to a person's **experience**, particularly when a child, to explain subsequent personality development. (See Chapter 2 for an introduction to learning theory.) It follows from this that parental figures are seen as having paramount importance.

Behaviour is seen as both the cause and effect of other behaviour. Thus primary drives—dependence, feeding, toileting, sex and aggression—are instrumental for initiating behaviour in a social world. Environmental responses shape that behaviour and lead to an **increasingly predictable repertoire** which constitutes personality. An out-and-out environmentalist acknowledges differences in the behaviour of boys and girls but sees these differences as springing from parental reactions rather than biological determinism.

Robert Sears, an experimental psychologist, took the view that psycho-analytic theory cannot be tested and cannot be regarded as scientific. However, he did not reject it out of hand, declaring: 'Instead of trying to ride on the tail of a kite that was never meant to carry such a load, experimentalists would probably be wise to get all the hunches, intuitions and experience possible from psychoanalysis and then for themselves start the laborious task of constructing a systematic psychology of personality. . . .'

Sears starts from basic learning theory. For him behaviour is a result of a need to reduce tension; looking for final causes is a waste of time. Every unit of behaviour that comes just before tension reduction becomes capable of reinforcing later behaviour. Personality is seen as **a product of a lifetime of relations with other people** which have taught one how to behave. Parents are crucial because they are the most important reinforcing agents during the child's early years. Development is a continuous chain of events, with phases dictated by social conditions:

Phase one: *Primary needs and the learning of early infancy.* During the first six months most behaviour is an effort to reduce **inner tensions** arising from the primary drives noted above. Reduction in the hunger drive leads to an association with the mother, or mother figure; dependency is an essential component to learning and much of the child's earliest development can be traced directly to the mother's personality. Aggression is learned early on in this stage, arising from the moment the infant first experiences a sense of frustration.

Mothers are seen as behaving towards their babies first within the general disposition towards children as such and then according to the infant's sex—'a social category that has enormous implications for training'. The child's position in the family is not ignored: the oldest receives the most direct parental training while others have older siblings to act as inter-mediaries. From this argument it follows that Sears sees **age spacing** as even more important than **ordinal position**, for the greater the gap the more free the parents will be to deal directly with each child.

Phase two: *Secondary motivational systems—family-centred learning.* This phase lasts roughly from six months to the age of school entry. Primary needs are gradually incorporated into reinforced secondary drives. An example of this is the way hunger is no longer dependent entirely on contractions felt in the stomach; it becomes associated with the sight of food or the opening of a refrigerator door. (One can observe this phenomenon in domestic pets as well.)

During this phase mothers look to a reduction in dependency and the child finds himself freer to compete with others. The child moves towards **partial self-control**. At about the third year children start to identify with their parents, their behaviour reflecting at first that of the mother. Sears does not see this as a result of specific child-rearing, rather it is a form of role playing. About a year later boys switch to imitating their father while girls continue with a maternal major identification.

Aggression, to Sears, is learned as much by accident as design. A child learns that screaming can bring a much-wanted toy, or ice-cream, or an adult's attention. The way early aggression is handled is seen as a crucial determinant of later behaviour.

Essentially this second phase sets the personality being developed under the direction of adults, with success or failure being dependent on their maintaining an adequate balance between control and permissiveness.

Phase three: *Secondary motivational systems—extrafamilial learning.* By school age children's personalities have so developed that they are able to cope with the learning experiences provided by a wider world. Dependency is shared with teachers who consciously or not teach far more than basic attainment skills. Gradually the horizons widen to include other children as models and it is during this phase that religious and political views are formed. Underlying all learning during this phase, though, is the value system first encountered from the child's original caregivers.

Personal Construct Psychology

One of the latest approaches to the study of personality is that of the psychologist **George Kelly** who published his book *Personal Constructs* in 1955. This is a two-volume work; anyone looking for a briefer introduction might start with *Inquiring Man* by Don Bannister and Fay Fransella (Penguin, 1971).

Strictly speaking Kelly preferred not to write of personality as distinct from other aspects of a person and his work on children was sparse. Nevertheless, the approach he put forward should be considered in any general round-up of theories.

The model of the scientist. Kelly was unhappy with both psychoanalytic and learning theory. In a memorable gloss on Kelly's views, Bannister declared that the former is reminiscent of mortal combat between a sex-crazed monkey and a maiden aunt while the latter sees man as a ping-pong ball with memory.

Kelly preferred to view man as a scientist. Scientists, he noted, consider something first. They then erect hypotheses about whatever it is they have considered. These hypotheses enable them to make scientific predictions. Next they carry out an experiment to test the hypotheses, which are either confirmed or not. If they are not confirmed the scientist has to go back to the original observations and think up something likely to be more adequate.

We all follow the same sequence. We make observations about our world and by the way we behave we test hypotheses. In this way each one of us builds up a kind of map of the psychological universe, known as a **construct system**. A key aspect of the system is the core role construct, the notion of the essence of one's self which is built up and modified throughout one's life.

In a discussion of **the role of the mother** in personality development Phillida Salmon has made two main points. The first is that the mother should be seen as providing **an enabling structure**: the child is not a passive recipient, not a ping-pong ball with a memory, but is constantly active, needing to be guided and encouraged. The second point arises from the first: children act on their mothers as well as mothers on their children, so an analysis of the influence of the mother on personality development should rest on a study of the mother–child pair, not the mother alone. She goes on to underline the importance of the mother in providing a basis for construct development, pointing out the necessity of the mother having some sense of shared content between her view of herself and her view of her baby. From this basis the baby can strike out.

There are, of course, some similarities between both overall approaches outlined above and personal construct theory. For Kelly a baby comes into the world active but with no formed system. At first the constructs are few and poorly organised since they can be built only with experience. They are built—especially those related to the core role system—largely as a result of the child's perception of the responses of significant others. As the system becomes more complex and better organised so the child is able to incorporate the views of people other than his parents and so too he is able to form constructs which apply in widening circles from his immediate home environment.

Questions

1. What is meant by the term 'personality'.
2. What is meant by an anal personality? Is the notion plausible?
3. Compare and contrast psychoanalytic with learning theory explanations of personality development.
4. How might the concept of Man as a Scientist explain personality development?

Exercises

1. Consider the validity of Sheldon's theory of body build and personality using ten children known to you.
2. Describe any child known to you in terms of Eriksonian stages.

19
Moral Development

Morals and Society

Moral behaviour means conformity with the moral code of the social group, the word moral coming from the Latin *mores* meaning manners or customs. True morality entails not only **an understanding of the external forces** on one to behave according to the group's wishes but also a **voluntary wish** to behave in this way. It is accomplished by a feeling of personal responsibility and involves putting the interests of others before oneself.

There are, therefore, four components to the concept:

1. **Conformity to social standards**, learning the laws, customs and rules of the group.

The **laws** of a group indicate those mores sufficiently important and clear-cut to have penalties attached.

Customs are equally binding mores which have no fixed penalties. For example, it is against the law to steal others' possessions; it is contrary to custom to handle them.

Rules are mores than are more particular to a family, a club or any small subgroup.

2. **The role of the conscience.** The conscience, defined by some as 'a conditioned anxiety response', acts as a mechanism for ensuring internal control.

3. **The role of emotions**, especially guilt and shame. Children who feel guilty acknowledge that their behaviour has fallen short of the standards they have set themselves. Before guilt can be experienced four conditions must exist:

Children must acknowledge notions of good and bad.

They must accept an obligation to regulate their own behaviour.

They must accept that they, not others, are to blame for lapses in behaviour.

They must be able to recognise a discrepancy between themselves as they would like to be and themselves as they are.

Shame is an unpleasant emotional reaction arising from an awareness of disapproval in others; it thus relies on external sanctions alone, unlike guilt which relies on internal and external factors.

4. **The role of social interactions.** Contact with others—an obviously

essential part of moral development—follows a pattern similar to that of social development in general: first the family is all-important, then the peer group and school and so on.

The Development of a Moral Sense

Children are born immoral or nonmoral—that is, they are not expected to have a conscience or to behave in a prosocial way. The earliest customs and rules they learn are usually to do with safety, followed by those concerned with politeness. By school age most are expected to have some concept of right or wrong, but few teachers of five-year-olds expect self-motivated social behaviour. Gradually the voluntary component develops until late adolescence by when more or less adult standards are at least expected if not always anticipated.

Summarising work done in this field, **Philip Graham**, writing in 1980, noted the following:

1. There is no clear-cut **sex effect** in the development of prosocial behaviour. Girls may have a greater tendency towards altruism but are less likely to display this trait because they are generally less assertive.

2. **Intelligence** and high levels of achievement are related to both helpfulness and honesty.

3. **Social class** is not consistently related to any aspect of moral development. This one of the very few areas where this is so.

4. **Maternal warmth** and good early experiences are associated with moral development. It is possible that these lead to high self-esteem and thus link with point 2 above on levels of achievement.

Theories of Moral Development

In Chapter 2 it was noted that no one theory of child development can be seen to explain all observed phenomena; so it is with moral develoment where three main approaches have addressed themselves to the subject. All three have made valuable contributions, yet none has so far provided a totally satisfactory conceptualisation.

Psychoanalytic theories can be seen to stem from Freud's original views put forward in his introduction to the concept of **narcissism**. (See Chapter 2 for a brief description of psychoanalytic theory in general.) The superego is the result of repressed hostility towards a frustrating parent: when the child feels that he has done something that the parent would disapprove of he is punished by a kind of internalised parent whose rules are adopted by the child. In Freud's original formulation the most strongly felt hostility was directed at the same-sex parent, thus that parent's attitudes became incorporated into the child's system. Since hostility is experienced at its most intense around the ages of 5–6, this is the crucial period for the development of the conscience, for it is at this time that the child wishes most to identify with the same-sex parent in order to cope with hostile feelings.

Neo-Freudians have modified this view. **Ian Suttie** turns the whole topic around and sees a mother–child love relationship as the basis for the development of conscience. To him the child identifies with what mother would approve of rather than fearing what the same-sex parent would forbid. **Melanie Klein**, on the other hand, dated the onset of conscience at a much earlier age. She saw it as arising in the first year of life as a result of the infant's destructive fantasies. These fantasies are so worrying that a caring response emerges as a way of making reparation for them.

Cognitive developmental theories began with Piaget's *The Moral Judgment of the Child*, published in 1932. His approach to the development of moral judgement was consistent with that used for cognition in general—that is, children pass through certain clearly defined, invariant stages of moral thought. (Note that Piaget wrote about the child's judgement; only in passing did he study moral behaviour.) Piaget based his conclusions on observations of play, on questions about the rules of play and on questions to children about stories he had told them. An example of the latter is the story of a child who cuts himself while sharpening a pencil using a knife he has been forbidden to touch. Children were asked whether the child in the story would have had this accident had the use of the knife not been forbidden, i.e. is there an unavoidable retribution for doing something forbidden by an adult? At six years, 86 per cent of children had the concept of unavoidable retribution, or 'immanent justice', whereas by 11–12 years only 34 per cent held this view. There is a similar age-related development of the just punishment. Younger children see punishment related to the extent of damage incurred; the older take intention or carelessness into account.

Piaget's conclusions were that before the age of about seven thought is egocentric and only after that does the concept of shared rules emerge. At this age rules are being based on powers outside the child. Later the child comes to understand that he too has a part to play in rule-making, as he realises that relationships with others are essentially reciprocal.

The person who has more than any other developed Piaget's views, using the same story-telling technique, is **Lawrence Kohlberg**, who has extended the age range of subjects to include young adults. An example of Kohlberg's stories for adults is one in which a man's wife is seriously ill. A local chemist has the drug that will save her life but is asking more than the man can afford. The question put to the listener is whether or not the man should steal the drug.

Kohlberg formulated three levels of moral judgement:

1. **Pre-moral**, when behaviour is governed by thoughts of rewards and punishments.
2. The morality of **conventional rule conformity** is that determined by thoughts of the approval or disapproval of others.
3. The morality of **self-accepted moral principles** emerges with notions of contact with others and a democratically determined set of rules.

Finally comes a stage which transcends laws, when **self-determined individual principles** are the determining factor.

The Piagetian approach to a study of moral development has been criticised on similar grounds to those concerning cognitive development generally. Children's responses have been shown to vary according to the content of the story: it seems to make a difference whether one is asking the child to judge refusal to share or a theft. There have been some examples of regressions rather than smooth stage-by-stage progress towards reciprocity and it is clear that this particular theoretical formulation does not explain all expressions of moral behaviour.

Learning theory, at first glance, seems to offer the most attractive explanation for moral behaviour. Both classical and operant conditioning models have been invoked to demonstrate the way that rewards and punishments mould behaviour to become socially acceptable. (See Chapter 2 for an explanation of the terms 'classical' and 'operant conditioning'.) Through experience of being rewarded for certain acts, or the expression of certain thoughts, the child builds up a repertoire of behaviours which he associates with pleasant or unpleasant consequences. **Hans Eysenck** has offered another dimension to the debate by suggesting that introverts condition more quickly than extraverts and so learn more readily to be well behaved. The introvert-extravert dichotomy is biologically based, according to Eysenck, and so moral behaviour is determined indirectly and in part by our genes.

M. L. Hoffman has drawn on cognitive and psychoanalytic and learning theories, postulating that moral behaviour is a result of the person's **gradually increasing capacity to take the role of the other**, i.e. to recognise that others have a point of view and certain rights. He develops this theory mainly to explain altruistic behaviour and from it one can detect the following stages:

1. By the end of the first year of life an infant may display **sympathetic distress**, i.e. he feels concern for another but his lack of role-taking ability prevents him from doing anything about it.

2. Between two and three years role-taking has developed sufficiently to allow the child to take some steps to aid someone else who is manifestly upset.

3. Between six and nine years the child can role-take more widely, and can appreciate general rather than immediately obvious distress.

4. In adolescence there may be some sense of guilt at others' sadness, even if there is no question of personal responsibility.

The Measurement of Moral Behaviour

So far an emphasis has been put on finding out what people think is right or wrong rather than asking what they actually do. Much of the work in this field has consisted of the collection of data based on observations of behaviour, although since many of the experimental studies have used simulated settings it might be argued that we are still some way from being able to make general statements about the relationship between what people say and what they do.

Prosocial behaviour, generosity, helpfulness and altruism have been studied by giving children an opportunity to behave prosocially when ostensibly being observed doing something else. Thus in one experiment children won tokens which could be exchanged for sweets. The experimenters then gave the children an opportunity to give their tokens to a charity. Other techniques have involved observing children, for example, in a nursery school when even two-year-olds can be seen to be helpful to others.

Antisocial behaviour is harder to define than prosocial since one has to look at it by definition within a social context and this implies a greater degree of value judgement on the part of the observer: what is antisocial in one group may be acceptable in another. A group of children may, for example, see nothing wrong in lying to adults but everything wrong in not telling the truth to their peers. The earliest large-scale enquiry into lying and cheating in a laboratory-based study was by **H. Hartshorne** and **M. May** in 1928. They investigated several thousand children aged eight to 16 in a range of simulated settings. Other later studies have built in opportunities for children to cheat during tests or games.

Moral Development and Discipline

'Speak roughly to your little boy
And beat him when he sneezes.
He only does it to annoy
Because he knows it teases.'

Lewis Caroll's lines may have been intended as humour but there is more than a touch of the nineteenth-century attitude to discipline in this verse: boys in particular had to be beaten into morality, and discipline was synonymous with punishment.

Today discipline, at least as defined in textbooks, is related to notions of the disciple or follower: the goal is to produce one who will voluntarily follow leadership. As **Benjamin Spock** has pointed out: 'Some people believe there are only two ways to raise children: with overpermissiveness which produces brats, or with sternness and punishment which makes good citizens. Neither of these extremes works well.'

Elizabeth Hurlock has identified **five needs of childhood** which are fulfilled by discipline:

1. A feeling of security is imparted to the child.
2. Enabling children to live according to the mores of their group brings them social approval.
3. Through discipline children learn to behave in a way that leads to praise.
4. Developmentally appropriate discipline (that is, discipline suited to that particular child) encourages children to achieve.
5. Discipline helps children develop a conscience and thus to regulate their own behaviour.

Punishment fulfils three functions in childhood: the first is to restrict, the second is to teach and the third is to instil some motivation to avoid socially disapproved behaviour.

The principle behind the use of punishment is based on learning theory: associate an unpleasant experience with a certain act and it is less likely that the act will be repeated. A good example of inevitable punishment comes from a burn got when a hot object is touched.

So far so good. Unfortunately much punishment manifestly does not have the desired effect. There are several reasons for this:

1. The unpleasant experience may come too late after the act in question. To slap a child the second he steps off the kerb when told not to is one thing; to say 'Wait till your dad comes home' is another.

2. The unpleasant experience may become associated with the punisher rather than the act.

3. The unpleasant experience may confer status on the recipient.

4. Any attention may be seen by a child as better than none.

Rewards are often cited as more powerful in controlling behaviour than punishment. (They should not, incidentally be confused with bribes which are given to induce someone to do something illegal or immoral.) They, too, have an educational function; like punishments, they also instil motivation to behave in a certain way and they reinforce socially approved behaviour. They are undoubtedly powerful but most societies function with a combination of both rewards and punishment.

Common Moral Transgressions of Childhood

Lying. Much so-called lying in young children does not deserve the name for up to as old as seven or eight they easily confuse fact with fantasy. So much is strange in the real world that it is hardly surprising that children invent brothers or sisters, or talk about tigers at the bottom of the garden. Much needless anxiety is caused to adults who fail to realise this point.

Most real lies are the result of children trying to avoid punishment, disapproval or ridicule.

Cheating either in games or in school work is directly related to the social esteem attached to winning or succeeding and to the level of self-esteem of the child in question.

Stealing is one of the earliest right and wrong differentiations taught children and one of the most commonly transgressed. The temptation to take an occasional sweet or small coin is easy to understand and such 'stealing' is not a cause for alarm if it remains occasional.

Destructiveness is rare in young children except as retaliation. Much of what is called destruction is probably due more to ignorance or clumsiness. Older children, however, may deliberately destroy something as an attack on the owner or as a perverse form of achievement: at least they can do something.

Questions

1. Consider the prerequisites of moral behaviour in an eight-year-old.

2. 'Remember,' said a mother to her two-year-old daughter, 'I am your superego and I am always with you.' Comment on this statement.

3. Compare the effect on subsequent behaviour of rewards and punishment.

4. Design an educational system based entirely on rewards.

5. How many forms of reward other than financial can you think of?

Exercise

Note, during one day, the rewards you give and receive.

20
The Self Concept

Concepts Age by Age

It seems, although one can never be certain, that very young children have no concept of being separate from the mother or whoever is looking after them. **Freud** discusses the **symbiotic relationship** between the two, arguing that the baby perceives self and mother as one unit. **Piaget**, too, agrees that there is no distinction between self and not-self during the first few months. However, by about eight months the notion of separate objects is developing and with it the idea of separateness as a person.

As with so many aspects of child development **language** plays a critically important role. Well before the age of two most children will respond when their names are called but it is not until two that most begin to use their own names. During the next year children are in an early stage of self-assertion, a stage characterised by vocal demands for autonomy: 'Jenny do it'. There are many factors going to make up this pattern of behaviour, one of which is likely to be a desire to demonstrate to oneself as well as others that this person called 'me' is capable of far more than might have been imagined.

By four there is **possessiveness**, a pride not so much in what the child can do but what the child has: 'That's my car ..., my mummy ...'. It seems as if the self is now defined by extension to what belongs to me. (Adult parallels are not difficult to find.)

By five or six, it is thought, the child has **adult-style** self concepts—that is, there is a range from positive to negative, high esteem to low esteem, which can be expressed verbally. I use the phrase 'it is thought' because it is possible that adult-style self concepts are present before then; what is lacking is techniques of getting at them. From then on until puberty the self concept develops, usually becoming more complex. At puberty there is often a drastic reappraisal (see Chapter 25).

Before discussing how the concept of self develops, a couple of general points: one is that some authorities argue that consciousness of **a sense of self is what sets off Man most distinctly from animals**. It is this ability to reflect on one's actions that releases homo sapiens from the chains of instinct and opens the doors of religion and morality. Another is that it may be misleading to talk about a person's self concept in the singular: it is possible to have a high opinion of one's brain and a low one of one's body. What is perhaps harder for the experimental psychologist to grapple with is that concepts may be **situation specific**. A child may see herself as a princess at home and a pauper at school.

Origins of Self Concepts

To some extent concepts develop as a result of what children observe they can do. Thus a child who can beat up everyone in the neighbourhood learns from his own actions that he is hard. But he learns also from the behaviour of other children and possibly in this case from their parents. This latter source—other people's opinions of one—is probably the most influential and the adult who constantly belittles a child is, in the opinion of some psychologists, doing incalculable harm.

It is not surprising that the root of self-esteem lies in family experiences. **Stanley Coopersmith**, working in America, found that children with high esteem came from families where the parents themselves had similar self concepts and where adults were able to treat children as responsible individuals. Parents of such children were more accepting, more affectionate and more positive towards their children. Above all, they were interested in them and they showed it. But, and this is a very big but, they also set firm limits to their children's behaviour, limits which they applied consistently.

An elaboration of this approach is found in the work of **Diana Baumrind**, who distinguished between three broad approaches in her study of pre-school children. The first approach is similar to that employed by the ideal Coopersmith parents noted above and is called, by Baumrind, **authoritative**. It is contrasted with the **authoritarian** (detached, controlling and less warm) and the **permissive** (affectionate and warm but non-controlling and undemanding). In this study the least self-reliant and effective children were likely to have permissive parents. Perhaps the message transmitted by such parents in their lack of boundary setting is that they do not, deep down, care much for or believe in their children. The most positive and competent children had authoritative parents, following Coopersmith, and the children of authoritarian parents fell in between.

Yet a further elaboration of this basic notion of Coopersmith and Baumrind is found in a study which started with children aged about 12 months. **W. C. Bronson** followed observations of children of this age through so that she could trace the effects of very early interactions with parents on later self-esteem. Her most interesting findings relate back to Coopersmith's point of the importance of treating children as individuals. Parents whose children grow up with high self-esteem seemed able to be sensitive to the messages given by their very young children. They let the children initiate and pace most of the interactions and gradually increased the complexity of their responses to suit the developing capacities of the children. In contrast to this the parents of low-esteem children dominated early interchanges and gave no message of acknowledging the child's capacities or wishes.

Sex, Social Class and the Self Concept

It has already been mentioned in Chapter 3 that concepts of one's **gender identity** are learned in early childhood: boys and girls are spoken to and played with differently. It was noted also that girls are thought by some to fail at maths because that fits their self concept. It is also generally agreed that children from poor homes do less well in school than those from richer families. From these statements it might be assumed that girls and poor children have generally poor self concepts.

Some studies do bear out the prediction about working-class children but not all do. One study by **N. Trowbridge** carried out in America in the early 1970s found that between the ages of eight and 14 children from lower social classes had consistently higher self-esteem. There is a similar lack of consistency in findings on sex differences. Teenage boys seem to be more confident in their ability to succeed and often feel more in control of their lives. They also see themselves as ambitious and energetic while girls' self concepts centre around more social qualities. It is possible, of course, that experimental evidence is simply reflecting current stereotypes; what is more certain is that there is no evidence of girls generally perceiving themselves as inferior to boys.

Questions

1. Trace the development of the concept of self from babyhood to the preadolescent stage.
2. How can one best judge other people's self concepts?
3. Is the study of a child's self concept likely to be of more or less value than the IQ in explaining learning difficulties?

Part 6
The Activities of Childhood

21
Play

An Example from Animals

Twenty-eight domestic cats were the subjects for one study of play. They were divided into three groups: one in a laboratory, one at home and one in the wild. From 14 days to maturity their play was observed and categorised using terms like 'pounce', 'horizontal leap' and 'chase'.

It may seem fanciful to study kittens at play and even more fanciful to quote these findings in a book on human development. Yet, as **Catherine Garvey** has pointed out in her book *Play* (Fontana, 1977), the pattern of play that was observed illustrates many of the basic principles underlying children's activities: at first play was solitary but it soon became social; once an activity was acquired it was practised repeatedly; play decreased as the kittens grew old enough to start hunting and foraging for food for themselves. This last point applied equally to the domestic as to the wild kittens, underlining the way that for all of them play appears to be an integral part of development.

Definitions of Play

Play, like intelligence and emotions, is another of those words we all use but cannot easily define. Before saying what it is, we can be sure of what it is not: it is not work, not even 'children's work'.

For some play is an instinctive **preparation for adulthood**; 'playing mothers and fathers' is an illustration of this view. Others note that play changes with age and propose a theory of **recapitulation**: children in play recapitulate the history of their race. A simpler interpretation is that play is a way of **expending surplus energy**.

Psychoanalysts see play as a method used by children to relive certain powerful experiences and thus to come to terms with them. More recent theories stress play's **adaptive function**, underlying man's distinctive use of tools.

None of these theories is acceptable as a total explanation of play and none can be, for play means different things to different people at different times. One way of defining play is to consider its components, as was done by **J. Huizinger** in his *Homo Ludens* (Routledge & Kegan Paul, 1947).

Components of Play

1. It is voluntary.
2. It is pleasurable.
3. It is tension-enhancing.
4. Its immediate consequences are not of biological necessity. This can be expanded to say that it has no goals other than the enjoyment found in the activity itself.
5. It contains elements of fantasy or quasi-reality.
6. It changes qualitatively and quantitatively with age.

To this list Garvey has added:

7. It involves some active engagement on the part of the player.
8. It has systematic relations to other activities, including social development, creativity, language-learning and problem-solving.

The Contribution of Play to Child Development

Point 8 above indicates some of the ways in which play is related to development. **Elizabeth Hurlock** has spelt out 11 contributions:

1. **Physical development.** Active play encourages both gross and fine motor development.
2. **Communication.** Children must learn to communicate with others if they are to play successfully and in turn they must learn to attend to communications from others.
3. **An outlet for pent-up emotional energy.** Inevitably there is some restriction on most children for at least part of their day. Play offers an outlet for energy built up.
4. **An outlet for needs and desires.** A child who has no opportunity to become a leader in life can meet this need in play.
5. **A source of learning.** Exploration of the environment is one example. Passive play like television-watching or reading are further sources. (Those who see play as involving active engagement may not accept the notion of passive play.)
6. **A stimulant to creativity.** Children can experiment in play and may then transfer activity to other situations.
7. **The development of self-insight.** Children learn something of their abilities and how they compare with their peers.
6. **Learning to be social.** Since so much play involves other children there must be some accommodation to others.
9. **Moral standards.** As play becomes more bound by rules so these become increasingly rigidly enforced and group norms of right and wrong, fair and unfair are learned.
10. **Learning to play appropriate sex roles.** Unlike the rules of a game, sex roles are rarely taught explicitly but children need to be aware of them if they are to move comfortably in their group. Play provides many opportunities for covert instruction. (No comment is made here on whether or not learning to play given sex roles is desirable in a more general sense.)

11. **The development of desirable personality traits.** If the play experience is successful children may learn to be cooperative, generous and truthful. (They may also learn to bully, to lie and to cheat.)

The Development of Play

Four reasonably well defined stages of play can be observed in most children.

First comes **exploratory play**, when babies look, touch, feel, bite, suck and bang. Once they are mobile they explore everything they possibly can. Second is **toy play**, beginning in the first year and reaching a peak in Western societies at any rate at about six years. Third comes a **widening repertoire** when games, sports and hobbies become part of a child's life. This lasts until puberty, when many previously enjoyed activities wane and **day-dreaming** increases.

The development of **social play** can be traced back to the baby's first interactions with the mother. Careful observations even of a neonate can yield a picture of something very close to play between adult and baby, especially around feeding or nappy changing.

Play with other children tends to be in parallel at first, with much looking rather than cooperation. By 19 or 20 months many children are playing with other children for about a quarter of their play time. Indeed, at this age they often play better when they have a companion, leading to the aphorism that the best toy for a child is another child. The observations on cooperative play on which this paragraph is based were made in the late 1970s. They illustrate the danger of relying on work of previous generations, for **M. B. Parten**, writing in 1934, did not note cooperative play in children under 3½ years.

Once cooperative play has begun young children will usually play with whoever is around, but when the gang age has been reached (see Chapter 16) the number of playmates decreases steadily.

Play also becomes increasingly sex appropriate or, as some would say, sex stereotyped with age as social forces impinge.

The **level of formality** of play also changes with age. At first children will play anything anywhere. Indeed, old pots and pans are often favourite 'toys'. Later, special toys, a special place and even special clothes may be demanded.

Cross-cultural Studies of Play

Economic necessity puts a severe constraint on play in some cultures. One group in Kenya, for example, have chores assigned by the age of three and time for play is restricted. (The phrase 'playing about' is used disparagingly in many cultures.) Economic poverty also restricts the number and quality of toys available to many children but it does not automatically follow that there is no play: children are adept at fashioning toys from wood, stone or mud. On the other hand, rich imaginative play is less often observed in cultures where adults live narrow, restricted lives.

It is possible that different play experiences explain many of the differences in ability and attainment that are found between children of differing cultures. This is a politically sensitive topic on which evidence is badly needed.

Questions

1. Why is it not possible to define play in a single definition?
2. Why is play important to a child?
3. Consider the notion of adult play.

Exercises

1. Observe a group of children and comment on the variation shown in their play. Try to give explanations for different forms of play that you see.
2. Advise the mother on the choice of toys and play activities for (*a*) a three-month-old, (*b*) a three-year-old.

22
Children's Art

'Once I drew like Raphael but it has taken a whole lifetime to learn to draw like children.'—Picasso

From a developmental point of view one can ask three fundamental questions about children's drawings: how do they do it? what do they do? why do they do it?

How Children Draw

In this context this is related to pencil control. At six to eight months they are likely to pick up a pencil or crayon and bang it on the table, put it in their mouth or throw it on the floor. Four to five months later they may begin to make some marks on paper, probably using a palmar grip—that is, the pencil will be held in a clenched fist, movement being with the whole arm from the shoulder. Next the grip will improve but the fingers may be midway along the pencil and control is still poor. Graudally control becomes finer until a sophisticated grip is attained with movement remaining only in the hand.

What Children Draw

This follows a reasonably consistent sequence. They begin by scribbling. To the uninitiated eye this is 'just scribble'. Children of 12 to 24 months or so enjoy making marks on paper and gradually learn to turn them into pictures. But **Rhoda Kellog**, who has made a special study of this stage, sees children having a desire to create order and balance even when they scribble. The apparently 'hit or miss' collection of lines falls into 20 basic types with 17 different placement patterns. A key shape at this time is the **mandala**. Mandala, a Sanskrit word for magical circle, is taken by some to mean any circular figure, while others take a stricter line and see it as a circle enclosing a rectilinear form. Children's drawings abound in mandalas. Often a circular form is the first recognisable element they produce and they go on to dot their later pictures with faces and the ubiquitous sun in one corner.

While there is no doubt about the frequency of the mandala there is no generally agreed interpretation of its place in a child's drawing. **Jung** saw it as a religious symbol of unity and a psychic expression of the identity of brain structure common to all members of the species. Some psychoanalysts see it as a breast. **Kellog** regarded it as part of a natural sequence of drawing that begins with scribbles growing into circles. **Howard Gardner**, whose book *Artful Scribbles* (Jill Norman, 1980) should be read by anyone wishing to pursue the whole topic of children's art in more depth, is close to Kellog in seeing the mandala as universal because it stands midway between the exploration of form and genuine representational depiction. 'It serves as an actively felt hint of pivotal events ahead.'

It must not be forgotten that children are to some extent constrained by the medium in which they work. Give them a pencil and they will draw lines; give them finger paints and they will produce a series of bold splashes of colour. Since most observation of children's work is based on line drawings it is these that will be discussed for the rest of this chapter. However, it should be noted that other forms of expression—for example, patterns—are open to discussion.

The **earliest attempts at representation** are often drawings of a human figure and the earliest of these is usually the familiar **tadpole person**, consisting of head and legs (see Fig. 23). There has been much speculation

Fig. 23. A trunkless man.

on why children omit the trunk; they may even depart from reality to such an extent that they put arms coming from the head. **Rudolf Arnheim** does not see this as a problem: he asserts that children are depicting both head and body when they draw a circle. Others have speculated that children draw only those parts which have emotional salience, and face, arms and legs fall into that category. **Gardner**, along with other authorities, notes that the absence of a body may be a problem only for the adult observer, not for the child. It is, following this argument, possible that children are drawing using consistent but non-adult rules. There may be a parallel here with language development (see Chapter 13). Just as children's first words often stand for a whole sentence so a simple drawing may have as much meaning for the child as the first words, and developmentally the first drawing may be as important. As Gardner put it, 'A general correspondence suffices between what is drawn and the object in the world.'

Norman Freeman has studied the phenomenon of the tadpole and attempts to answer the trunk question using techniques and observations borrowed from experimental psychology. He carried out one study in which children were asked to complete drawings by adding arms to a series of figures,

Fig. 24. Freeman's tadpole-like figures.
From G. Butterworth (ed), *The Child's Representation of the World*, Plenum (1977).

some of which had heads bigger than the circle below, and some of which were the other way round (see Fig. 24). Preschool children tended to put arms on whichever part was larger, suggesting that arm positioning is determined by the child's perception of the relationship between parts. Freeman also notes that we should consider the **task demands** of drawing a figure. A critical feature of such drawing is its serial nature: there is a recognisable **sequence** in the depiction of a human figure. Further theoretical consideration comes if one steps aside from drawing and goes to psychology to study **end anchoring**—that is, the tendency to emphasise the beginning and end of a series, whatever the series may be. (An example of this is the way that people are likely to remember the first and the last number when asked to remember several.) It may follow that children are using end anchoring when they draw, for head and legs are the two end points. In this context it is worth noting that while arms are frequently omitted legs are almost always included in even the most rudimentary figure.

Sequences within drawing can be observed in much the same way that one can observe a sequence in skills like walking, spelling or driving a car. Children tend to draw in consistent sequences even as young as three years old. They are likely to start at the top of the figure and work down; they may use 'subroutines' and treat pairs, of arms or legs, as units. At first they are likely to produce circles in a clockwise direction, changing when they learn to write at school.

The change in direction of the circle and the addition of bits of the human body can easily lead to a judgement of a child's level of maturity from a single drawing. The **Draw a Man test** gained great popularity in the 1930s: marks are given for the number of features and the detail included in a drawing. It is a seductively simple test. True, there are developmental sequences; true, most 10-year-olds produce pictures which are qualitatively different from those drawn by most five-year-olds. Nevertheless, the amount of variation between one drawing and the next makes any 'maturity score' extremely suspect. Equally questionable is the reliance on unaided drawing. It is always possible that a child has a conceptual store richer than that readily apparent from a drawing produced to the simple order 'Draw a person'.

Once the tadpole stage has been passed other subjects are rapidly added to the typical child's pictures. The mandala-like sun may be shown to be smiling, demonstrating a degree of animism, a dog may be included, looking rather like a human on its side with four legs, and—in cultures where doors and windows are rectangular—a square house with four windows and central front door is also likely to appear frequently. These are schematic figures, with children drawing representations of all dogs, all houses, in much the same way that they refer to all men as daddy. The figures are also partly determined by the child's environment; a culture with only rounded huts is unlikely to lead to children drawing square houses, unless the child has learned that this is 'correct' from someone else.

By **school age** children's drawing and painting has reached what some would see as art—see Picasso's comment at the beginning of this chapter. Gardner describes the products of this five to seven year stage as '... lively, organised and almost unfailingly pleasing to behold'. Not everyone agrees with this view. **Maria Montessori** stated, 'The eye of the child is uneducated, the hand inert, the mind insensible alike to the beautiful and the ugly.' **Paul Klee** admonished, 'Never forget the child knows nothing of art.'

Eight- to nine-year-olds seek realism in their pictures. It is sometimes said that young children try to draw what they know to be there, older ones draw what they can see. For many children this stage is a watershed for they cannot achieve satisfactory realism and so lose interest in the whole enterprise. Others allow their search for realism to constrain their output and lose earlier spontaneity.

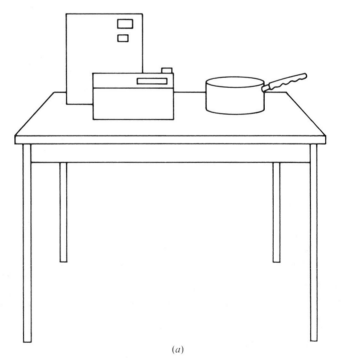

(*a*)

Fig. 25. (*a*) The original drawing.
From *Quarterly Journal of Experimental Psychology* (1977).

(*b*) No attempt at perspective.

But there is some progress during this search after realism period and that is the interest in and development of the skill of perspective drawing. One study, by **John Willats**, investigated the development of an ability to use perspective in the representation of a table containing several everyday objects (Fig. 25(*a*)). Six-year-olds made no attempt at a perspective reproduction, they typically drew a rectangular box with objects above it (Fig. 25(*b*)). An intermediary stage was the use of **isometric perspective**, with the sides of the table not converging (Fig. 25(*c*)). Finally the table and contents were correctly reproduced (Fig. 25(*d*)).

Using these sequences one can come to some conclusions about the process of development here. Children are not simply imitating, for those in the intermediary stage are not producing a copy of a model. Rather it seems that there is an interaction between the skills that evolve within the child

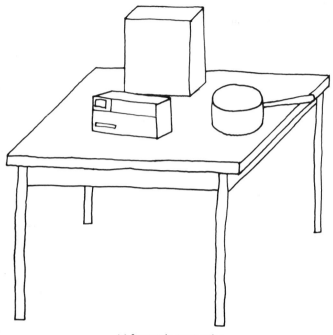

(*c*) Isometric perspective.

(*d*) Accurate convergence in true perspective.

and his everyday perceptions of models encountered from older people's work. One can also see in the development of perspective a visual grammar at work. The parallel with language is again apparent.

Why Children Draw

Aristotle: '... the soul never thinks without an image.'

Drawing has been described by a contemporary psychologist, following Aristotle, as 'visible thinking'. The universality of drawing supports the notion that it is of such fundamental importance as a means of expression that it can be seen to rank alongside language as one of those activities that go to define homo sapiens. At the risk of some circularity a simple answer to the question is: children draw because they are children.

Questions

1. Do children learn to draw or do they draw to learn?
2. Consider the notion that children draw in shorthand.
3. 'Drawing has its own grammar.' Is this statement (a) meaningful and (b) helpful?

Exercises

1. Examine children's drawings for mandalas and comment on their use.
2. Ask any group of children aged four, six and eight to draw a man or woman. Compare the results developmentally.

Part 7
Adolescence

23
Physical Development in Adolescence

Introduction

Perceiving adolescence as a time of physical and emotional turmoil is common. But commonly held views are not always correct. In the next two chapters the phase from the onset of puberty to the end of adolescence will be considered with as much emphasis as possible on conclusions to be drawn from systematic evidence, much of which has been collected in the last decade. There may then be a revision of the common view.

The Onset of Puberty

Coming from the Latin word **pubertas** meaning the age of manhood, puberty dates from the onset of menstruation (menarche) in girls and the emergence of pubic hair in boys. It is misleading, though, to see pubertal development only in terms of sexual characteristics; changes take place also in the heart, the lungs and many muscles.

Adolescence is heralded by the **growth spurt**, the accelerated increase in height and weight that turns children into youths. A critical point to bear in mind is that the age of the growth spurt varies widely. One boy whose father was 6′ 2″ and who himself eventually grew to the same height was asked, when he was 14 and still small, whether his father was 'little like you'. In boys the spurt may occur as early as eight or be delayed until 14. In very rare cases, known as **precocious puberty**, there is pubertal development in the child of six or seven. Typical growth curves are shown in Fig. 26, in which it can be seen that the average peak of increase in height is about the twelfth year for girls and the fourteenth for boys.

There are certain **sex differences in the pattern of the growth spurt**, a point that older texts do not include. Girls have their growth spurt before the appearance of their breasts, while boys typically begin to grow after they have developed pubic hair. So a tall girl who has only just begun to menstruate can be reassured that she is unlikely to grow much more, while a short boy who is a late developer can be told that increased height is almost certainly yet to come.

Changes in **sexual functioning** can be traced to hormonal activity. The hypothalamus signals to the pituitary gland which releases activating hormones. These in turn affect other glands which release further hormones,

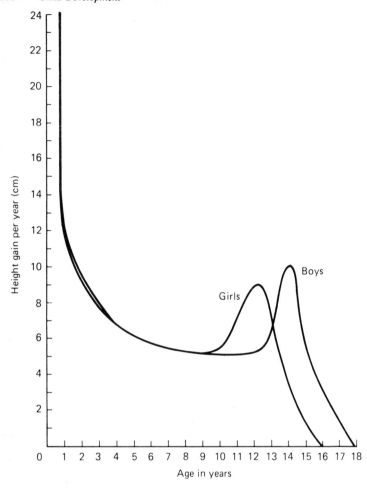

Fig. 26. Typical velocity curves for supine length or height.
From J. M. Tanner, R. H. Whitehouse and M. Takaishi, *Archives of Disease in Childhood* (1966).

among which are **oestrogen** stimulating the growth of ova and **testosterone** stimulating the development of mature sperm. They combine with other hormones to activate the growth of bones and muscle.

During this time the weight of the **heart** almost doubles with a corresponding increase in the power of the cardio-vascular system. There is a significantly higher increase in systolic blood pressure in boys than in girls, as Fig. 27 shows.

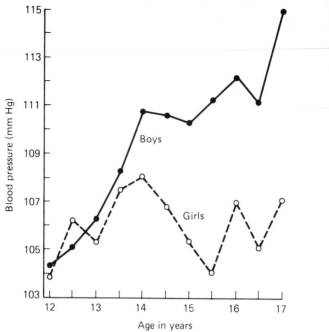

Fig. 27. Differences in systolic blood pressure between boys and girls at puberty. From W. Montagna and W. A. Sadler (eds), *Reproductive Behaviour*, Plenum (1974).

The Age of Development and Associated Factors

The physical growth and development occurring at puberty are so striking that it is hardly surprising that much follows in their train. In particular it is possible to make certain predictions about psychological phenomena from observations on physical changes.

Early maturers tend to do better on tests of mental ability and to do better at school. This finding is not confined to post adolescent development: it holds for all ages from about six onwards. **Late developing boys** tend to be more self-assertive, restless and less attractive with a lower level of self-esteem. In contrast, **early maturing girls** are reported to tend towards feeling socially at a disadvantage although this passes by the age of 14 or so. Equally the very **late maturing girl** often lacks self-confidence.

A word of warning, though: much of the psychological effect of the age of onset of adolescence is culturally determined and in any case all the trends noted above are relatively weak, based on studies of large samples. It would be wrong to assume that all late developing boys will be bossy and stupid, or that all early developers are intelligent.

One aspect of psychical development which is also culturally determined is the so-called **secular trend**, the increase in height and the acceleration in puberty which has been observed throughout the Western world in the last century. For example, the average height of boys attending one public school in Britain rose by 4.1 in. between 1873 and 1953; the average American foot has increased by $\frac{1}{8}$ in. for several generations; the age of menarche in Western Europe has dropped by about four months since 1850. The causes of the trend, according to the British authority **James Tanner**, are to be found in improvements in general health care, nutrition and housing.

The indications are that the curve of this trend is flattening out as sooner or later it must. If the fall in the age of menarche were to continue on its recent trajectory we could expect puberty to begin at four years by the year 2200. Tanner has pointed out that there are almost certainly biological limits for a given population: he sees that for menarche in European females being set at an average of $12\frac{1}{4}$ years.

Questions

1. Define the following: precocious puberty; the secular trend; oestrogen.
2. What main points would you like to see included in a lesson on physical aspects of puberty planned for a class of 9–10-year-olds?
3. Consider the importance of understanding sex differences in the growth spurt.
4. Is a study of physical development at puberty of any value in determining the value of coeducational rather than single-sex schools?

24

Personal Development in Adolescence

Theories of Adolescent Development

In the past two main theories have been put forward to explain the developmental process of transition known as adolescence.

Psychoanalytic Theory

Psychoanalytic theory has been discussed in outline in Chapter 2. The starting point for the psychoanalytic view of adolescence is the upsurge of instincts which occur with puberty. Immediately before this, it is asserted, is a quiet period of latency, a period of psychic balance. With puberty comes a new found sexuality and the adolescent seeks 'love objects' outside the family. (To seek them inside violates the incest taboo.) The adolescent personality is vulnerable at this time and is made anxious by the process of seeking a sexual partner, hence the development of defences.

Peter Blos has described adolescence as a **second individuation process**, the first having closed towards the end of the third year. If this view is correct there should be certain features in common between the three-year-old and the teenager. At first this may seem rather farfetched, but Blos argues that at both times there is a need for psychological change to help the individual along the path of maturation; there is increased vulnerability in the personality; both times witness an increase in independence.

Psychoanalysts see a crucial aspect of adolescence in the process known as **disengagement**, the freeing of oneself from the influence of the mother. This process is accompanied by a period of **regression**, when people behave as though younger. Blos explains the paradox of how anyone can become more adult by returning to childlike ways, asserting that the adolescent must 'come into emotional contact with the passions of his infancy and early childhood' to enable a shedding of accumulated mental energy: '... Only then can the past fall into conscious and unconscious memories.'

Regression in childhood usually refers to babyish behaviour; in adolescence it is less obvious. Blos cites the following examples:

1. The **idolisation** of famous people, notably pop stars and sportsmen. This is a regression to the time when parents were idolised.

2. **Ambivalence**, with rapidly changing interests and relationships, with a veering from a desire for independence and a need for dependence, reflects

the younger child's fluctuation between loving and hating, acceptance and rejection.

3. **Nonconformity and rebellion** are explained in psychoanalytic theory as rationalisation; that is, the young person is faced with a pull away from parents and all that they stand for. If this movement away can be made rational it will be more comfortable: the rationalisation process is one in which parental values are construed as worthless so that discarding them follows naturally. An illustration of this type of rebellion is the frequency with which teenagers appear to do not just what they want but what they perceive as the opposite of what their parents want. They seem driven to perversity.

The last aspect of the process dealt with in psychoanalytic theory is **loss**. The cutting of emotional ties noted above leads to a sense of loss akin to that felt after a death. There ensues an emptiness which has to be filled, which often is filled by intense emotional states, crushes, drug experiences, delinquency, religious fervour and all the kicks available.

Sociological Theory

Sociologists agree with psychoanalysts that adolescence is a process of transition and both lay stress on the importance of this phase. They differ in the way they look at the *causes* of the process. Psychoanalysts, as exemplified by Peter Blos, concentrate on intra-psychic phenomena; that is, they are most concerned with events going on **within the person**. Sociologists, on the other hand, look to factors **within society** as a whole.

Two key concepts in the sociological approach are **socialisation** and **role**. Socialisation has already been discussed in Chapter 16. To recapitulate: it refers to the process whereby individuals adapt to their social environment, absorbing the values, standards and beliefs surrounding them. Part of the socialisation process is learning about roles: each society has well recognised expectations of the role behaviour appropriate to a toddler, to a 10–11-year-old, to a father, grandmother and so on.

During early childhood roles are more or less imposed on children. The use of the phrase 'more or less' is critical since in most Western societies role expectations are not rigid and there are many subcultures within one overall societal group. As children approach adulthood they have increasing **freedom in their choice of role**; adolescence is a period which marks the transition to more or less complete freedom of choice. There are three main reasons why this period is marked by unique difficulties.

The first is that the transition from childhood roles to adult roles produces a **sense of discontinuity** and discontinuity usually spells distress. (Examples of the distress in other contexts are the problems encountered by a child who is admitted to hospital, by a move to a new town or more extremely by a move to a new country.)

The second is the notion that any inner uncertainty increases the need for dependence on others, leading to a **search for reassurance**. (This idea also is not unique to adolescence; one can see it operating at any time of uncertainty.)

The third is that adolescence is characterised by a series of **new expectations** many of which are greater than have hitherto been experienced. Changes in school, choices of what to do as school leaving approaches, leaving home— all present the young person with demands involving coming to terms with new sets of relationships.

A development of role theory distinguishes between two types of change. The first is **intra-role development**: the role is the same but different expectations are imposed. For example, a pupil in school will remain a pupil but will be expected to tackle harder work with increasingly less direct help. The second is the development of **entirely new roles**, an example being the abrupt change from being at school to being at work. The very young worker often shows signs of dependence, as predicted by sociological theory.

But role change is only part of the story. Within the pattern of role behaviour there are several potential **stress areas**, adolescents being vulnerable to some or all of them.

The first is **role conflict**. An individual may find that he or she is playing two or more roles simultaneously. An example is the teenage girl who finds herself both daughter and girlfriend. Two sets of people will then expect two sets of behaviour. One way of resolving this conflict is a rapid acceleration of the daughter role, with assistance from the mother so that mother and daughter adopt sister-like roles towards each other.

Role discontinuity is the second stress area, a notion already discussed above. Role discontinuity occurs when there is no bridge between one role and the next. An example of such a bridge is the work experience projects that many British school children are offered in their final year at school.

The third is **role incongruence**, when there are expectations from others that the individual cannot meet. An example of this is the person hopeless at games in a school where sport is held in high esteem. A less obvious example occurs when parents try hard to keep their children as children, refusing to allow them appropriate independence.

Sociological theory, then, looks firmly towards **interactions** between the individual and significant adults to explain both the process of transition and the possible stresses that may occur during the process. It looks also at aspects of socialisation wider than role adoption. Two changes have occurred in Western society in the last twenty years or so which are seen to have had a profound effect on adolescent development.

One is that young people have had their period of dependence increased by the prolonging of full-time education; leaving school at 14 was once the norm for British children. The other is the perceived decline in the role of the family as a powerful socialising force, leading to a segregation of the age groups. In societies where this segregation happens, and it is far from universal even in Western culture, adults spend less and less time with their children and the peer group attains proportionately greater influence.

This last point has been studied in some depth by **Urie Bronfenbrenner** who, along with others, has argued that the changes in the structure of society witnessed in the last couple of decades have brought increasing stress to Western youth and as a result young people have become more and more alienated from the older generation (see Chapter 3 also).

Whether or not Bronfenbrenner is correct, and whether psychoanalytic or sociological views are more pertinent to an understanding of adolescent behaviour, are matters for the reader to consider. Some evidence of what young people actually do and think is reported in the next part of this chapter, to be followed by a consideration of a third theory developed in the light of this evidence.

Thought and Reasoning and the Adolescent

Of all the changes that occur at adolescence the development of powers of reasoning is the least visible. Physical changes are obvious, behavioural changes are readily apparent but powers of thought alter also although this area of development is often neglected, perhaps because it is less striking than others.

Formal Operational Thought

The work of **Piaget** has already been discussed in Chapters 2 and 9. At or just before adolescence is the time that formal operational thought becomes possible; that is, there is a qualitative change in cognitive abilities which has far-reaching effects. One of the most crucial results of this is a shift in emphasis **from the real to the possible**. The young person can now manipulate mental constructs, whereas before only objects could be worked on, and so for the first time there is the power to consider notions of **propositional logic**, of **probability** and of **belief**.

A study by **David Elkind** illustrates Piaget's point. There were two groups of subjects: one age 8–9 and the other 13–14. A series of pictures was presented in pairs and the task was to decide which of the two was the 'correct' one. In other words, it was necessary to work out from early trials what rule or rules governed the game. In fact the pictures were in two sets, one of which was of tools or vehicles with wheels, the other being tools or vehicles without wheels. When a wheeled object was chosen a light went on. Only half the younger group achieved an understanding of the rule. Many of them formed a hypothesis early on and stuck to it blindly, seeming unable to realise that the testing of different hypotheses was possible. All the adolescents solved the problem.

Piaget proposed the age of 12 or 13 as a time by which formal thought might be attained but, as **John Coleman** has pointed out, he was optimistic in this suggestion; even at 16 only a minority have reached the most advanced level of formal operations, although the early levels might have been passed by a greater percentage. (For a further discussion of this and, indeed, many other points raised in this chapter see Coleman's book *The Nature of Adolescence* (Methuen, 1980), on which much of the present chapter has drawn.)

The observed variation in physical growth is mirrored in the **development of cognitive skills**. One child will be able to think in abstract terms at 12 or earlier, another may not reach this stage until 16. There is no one reason for this variation. Intelligence, as indicated by the IQ, is not strongly associated with the development of formal thought. There is a weak link with physical maturation but this is not strong enough to provide a complete explanation. Piaget himself saw social factors as the most important determinant but there is little evidence to support or refute this view. For the moment we must remain content in the knowledge that a shift occurs.

One final point must be remembered: some people never reach full operational thought at any age. An example of **egocentric thought in the adult** is the telling of an event entirely from one person's viewpoint. Compare 'I was standing by the window looking out like I always do last thing and I saw this red glow in the sky and I thought, that's funny, I've never seen that before' with 'Last night the house opposite caught fire'. Or consider the person who never, ever, discusses generalities, but talks only in concrete everyday terms.

Reasoning

The adult quoted above, who can perceive only from an egocentric point of view, is trapped in this mode of thinking. An outcome for the adolescent who manages to shift to formal operational patterns is a certain freedom from the earlier felt constraints. But, as Elkind has pointed out, despite the new-found ability to use mental constructs, despite the ability to move ground so that one can consider what is before one without always being bound by the immediate and the concrete, the adolescent is not always free from thinking about himself. Far from it: he is able to consider others' views, to put himself in their shoes and he does this only too firmly. Adolescents can be paralysed with embarrassment precisely because they are convinced that others are as preoccupied with the same thoughts that they are. So if a 16-year-old has a spot and is conscious of it then everyone who sees the spot must, it is assumed, share this awareness.

Elkind invokes a concept of the **imaginary audience** to explain much adolescent behaviour. Because the young person imagines that everyone shares his preoccupations he is driven by his constructions of what others think—hence the hours in front of a mirror, the intensive anxiety about clothes and the need always to say the right thing.

Elkind uses another concept to throw light on adolescents' egocentricity: the **personal fable**. The adolescent comes, it is argued, to see himself as so important that he jumps to the conclusion that he must be unique, and his waking thoughts are full of fantasies of omnipotence.

A different approach to teenage reasoning comes in a study carried out in the 1970s by **E. A. Peel**. He distinguished between three levels of judgement:

Level one: inadequate reasoning based on irrelevant information.
Level two: adequate but highly specific reasoning.
Level three: adequate reasoning which goes beyond the specific content of what is presented and considers a range of possibilities.

An example of the method of enquiry Peel gives to tap the level at which a person is working is the following:

All large cities have art galleries and Italy is exceptionally rich in art treasures. Many people travel to Italy, especially to enjoy these old paintings, books and sculptures. Floods in the Florence area recently damaged many of these great works. Old paintings are rare, valuable and beautiful, and should be kept safely stored.

Question: Are the Italians to blame for the loss of paintings and art treasures?

Using this question Peel found a marked change took place between 13 and 15. By the later age most of his subjects had reached his level three.

Adolescents' Relations with Adults

The adolescent to Shakespeare stood twixt man and boy. Few would disagree with this: the achievement of adulthood is the outward sign that adolescence is over. Adulthood can mean many things but one common factor to all definitions is likely to be **independence**. The adolescent feels the pulls towards a state in which most major decisions are no longer the sole province of parents but at the same time there is still some influence from home and family. Up to a point adolescents in some societies can have it both ways: while still physically a member of the family unit they can gradually gain independence of action, returning to old ways from time to time when the move towards the adult world becomes frightening.

The result of this gradual shift is a greater conflict than would occur if there were a sudden, complete break. Teenagers find themselves prey to mood swings, when the world is full of uncertainty and they do not know which of many possible roles to play. Parents, too, complicate the issue for they may feel a rather different ambivalence as they see their child disappear and a new person take his place. They may regard the child's move to independence while staying at home as particularly galling, finding themselves using the cliché accusation about the adolescent using the house like a hotel. What is more, *parents have to make some adjustments themselves.* They may have reached a stage in life when the hoped-for promotion is clearly not coming, when marital difficulties arise and are exacerbated by the prospect of a future without young children to provide a reason for staying together, when retirement begins to become a reality. Throughout this book there has been an emphasis on the importance of looking at two-way processes; adolescence is no exception.

Transition or Turmoil?

It is tempting to look at adolescents with a sense of desperation. They all try so hard to be outlandish, they all wear ludicrous clothes and take drugs and listen to offensive music at unsuitable hours. Clearly they must live in a world of their own and it must be as uncomfortable for them as they make us feel. There are, of course, several fallacies in all this: only a minority actually wear such odd clothes and by no means all set themselves apart as much as many adults imagine. When an attempt is made to examine the picture systematically the facts are not at all in accord with received opinion.

Evidence on the so-called generation gap and its dire consequences was collected in America in the 1950s. Since then there has built up a remarkably consistent picture from the work, among others, of **A. Bandura** in America and **K. Fogelman** in Britain, on both sides of the Atlantic which dispels a number of myths:

Myth number one: During adolescence parents are forced to be more controlling. The exact opposite seems to be the case. As children get older so the tendency is for **mutual trust** to develop.

Myth number two: Adolescents are perpetually struggling to emancipate themselves from parental authority. Again, there is no evidence for this, rather there is a suggestion that adolescents move easily from parental over-sight: the trauma is felt more by parents, especially fathers.

Myth number three: The adolescent blindly follows a peer group. Peer group identity is undoubtedly of importance and the support given by peers is real; but evidence suggests that teenagers choose which of many peer groups they will take as a reference and in most cases there is little conflict over this with their parents.

There are minor differences, usually centring on hair or clothes, but major issues of morality, religious or political beliefs and attitudes to sex seem rarely to be a problem.

It is important to emphasise at this point that it is major, cataclysmic, intergenerational battles that are in a small minority. It would be foolish to pretend that there are never minor clashes. An example of the evidence on this was a result from the Isle of Wight Survey carried out by **Michael Rutter** and colleagues. In 1976 came a report on alienation between parents and 14-year-olds. In only 4 per cent did parents record such a feeling and only 5 per cent of the teenagers noted it. However, 25 per cent of the children reported *some degree* of criticism of their parents.

Fig. 28. Proportions of each age group expressing themes of conflict with parents on one item of a sentence completion test.
From J. C. Coleman, *Relationships in Adolescence*, Routledge & Kegan Paul (1974).

There are, though, shades within even the relatively mild intergenerational conflict. There are some differences between cultures: American teenagers seem, for example, to be given less independence than their Danish counterparts. Young people's feelings of conflict reach different peaks according to age and sex, as Fig. 28 shows.

A study of the **social class effects** carried out in Britain in the late 1970s shows that middle-class parents of 16-year-olds expressed more favourable views of their children than did working-class parents, bearing out what has been touched on above: in many cases *adults are more hostile to teenagers* than vice versa.

One explanation for the discrepancy between received opinion and research data is that there is a difference between views about one's own family members and views about others. So a parent may castigate youth, but be sympathetic towards his own children. Children have to find their own feet; in doing so they may push the walls rather as they did when two or three years old, but pushing walls means friction, not necessarily a battle.

Authority and Adolescent Development

The attitude of reverence towards paterfamilias of the nineteenth century, the older statesman of the hearth who represented Authority, can still be found in some cultures but it is fast declining in the West. Unemployment in the 1980s, overpopulation, the perceived threat of nuclear war, the actual horrors in Vietnam, the nagging pain in Northern Ireland have combined to lead many young people to a cynicism about adults' powers. As one commentator put it, 'the major challenge to authority today is not that the young have no respect for authority but that they have little reason to have respect for authority' (Diana Baumrind, 1968).

Again one must beware of jumping to conclusions, in this case that a general decline in respect for authority means that parental models are no longer of importance. Rather the focus is on *what kind of models* are critical and how they operate. Several studies have looked at the effects of three different ways of exercising authority and all have come up with more or less the same results.

If one judges the effectiveness of authority by criteria like the achievement of adolescent independence coupled with a comfortable relationship with one's parents then two ways of exercising authority seem to be inappropriate. The first is **authoritarianism**, in which the parent attempts to shape the growing child according to a set standard of behaviour. The second is total **permissiveness** when children are allowed to get on with their own lives in their own way.

In contrast to these two is the **authoritative** approach, when parents encourage children to develop their own views while simultaneously insisting on socially acceptable behaviour. The distinction in outcome between these three is not confined to adolescence—see the reference to Baumrind's work in Chapter 20.

The Parent as a Model

It is possible that ultra-permissive parents behave as they do either through laziness or irresponsibility or because they have some ill-digested knowledge of child psychology and think that they are doing the right thing. Authoritarian parents are likely also to adopt that approach consciously and impose their ideas accordingly. The authoritative parent, on the other hand, is more likely to transmit a set of values less directly, with the children being more influenced by the role played by adults.

Adults in general and parents in particular provide a myriad of role models for the developing child. The models encompass among others the relationship between the sexes, attitudes to work, to ethical behaviour and attitudes to money. At adolescence young people become aware of the need to play certain roles themselves and they tend to look to those adopted by their parents or other significant adults as prototypes.

A critical factor in the influence of the adult is the degree to which the child has identified with that person; that is, the extent to which the adult's attitudes and characteristics have been incorporated by the younger one. (See Chapter 16 for a fuller discussion of this process.)

Sex roles have been studied in some detail in America, with complex results. During adolescence it seems supportive for boys to have a father who himself adopts strong stereotyped masculine behaviour. These boys have high self-esteem and are popular. But ten years later they are less well adjusted than those boys whose fathers displayed a greater range of role, including some so-called feminine interests. Girls are less easy to generalise about since the advent of the Women's Movement has brought about a shaking up of stereotypes. Here it seems that the most well adjusted girls are those whose mothers are comfortable in their role, whatever it may be.

Much less evidence is available on **work roles**. There are two studies of relevance, both of which suggest that the transmission of an **attitude to work** is more influential than simple occupation modelling: that is, it is not so much that a girl become a doctor like her mother, more that she adopt her mother's *values* about higher education and the use to which it is put.

According to one longitudinal study, 17-year-old boys who valued their father's occupation highly were most likely to do well in their own early careers. But this success waned unless the father influence was replaced by that of another significant adult by the middle twenties. In another study, women's attitudes towards work in general, the ability of a woman to hold down a job and the conflicts caused by the possibility of a dual career including work and motherhood were all shown to be directly related, at least in women between 19 and 22, to the role played by the mother.

For a further discussion on parental influences, direct and indirect, see Chapter 3.

Attitudes to Authority

Of all the topics touched on in this section this is the least well researched. There have been studies but they have looked at limited areas and have used only small samples. One tentative conclusion is that attitudes to authority undergo a marked change at about the age of 13 for both boys and girls. This is rather earlier than many commentators had imagined and it is possible that future enquiry will produce a modification of this view. Later workers may, for example, address themselves to a wider range of attitude-tapping techniques than has been used so far.

Another conclusion is that conformity among young people tends to be *greatest* within a peer group and *least* at home, with some association between social class and conformity, at least for boys, the more middle class being the more conforming.

A study carried out in Britain looked at stated demands of teenagers and came up with the finding—not altogether unexpected to anyone who has worked with this age group—that their greatest perceived need from adults was **support**. There was then a **gradient of control expectations**. The good teacher was seen as offering more control than autonomy. The good father offered both equally and the good mother offered more autonomy and less control.

Friendships

One definition of an adolescent is someone who wants to be different from everyone except his friends. Certainly friends come into their own at this time not only in dictating what should be worn but also in giving a lead on what should be thought and how one should behave. There are a number of reasons for this burgeoning power:

1. Adolescence is a time when, by definition, young people move away from the umbrella influence of the family, with the result that an **emotional gap** is left. This gap has to be filled somehow.

2. **Common experiences** provide a powerful bond. One has to look no further than the school Old Boys' Association or clubs for foreign nationals for examples.

3. Related to the second point made above is the need of some adolescents to feel **supported** as they venture into new roles and are exposed to new expectations. Someone else who is undergoing the same kind of experience will provide unique support.

4. In some cultures there is an increasing **age segregation** wherein the young are treated as a separate category of person, not only by their parents but also by commercially based pressures of advertising and magazines.

Developmental Trends in Friendship Patterns

Some have argued that there is a steady and regular increase in **stability of friendship patterns** over time: that the older one gets, between the ages of five to 18 or so, the more one is likely to name the same people as one's close friends.

Others have not disagreed with this but have pointed to different characteristics of friendship patterns which occur according to age. One study of girls' relationships, for example, noted three phases of friendship associated with three phases of adolescence:

1. **Early adolescence** (approximately 11–13 years) sees friendships based more on shared activities rather than on the interactions between people.

2. **Middle adolescence** (14–16 years) brings a stress on security: the best friend should be someone who can be trusted with secrets.

3. **Late adolescence** (17+ years) is a more relaxed time when girls seem less worried about being betrayed and abandoned by their friends. At this time many girls are beginning to form more or less permanent relationships with boys, which might explain some of the qualitative differences in attitudes to girls.

Other work has borne out this general finding of different needs at different ages. In particular the middle phase has been confirmed as a time when friendships are of paramount importance.

Some **sex differences** have been shown in friendship patterns, reflecting perhaps the difference in socialisation pressures exerted from an early age. In summary it can be said that girls show more anxiety about their relationships and that these relationships are both more intimate and dependent than those observed in boys. Boys look for shared pursuits for gang activities and for help when in trouble.

Popularity and Status

As a preliminary exercise before reading the rest of this section, make a list of five attributes that you would expect to be associated with popularity among teenagers. Consider whether boys and girls have separate attributes.

Work carried out in America and Britain in the 1950s and 60s has been reasonably consistent in finding that for both sexes **popularity** is associated with

cheerfulness, friendliness, enthusiasm, a sense of humour, enterprise in initiating activities and good looks.

Status has been shown to be associated with:

For girls: good looks, an attractive personality and good clothes.
For boys: either ability at sport or a deep knowledge of it.

The elevation of sport to a unique pinnacle for boys should not go without question. Even in the 1960s there was a suggestion that academic ability plus sporting prowess produced a super élite and with the recent economic decline it is likely that this trend will continue.

Conformity

Different from everyone except their friends: at a time of ascribed maximum rebellion there is, paradoxically, a peak of conformity to peer group fashions, particularly of dress. Indeed, it can be argued that the greater the move from parental norms the more need there is for the support that comes from contemporaries.

Two points need to be clarified. The first is that there are, in this as in other areas, significant age differences in conformity patterns. The peak age for conformity, for both boys and girls in Western societies, is 13–14, with very little evident sex difference, although what differences there are point to girls being somewhat more conforming than boys. The second is that one should not be misled into imagining that teenagers who dress alike necessarily behave in the same way. There may be a herd mentality extending to jeans and hair length but not all who dress in this way flout authority.

The role of the peer group in exerting pressure on someone to misbehave is often invoked: he/she was led astray by the dreadful company he/she has been keeping. This is clearly an important social issue and in contrast to much of the experimental evidence quoted in this chapter the conclusions on this topic are not all in the same general direction.

One view sees adolescents seeking peer groups who will do no more than **reinforce many of the values of the adult**. This argument regards teenage drinking, for example, as influenced not by peer group pressure but by a process of identification with adults. 'The majority of adolescents in our society would in all probability come to use alcohol eventually even if there were no peer group experience at all since young people tend to perceive drinking as an integral part of adult behaviour.' (**R. L. Akers**, writing in 1970.)

The other view looks at **peer group pressure** as paramount. A study on drug-taking in Great Britain noted that almost all the respondents said that their first drug-taking experience was a direct result of encouragement from friends, who themselves saw drug abuse as imparting status within the group.

Parents versus Peers

The heading to this section is actually a misnomer for the position is not a simple either/or conflict. Here research evidence is more or less consistent in arguing that both parents and peers exert influence but in different situations. Thus it seems that when the question to be decided has long-term implications for the future, parents' wishes are more likely to be paramount, compared to times when the matter at hand concerns immediate status.

One school of thought goes beyond this situational hypothesis and argues that in critical areas young people tend to seek a course of action which will be in accord with pressures from both parents and peers. **John Congree**, in *Adolescence and Youth* (Harper and Row, 1977), takes this possible overlap between parents and peers as the first of his five points to be considered in the parent–peer context. The other four are: parents are not always confident in their attitudes—they may be happy to allow peers some influence in fields beyond their competence; there is general recognition of situationally determined influence, with peers having the major say at some times, parents at others; peer group influence is at its height when parental interest is lowest; the need to conform varies from individual to individual.

Faced with conflicting evidence of this sort one can take one of two courses. The first is to accept one and discount the other, using other evidence to determine which is accepted. The other is to argue that either could be correct for some subjects, but that this is far too complex a topic to be totally illuminated by a single study. Anyone who has read earlier chapters of this book will by now be in no doubt which is the more likely course to be taken here.

The first dimension of complexity is the **diversity of social influence**. Some people are influenced by actual role models with whom they identify—'the chip off the old block'; others are influenced by an ideal and try to behave in the way they imagine this ideal would—hence the outbreak of certain types of hair style copying the world famous ideal-type figures. The group can influence by threats of violence or ostracisation if their norms are not adhered to; there is no doubt that fear of ridicule and rejection by peers acts powerfully on the young person. One result of this complexity may be a reconciliation of the two views expressed above. An American study of drug-taking teenagers reported that peers were influential; but it was also noted that the parents of the drug-takers, although expressing disapproval of drug abuse, were themselves heavy drinkers or smokers. So perhaps these were youngsters who found peers whose influence would in some way reinforce examples set at home. We must not forget that there is usually more than one group available to most young people; there is an element of choice.

The second dimension is the **link between certain forces and certain outcomes**. It is highly probable that choice of clothes is heavily influenced by peers; choice in matters of morality, on the other hand, may be due far more to adult influence.

The third dimension is that of **vulnerability**. This is a concept that has received some attention from researchers lately and is likely to receive more in the near future. The principle is simple: some people are more vulnerable to certain pressures than others. One can see this at work in families where only one person deviates and becomes the black sheep or, in another terminology, the scapegoat. On the other hand, there are some families where one person manages somehow to withstand the effects of neglect or overt ill-treatment. So it is with adolescents.

An example of several points made above is found in a study of teenage drinking habits in Scotland: 82 per cent of the young people began drinking in the house, the other 18 per cent having their first experience in parks, playgrounds and clubs, with friends rather than family. But when the heaviest drinkers were singled out it was found that they all came from the 18 per cent who had been influenced by friends. What is more, all were on bad terms with their parents and had little time for authority.

The final dimension is that of **time**. One view, based on drug-abusing teenagers, is that situational factors affect *initiation* into the group but intrapsychic factors determine whether or not the group's ways will *continue* to be an influence. If this view is valid then family composition, the nature of the school and the environment in which someone grows up will be influential in the young person joining a group; whether or not he stays there will depend more on his personality.

This last point illustrates the futility of seeking a single explanatory factor, for the young person's personality must to some extent have been formed as a result of influences from the home and the environment. We go round in circles only too easily.

Sexuality

In a book published a generation ago the author noted that people living on the Continent have sex; the English have hot-water bottles. The 1980s teenager would not be amused for two reasons: one is that the word sex no longer brings an automatic response related to naughtiness in this age group; the other is that the statement is no longer true. Today contraception is widely available, abortion is no longer illegal, homosexuals can come out and declare themselves and the prevailing attitude among the young towards sexual matters seems to be based on the precept that one works out one's own individual morality rather than being tied by universally applicable laws.

Sexual Behaviour

Our understanding of the behaviour of young people is based almost entirely on surveys. There is an immediate question mark over any data thus obtained for there will be a temptation either to boast of conquests more hoped for than achieved or a desire to hide behaviour that might be perceived as shaming. So American work, from that of **A.C. Kinsey** in the 1950s, and British surveys, notably those of **Michael Schofield** in 1965 and **C. Farrell** in 1978, must be taken with a grain of caution. One way of gaining some sense of validity is to see if all results go more or less in the same direction, which on the whole they do (see Table 15).

Table 15. Percentage of populations studied claiming to have had sexual intercourse.

Country of origin	Authors	Age in years	Percentage	
			Girls	Boys
USA	Kinsey *et al.* (1948/1953)	17	10	61
		20	18	72
	Kantner and Zelnick (1972)	17	27	
		19	46	
	Finkel and Finkel (1975)	17		69
UK	Schofield (1965)	17	11	25
		19	23	37
	Farrell (1978)	17	39	50
		19	67	74

Producing totals broken down crudely by age group is only one way of considering behavioural trends: another is to look in some detail at individual and group differences. Taking this approach we can say that it seems that in the USA at least, black teenagers are more experienced than white, and in Britain working-class boys are more experienced than those from the middle classes. One study published in 1969 comparing university students in different countries came up with the finding that English students, both male and female, were the most experienced, followed by, for females, Germany, Norway, USA and Canada, and for males by Norway, USA, Canada and Germany. It must be noted that this study collected data by post and may say more about anonymous boasting than actual behaviour.

Coleman's Focal Theory of Adolescence

John Coleman has examined psychoanalytic and sociological theories in the light of the evidence about what young people say and do and has found both wanting. There is, he asserts, a gap between theory and practice. Both the two major theories view adolescence as a time of transition and turmoil, of identity crisis and rebellion. Empirical evidence from systematic enquiries of young people in America and Europe supports the notion that this is a time of transition but lend no support for the automatic assumption of universal continuing distress and alienation from adults. Coleman, in his 1980 book, quotes from an American psychiatrist, **David Offer**:

'The transitional period of adolescence does present the adolescent with a special burden, a challenge and an opportunity. He has to individualise, build up confidence in himself and his abilities, make important decisions concerning his future, and free himself of his earlier attachments to his parents. Our observations have led us to conclude that the majority of the teenagers in our sample coped with these tasks successfully.'

Perhaps the early psychoanalysts relied too much on their observations from patients sent to them. Perhaps sociologists have seen youth as a metaphor for change and therefore ascribed too much to ordinary normal young people. Coleman argues that we need a theory of adolescence based not on the abnormal few but on the normal many. He proposes a **focal theory**.

This explanation encompasses both the critical factors that emerge from empirical research: *first* that there are undoubted elements of stress associated with certain aspects of the developmental process and *second* that overall the majority of people get through without undue turmoil. The key to Coleman's theory is in the phrase used above: stress associated with *certain aspects* of the process. He sees young people encountering aspects in turn, focusing first on one, then on the next. So an adolescent might cope first with anxiety over sexual relationships. Then, when that is more or less under control, it is possible to grapple with peer group membership, after which there is psychological space to manage a break from parents.

Coleman does not suggest that all crises come in this or any other sequence, nor is his a stage theory. Stage theory, exemplified in work on cognitive psychology, demands that stage one is gone through before stage two can begin.

Conclusion. Coleman's theory has much to commend it. Based on evidence from systematically collected data it augments and illuminates earlier theories and goes a long way in explaining some apparent contradictions.

Questions

1. Critically consider the notion that adolescence is a period of turmoil.
2. What has been the contribution of the following to our understanding of adolescence: psychoanalysis, sociology, biology?
3. What is meant by role conflict? Illustrate your answer with at least two examples.
4. Describe the typical thought processes of any adolescent known to you.
5. Is adolescence more difficult for parents than teenagers?

Part 8
Developmental Disorders

25
Developmental Disorders: Nature and Treatment

Introduction

There are many ways in which children's behaviour gives rise to anxiety, not all of which are properly the concern of the student of child development. In this chapter, for which I have drawn heavily on Philip Barker's *Basic Child Psychiatry* (Staples Press, 1979). I have confined myself to a consideration of some of the most common disorders related to change over time. In their early months all children are incontinent, waking and sleeping fitfully, unable to talk or to read. When appropriate skills are not achieved by what has come to be regarded as an age-appropriate time we talk of a **disorder**.

Enuresis

Enuresis is a general term referring to **wetting** and is usually subdivided into **nocturnal enuresis**, or bedwetting, and **diurnal enuresis**, or daytime wetting. Further ways of classifying the condition are **primary enuresis**, when a child has never yet been dry, and **secondary enuresis**, which is wetting occurring after the child has been dry for a period of a year or more.

Bedwetting is common: about 10 per cent of children still wet at five years, the figure falling to about 5 per cent by the age of 10. By the teens the number has dropped to 2 per cent. Boys are more affected than girls.

Aetiology

Occasionally enuresis is due to a structural abnormality of the urinary tract and it may be associated with urinary infection. Other physical conditions associated with enuresis are epilepsy and any which cause the passage of increased quantities of urine, an example being diabetes, fortunately a rare condition.

Developmental delay accounts for the great majority of cases of primary enuresis. The postulated delay is in the maturation of the nervous system (see Chapter 7) or at least in certain parts of the system. Support for a constitutional basis for enuresis comes from the finding that there is a positive family history in up to 70 per cent of cases of the primary condition.

On the other hand there are, undoubtedly, other factors at work. Primary enuresis is more common in lower socioeconomic groups than high ones. Family disorganisation and inconsistent training are both related to enuresis and a plausible hypothesis is that these two combine with delayed neurological maturation to produce the end result of wetting. Emotional disturbance is rarely a cause of primary enuresis although it may easily be a result; much depends on the sensitivity of the adults concerned.

Emotional disturbance is usually the cause of secondary enuresis. Children under stress often regress to the habits of an earlier age, an age when perhaps they were more secure because less was expected of them. Common examples of this stress are admission to hospital, the birth of a sibling and family turmoil associated with parental discord.

There is no evidence to support the notion that children who wet sleep more heavily than those who do not.

Treatment

The two forms of treatment for developmental enuresis most often used are training—technically known as conditioning—and the use of drugs.

In some cases there appears to be a need to train the relevant muscles. Children can be encouraged to control their micturition voluntarily: stop-start-stop-start. Nocturnal enuresis may respond to a bell and pad: a specially constructed pad is folded into the child's bed, attached to a bell or buzzer. As soon as the pad becomes moist the bell rings and continues to ring until switched off. The sequence then is

child begins to wet—bell rings—child wakes within a few moments—child turns off bell and empties bladder in an appropriate place—bell is reset—child returns to bed.

In this way a habit of waking to empty the bladder is established.

The most commonly used drug is imipramine, the action of which when used with enuresis is uncertain. It is an antidepressant but it is thought that it owes its success more to its side effects on the nervous system than to its function as an antidepressant.

Prognosis

There is a tendency for children to grow out of enuresis anyway and so the outlook is good. However, spontaneous recovery may take quite a long time and there is every reason to attempt to work with the child. Results of treatment between the ages of six and nine years are normally good although they are less satisfactory if left later than this.

Encopresis

This term refers to faecal soiling, the passing of faeces in the clothes. Usually this refers to soiling of pants but the symptom can occur at night. Most children are clean by the age of three; soiling beyond the age of four is abnormal.

Continuous soiling refers to that which has been present from birth; **discontinuous** to that which appears after a period of continence.

The Isle of Wight Study published in 1970 reported that 1.3 per cent of 10–12-year-old boys and 0.3 per cent of girls soiled at least once a month. The higher rate among boys is constantly found.

Aetiology

A rare physical condition known as Hirschprung's disease is one cause of encopresis. There is an absence of nerve ganglia from the colon which means that faeces cannot be moved on in the usual way. The result is that the colon becomes loaded with faeces and overflow occurs. An anal fissure may also cause pain or defecation which can result in the child learning to retain, learning which can persist well after the fissure has healed.

Far more frequently encopresis is not related directly to physical conditions such as Hirschprung's disease; it is a result of lack of training as in a very disorganised family or, more commonly, of emotional disturbance. There is generally more than one factor involved.

Children under stress may, as was noted in the section on enuresis above, regress to a more dependent stage of emotional development.

Children may also use encopresis as a weapon, a very powerful weapon, in a war with adults. An often observed picture is of an over-controlling parent who might have achieved toilet training by the time the child is 12 months old. Normal outlets of aggression are denied and there is an unconscious appreciation that soiling will produce a devasting effect. It does.

Aggressive soiling may be retentive, when the child becomes constipated leading to overflow, or non-retentive when faeces are deposited anywhere but the appropriate place.

Treatment

If the condition is one of constipation or retention then a physical examination is required. Whatever the nature of the symptom some form of psychologically based approach to the child and parents is indicated.

Prognosis

The outlook is good; encopresis in a physically and mentally normal adult is virtually unknown. It has been noted though that some children respond to treatment by becoming clean but then express their emotions in other ways.

Feeding Problems

Children can eat or drink too little or too much. They may be excessively faddy, like the girl who would eat nothing but Mars bars and Complan, or they may eat the inedible, a habit known as **pica**.

The conditions discussed in this section are those with a developmental aspect; anorexia nervosa does not come into this category.

Food refusal can often be traced to causes similar to those noted above in the section on soiling. A rigid, over-controlling parent may have exaggereated views on the importance of a certain kind of diet and the child's unconscious unerringly homes in on this weak spot.

Overeating and obesity. If a child of normal weight for height is reported as eating too much he may be suffering from a physical condition requiring medical attention or he may simply have parents who are unaware of a child's needs. An obese child is, however, a different matter. Not all obesity is a direct result of emotional disturbance, but psychological factors which can lead to comfort-providing overeating should always be considered.

Pica. The eating of, for example, wood, soil, paint, wool, paper or pebbles is developmentally normal in toddlers who experiment with eating but becomes abnormal if it persists. It is often, but not always, associated with subnormality.

Early Experience and Feeding Problems

Breast feeding is likely to be more successful if the baby is put to the breast within four hours of birth. It is difficult to generalise on the relationship between breast feeding and later developmental feeding problems since the incidence and duration of breast feeding varies so much by social class, by region, by culture and by community.

Feeding problems are frequently encountered among preschool children. One study noted that 13 per cent of three-year-olds in London were reported by their parents to have food fads, while another, in Nottingham, found that 42 per cent of the mothers interviewed were at least mildly concerned about the amount their four-year-old child was eating.

From these and similar findings it is easy to jump to the conclusion that there is a continuity of causes of the problem from infancy to later childhood. There are two reasons for caution before such a conclusion is accepted. The first is that there are wide individual differences between babies in their feeding habits and retrospective studies based only on those who have later presented with symptoms are likely to give a distorted view of normality. The second is the difficulty in disentangling genetic from environmental factors. It is known, for example from twin studies, that genetic factors should always be considered in cases of obesity, but continuity in weight from one generation to another may reflect cultural habits as much as genes.

Treatment

Food refusal is best treated by ignoring the symptom, a normal diet being offered to the child on a 'take it or leave it' basis. This is easier said than done and parents may need help in understanding themselves and their child.

Obesity is much harder to treat. Children usually lose weight rapidly when admitted to hospital but this loss is rarely maintained once they return home.

Pica is best treated by an approach to the underlying disorder present in the family.

Prognosis

The outlook for **food faddiness** is good. It is often no more than a manifestation of a developmental phase and providing the family background is relatively healthy it is likely to pass.

The outlook for severe **obesity** is poor, although one cannot be certain that a fat child will undoubtedly be a fat adult. Studies based on past generations are not always valid in this context since dietary habits can change over a 10–20-year period

Speech and Language Disorders

A discussion of language development has been given in Chapter 13. In this section some commonly occurring developmental disorders will be considered. They may be classified as disorders of language or of articulation or both.

Language Disorders

These may be **receptive**, when there is difficulty in understanding language, or **expressive**, or both. Such disorders are often referred to as **aphasia** (a disorder of language due to cortical damage) or **dysphasia** (impairment of language). These two terms are sometimes used, incorrectly, as though they were synonymous.

Aetiology

Children may fail to develop language because they are deaf, severely subnormal or abnormally withdrawn. The term aphasic should not properly be applied to them since their language difficulty is secondary to another condition.

Most diagnosed aphasia seems to be a result of some abnormality in the central nervous system, with the additional possibility of an interaction between such a deficit and other adverse conditions such as subnormality.

Treatment and Prognosis

Severe cases of receptive aphasia are very difficult to treat and speech may never be acquired. Milder cases respond to speech therapy, which enables the child to be in an optimal environment as neurological maturation occurs.

Articulation Disorders

Disordered articulation may be classified as **dysarthria** (implying a defect in the structure or function of the muscles and other organs involved in speech sounds) or **dyslalia** (the unduly prolonged persistence of infantile modes of pronunciation).

Developmental articulatory disorders may, like aphasia, be related to a delay in neurological development. Emotional factors may be associated, the baby talk being a symptom of regression in the face of stress. If there is evidence of normal articulation in the past or if baby talk occurs only in certain situations then emotional causes are likely.

Stammering is the repeated interruption of the flow of speech by repetition, prolongation or blocking of sounds. It is common when children are learning to talk—that is, between the ages of two and four—and usually passes with time. In some children the patterns of early childhood persist and become a disorder: stammering is found in about 1 per cent of British school children. It is four times more common among boys than girls.

The aetiology of stammering is not fully understood. There is some evidence of a hereditary disposition but brain injury, mental subnormality, emotional stress and anxiety may be implicated. Some children can speak normally in one situation but stammer in others; some can sing without stammering; not all stammerers are obviously worse when they are anxious.

Treatment is usually in the hands of a speech therapist and the prognosis is variable.

Sleep Disorders

During the first few months of life babies settle into some pattern of sleep, with *wide individual differences* being observed. Generally the pattern involves longer periods of sustained sleep, most of which occurs at night. The ability to maintain a period of sustained sleep increases markedly with maturation. However, mothers of three-year-olds studied in London by **Naomi Richman** reported that 13 per cent had difficulty in getting to sleep and 14 per cent woke during the night. Other studies of younger children have reported a rate of disturbance of up to a quarter of the sample in question.

Settling and Night Waking

Settling problems have been seen as a symptom of separation anxiety: children may have many night fears that parents never learn about. In some cultures this is recognised by having children share a bed with an adult or another child until they reach their mid teens. Settling problems can also arise if being up is more enjoyable than going to bed.

There appears to be a high degree of continuity in waking patterns from infancy to early childhood. The frequently waking 2–3-year-old is likely to have been an irritable baby, who slept little and cried often. This finding argues against automatically looking for a single event causing night waking, tempting though that search may be.

The first response of many advisers to a parent is 'let the baby cry'. This advice is easy to give but less easy to follow, especially if one lives in a flat with thin walls and awkward neighbours. A second response is to try some form of medicine which may or may not help. Recent work in London has suggested that an effective treatment approach is to help parents to be consistent in their behaviour and clear in the messages they convey to the child, providing the child with a kindly administered, firm routine in which there are rewards for being in bed.

Sleepwalking

Up to 15 per cent of children aged five to 12 years have had at least one episode of sleepwalking, the behaviour being more common in boys.

Twin studies suggest that genetic factors contribute in part and it is thought that both sleepwalking and sleeptalking are related to stress. They are both examples of behaviours that children sometimes revert to.

Nightmares and Night Terrors

Nightmares are unpleasant or frightening dreams. Children are not overtly disturbed while having them and if woken they react normally and can usually recount the dream.

Night terrors are alarming in the extreme to parents. The child usually shouts out, apparently in terror and may seem to be hallucinating, seeing or hearing people or things that are not physically present. Children are not accessible during this period and do not respond when spoken to. In the morning they have no recollection of the event. There is no evidence that night terrors are associated with any form of emotional disturbance when they occur in childhood.

Prognosis of Sleepwalking, Nightmares and Night Terrors

Most pass with age. If they persist or if they appear to be related to a specific event or area of anxiety professional help should be sought.

Dyslexia

There are many possible causes underlying a child's failure to learn to read or to spell. Children may be mentally subnormal, emotionally disturbed, deaf or visually handicapped. They might have been exposed to a variety of teaching methods or they might not have been to school because of illness or because their parents were continually travelling.

If none of the above causes pertains it is sometimes assumed that the child can be called dyslexic. Much argument has turned on the definition of this term. One of the most recent, formulated in the light of previous criticisms, is:

'... A learning disability which initially shows itself by difficulty in learning to read and later by erratic spelling and by lack of facility in manipulating written as opposed to spoken words. The condition is cognitive in essence, and normally genetically determined. It is not due to intellectual inadequacy or to lack of socio-cultural opportunity or to faults in the technique of teaching, or to emotional factors or to any known structural brain defect. It probably represents a specific maturational defect which tends to lessen as the child gets older, and is capable of considerable improvement, especially when appropriate remedial help is afforded at the earliest opportunity.' (M. Critchley and E. A. Critchley, 1978)

Because of the variability in definition it is not possible to give a generally acceptable estimate of how many dyslexic children there are; a conservative figures is 4 per cent. More boys than girls are affected.

Aetiology

The adjective 'developmental' frequently precedes the word 'dyslexia' and gives a clue to assumed aetiology. The assumption is that there is some form of delay in neurological development which leads to difficulty in processing visual material (visual dyslexia) or auditory input (auditory dyslexia). Thus it is perhaps more proper to talk of the dyslexias rather than dyslexia.

One common observation is that children with reading difficulty are slow to develop the ability readily to discriminate between **left and right**. This apparent stupidity is maddening to those who learn the skill easily but it seems to underlie some of the problems of children who read *on* for *no* or *was* for *saw*. There is no evidence, however, that **crossed laterality**, i.e. the preference for the right hand and the left eye (or vice versa), has any association with difficulties with reading or spelling. Neither is left-handedness a cause of problems in this area.

Another common observation is that dyslexic children frequently have a history of **language delay**.

Genetic factors have been invoked in discussions of aetiology. One of the most recent studies is by **Jim Stevenson** and colleagues in London. They found, using twins, that genetic factors appear to be associated with spelling but not with reading alone.

Teaching Dyslexic Children

Since this is primarily an educational rather than a medical problem 'teaching' is preferred to 'treatment' as a term to head this section.

No one method of teaching has been found unquestionably superior to all others. The key to those that do produce good results is that they take a systematic approach, working slowly but steadily. Part of the secret of success lies in maintaining the child's interest and motivation. Not to be able to read by the age of eight or nine is a serious social handicap and can easily lead to emotional disturbance.

Prognosis

The outlook for those who fall into this category is mixed. With a great deal of high-level teaching many learn to read adequately but most continue to have spelling difficulties throughout their life.

Questions

1. Encopresis is usually multifactorially determined. What are the possible factors?
2. Is dyslexia a 'middle-class disease'?
3. Can any developmental disorders be prevented?
4. How would you attempt to deal with a child who refused to eat school food?
5. How are night terrors different from nightmares?

Part 9
Technical Aspects of Study

26
Statistical Concepts

Introduction

This book has been written primarily for those working with children rather than those undertaking research. Unfortunately very few people who find themselves in daily contact with children read research reports, and it seems as if a gulf divides two camps. On the one hand are people in colleges and universities beavering away at erudite, elegantly designed studies; on the other are the field workers carrying on as though the former did not exist. In part this is the fault of the language used to report research but in part it is also because few field workers have been trained to read research with a critical appraisal of design and statistics. This chapter and the one that follows has been written to introduce some of the basic concepts of both.

Mean and Standard Deviation

Mean is easy: it is the average worked out by totalling items and dividing the total by the number of items.

Standard deviation is less easy: it refers to the average of deviation around a mean. So if a group of children have a mean height of 4 ft. and a standard deviation of 3 in. that means that about two thirds of them are within 3 in. of being 4 ft. Another group might have a mean of 4 ft. and a standard deviation of 12. The second will have far more very tall or very short children than the first.

The importance of this measure arises when one is comparing differences between groups. It often occurs that two means are very different. But when the groups' scores are tested statistically there may be even greater variation *within* each group than there is *between* the groups.

An example of this kind of difference can often be found in comparisons between schools in children's performance in examinations. It is not enough to cite the average pass or fail rate; one must look also at the spread of passes within each school.

Probability

A precise way of describing differences between scores is to work out the probability of a certain result having occurred by chance. So if a probability figure (usually written as a *p* value) is 0.01 this means there is a 1 per cent probability of that result having occurred by chance. A *p* of 0.05 indicates a 5 per cent probability. Anything greater than 0.05 is usually regarded as statistically non-significant—that is, the observed results are so likely to have happened by chance that they are regarded with extreme caution. The *p* value is sometimes referred to as the significance level.

Examples of the use of probability to indicate statistical significance are found in many studies in the psychological literature. One is that of **E. M. Hetherington** who looked at the effects of father absence on the behaviour of teenage girls. Comparing those whose parents were divorced and those whose father had died with those whose father was present she found considerable differences both in the girls' sense of security around male peers and around male adults. But the differences between the former comparison had a probability of 0.010, while that of the latter was 0.001. In other words, the lack of security around male adults was statistically of much greater significance.

Correlations and Causality

A coefficient of correlation yields a measure of the extent to which two scores are associated. The closer to 1.0 the coefficient is, the closer the association.

The two crucial points to note in this context are that correlations refer to scores and to associations. They do not in themselves say anything about the *cause* of an association or its *direction*.

Three examples will illustrate some of the pitfalls.

1. There is a statistically significant correlation between the incidence of heart disease in middle-aged men in Britain and the import of bananas. This is an example of an association which, despite the level of statistical significance, has occurred by chance.

2. There is a positive correlation between the sale of colour televisions and the sale of central-heating systems in Britain. Here is an association but one can hardly say that one has caused the other: rather the likely explanation is that a third factor of prosperity has affected both.

3. There is a correlation between reading backwardness and behaviour problems. Here the association seems plausible, but there remains the question of direction: does reading difficulty cause backwardness or vice versa?

Further points of possible misunderstanding are that the degree of relationship is not proportional to the size of the coefficient. A coefficient of $+0.6$ does not mean the association is twice as strong as one of $+0.3$. The coefficient is an *index*, not a measurement like centimetres or inches. The interpretation given to the figure will depend on the nature of the sample being investigated and the problem under consideration.

Reliability

A coefficient of reliability gives a measure indicating the extent to which one can assume that if a measure were immediately repeated on the same subject it would give the same result. Measurement of weight, providing the scales are working, is highly reliable; most psychological tests are expected to have a reliability of at least $+0.85$. If a research report discusses a new test without giving its reliability it is to be regarded with caution.

Measurement of Heritability

Some of the argument that has raged about the interpretation of twin studies is to do with the statistical analysis of the results. Older studies used the Holzinger formula

$$H = \frac{r_{MZ} - r_{DZ}}{1 - r_{DZ}}$$

where H is the heritability index, r_{MZ} the correlation between monozygotic twins, and r_{DZ} the correlation between dizygotic twins.

This has been criticised as a 'confusing statistic' since it makes certain assumptions about differences between families. A preferred formula now is the simpler

$$2\,(r_{MZ} - r_{DZ})$$

P. E. Vernon, in his *Intelligence: Heredity and Environment* (W. H. Freeman, 1979), discusses these formulae with the following correlations in mind.

MZ twins 0.87   DZ twins 0.56

Holzinger's formula gives an H of 0.70, while the second formula gives a figure of 0.62. The importance of this difference can be appreciated when it is realised that percentage estimates of the contribution of inheritance are reached by multiplying the H figure by 100. So one formula gives 70 per cent to inheritance, the other gives 62 per cent.

There are further qualifications to the acceptance of even the simple formula as it stands since it, too, makes assumptions:

1. It assumes that the environments have been equal.
2. It assumes non-assortative mating between the parents, i.e. the statistic is questioned if parents with assumedly similar genetic backgrounds mate since this will increase the genetic similarity between DZ twins.

Questions appear at the end of Chapter 27.

27
Research Design

Nothing can be Proved ...

Nothing, that is, within the context of scientific thought as it is currently found in centres dealing with child development. This is because we can never be completely certain of any prediction we make. To take an extreme example: we can say that the sun rises in the East and sets in the West. As far as we know it has always been thus and observations and measurements of direction that I have carried out for the last week (or for the last five million weeks) have confirmed the statement. But it is just possible that the earth will turn on its axis this evening and then tomorrow the sun will rise in the North.

Arising from this admittedly fanciful example we speak, scientifically, only of observations which support or contradict a theory and we properly speak in terms of probabilities rather than proof.

Children are Complex: the Notion of Multifactorial Causation Rules

There is an alluring temptation to take a complex problem and attempt to erect a simple theory to explain it. Any research into any aspect of child development should take this into account. An example of complexity is the acknowledged difference in mathematical attainment between the sexes. The simple-minded researcher measures maths skills in boys and girls matched for overall IQ and social class and concludes that since boys are better there must be a genetically determined factor operating. The researcher aware of more complex causes tries to examine the attitudes of the children, notably their expectation of success, and builds this into the equation. The simple-minded one may be right, of course, but the second student can write with greater confidence.

In the example quoted above it is assumed that high expectations in boys and correspondingly low expectations in girls directly affect maths performance. There are some cases where an apparent similarity is caused not by what seems to be the relevant factor but by another, so-called, **confounding variable**. For example, in recent years there have been many studies on the association between lead in children's bodies and their intelligence. Some have reported that children with higher levels of lead are less good on tests of intelligence and so it is concluded that the lead causes the lowered IQ score. In fact it is also known that lead tends to be higher in the bodies of children from lower social classes. And the measured intelligence of children from lower social classes is generally lower anyway so perhaps lead is irrelevant. I stress the word 'perhaps' here, no certainty is implied.

The Need for Random and Representative Samples

If anyone wants to study, say, the effect of being left-handed on spelling skills in children in Britain the ideal way to obtain a result would be to test every child in the country. Since no study can contemplate this researchers rely on samples.

Perhaps they take all the children of their friends? This will be of little value since it will hardly be a representative group.

Perhaps they take all the children in the nearby school? Again, this will tell us something about that school but since schools vary so much in their approach to spelling it will not necessarily enable us to have views on another school.

Perhaps they take all the children in the town? What then can we conclude about rural children?

The normal answer to the above problem is to select a **random sample** aimed at yielding a **representative group**. Twenty schools in different parts of the country might be approached to give a picture of rich and poor, urban and rural. Then to save time one in five children are tested in each school, the one child being chosen each time by a random technique—say, the fifth child on the register, then the tenth, then the fifteenth and so on. If this is strictly adhered to then there is a far greater chance of being able to generalise from the results than we would have from the same number of children drawn from a single school or town.

The Need for Replication

Levels of statistical significance are not more than a guide to the degree to which reported results can be taken as not having occurred by chance. After all, if a p figure of 0.01 means the probability of a result being by chance is 1 per cent then every so often this result will be found. Greater certainty is obtained if two separate studies yield similar results. For some research workers replication is essential if any conclusion is to be taken seriously.

The Notion of Interaction

An interaction occurs when two factors combine to produce a certain effect. For example, a researcher might be interested in the influence of noise on performance. It may be found that increasing background noise in a room makes little difference to the way subjects complete a test. But if anxiety levels are raised among the subjects then the effects of noise become significant. There has been an interaction between noise and anxiety.

Questions

1. Comment on the following: Blankshire Education Committee voted £20,000 last night to provide refrigerators in every class attended by a left-handed teenager. They did this following a report from an educational researcher who tested the reading of all the children in three secondary schools. It was found that left-handers did less well than right-handers when they were originally tested in June. Six months later their average reading age had increased. The correlation between reading and temperature was statistically significant. Refrigerators will provide ice to cool the hands of all dyslexic left-handers.

2. Why is the notion of reliability of such importance in psychological measurement?

3. Consider the place of the following in research design: (*a*) random sampling, (*b*) replication.

Appendix 1
An Overview of Development by Age

Introduction and Warning

The warning should not be required by anyone who has read the earlier chapters of this book, but for those dipping in and starting here it may be needed:

There is very wide individual variation between normal children and the ages given below are not more than a rough guide to what can be expected.

The age levels are based largely on the work of **Mary Sheridan**, whose booklet *The Developmental Progress of Infants and Young Children* published by HMSO in London remains an invaluable source.

Posture and Large Movement (sometimes referred to as gross motor)

1 month

Large, jerky limb movements, arms more active than legs.
When child placed downwards on tummy head turns to side.

3 months

Movements more smooth and symmetrical.
When on tummy can lift head and upper chest.

6 months

Raises head from pillow when lying on back.
When held sitting head is firmly erect and back straight. May sit unsupported for a few moments.
Feet bounce up and down when child held appropriately on hard surface.

9 months

Sits alone for 10–15 minutes.
Moves around floor by one means or another.
Can stand supported for a few moments but cannot lower self.

12 months

Moves about the floor rapidly.
May stand alone for a few moments.
Can rise to sitting position from lying.

15 months

Walks unsteadily with feet wide apart.
Goes upstairs by one means or another.
Can get onto feet unaided.

18 months

Walks well with feet only slightly apart.
Pushes and pulls large toys and other objects.
Walks upstairs with help.

2 years

Runs safely but rather clumsily.
Walks up and down stairs, two feet to a step.
Throws small ball.

2½ years

Runs well straight forward.
Can stand on tip-toe.

3 years

May climb nursery apparatus.
Can ride tricycle, steering rather wide corners.

4 years

Walks alone, one step at a time, up and down stairs.
Rides tricycle well.
Can climb ladder.

5 years

Runs lightly on toes.
Active and skilful on apparatus.

6 years

Catches ball bounced twice out of three attempts.
Can balance on one foot for 10 seconds.

Vision and Fine Movement

1 month

Turns head and eyes toward light.
Notices dangling object 6–8 inches away when shaken or rattled.

3 months

Visually alert, pays attention to nearby human face.
Watches movements of own hands.
Makes eager welcoming movements at breast or bottle.

6 months

Eyes move in unison.
Uses whole hand to grasp.
Reaches for object.

9 months

Stretches out to reach and grasp objects.
Manipulates objects and passes them from hand to hand.

12 months

Picks up small objects with thumb and first finger.
Watches people and cars out of doors with apparent interest.
May show preference for one hand.

15 months

Grasps pencil or crayon and scribbles in imitation.
Looks at pictures in book with interest.
Can put one brick on top of another in imitation.

18 months

Scribbles spontaneously using preferred hand.
Tower of three bricks built.
Enjoys simple picture book, may recognise some pictures.

2 years

Tower of six bricks.
Scribbles circular pattern spontaneously.
One hand now preferred.

2½ years

Recognises minute details in picture books.
Can line up bricks to form 'train'.

3 years

Copies circle.
Matches two or three colours (usually

red and yellow but may confuse blue and green).

4 years

Copies cross.
Draws man with head and legs and trunk and/or features.
Matches and names four or five colours.

5 years

Draws a recognisable man and simple house with door and windows.
Copies square and triangle.

6 years

Draws man with about six parts included.

Hearing and Speech

1 month

Startled by sudden loud noises.
If whimpering can be soothed by human voice.

3 months

Vocalises when spoken to or when content.
Quietens to rattle or bell or spoon in cup sounds.
May turn head towards sound.

6 months

. Vocalises using single and double syllables: *ka, muh, adah.*
Shows evidence of understanding different tones of voice.
Turns immediately to mother's voice.

9 months

Shouts to gain attention.
Babbles using string of sounds: *bab-bab-bab-*, etc.
Understand 'no' and 'bye-bye'.

12 months

Turns to own name, understands some words in context.
Bables tunefully and incessantly.
May hand common objects to adult on request.

15 months

Speaks up to six recognisable words.
Points to familiar objects or people on request.

18 months

Jabbers to self when playing.
Will point to hair, nose and shoe, self or doll.
Attempts to sing.

2 years

Uses up to 50 recognisable words; understands far more.
Two or more words used together.
Joins in nursery rhymes and songs.

2½ years

Knows full name.
Uses pronouns I, me and you.
Stammering not uncommon.
Enjoys listening to simple stories.

3 years

Uses plurals and pronouns.
Still monologues.
Asks 'what, where, who' questions.
Demands favourite stories repeatedly.

4 years

Speech generally intelligible but not perfect.
Can give account of recent experiences.
Asks 'why, when, how' questions.
Sometimes confuses fact and fantasy.

5 years

Speech fluent and generally correct with
only a few confusions.
Can give age and home address.

Self-help Skills

3 months

Can hold rattle for few moments.

6 months

Takes everything to mouth.

9 months

Holds and chews biscuit.
Tries to grasp spoon, puts hand round
cup or bottle.
May still take everything to mouth.

12 months

Drinks from cup with little assistance.
Helps with dressing by holding out arms.

15 months

Holds spoon well but cannot manipulate
it fully.
Indicates when pants wet.
Rarely takes objects to mouth.
Needs constant supervision.

18 months

Lifts and holds cup, two hands.
Gets food on spoon to mouth.
Takes off shoes and socks.
Indicates toilet needs, bowel control may
be complete.

2 years

Spoon feeds with little or no spilling.
Asks for food and drink.
Dry during day.

2½ years

Pulls down pants but may not be able to
replace them.
Eats well with spoon and possibly with
fork.

3 years

Washes hands but may need help with
drying.
Eats well with spoon and fork.
Can manage pants but needs help with
buttons.
Dry through the night.

4 years

Washes and dries hands and cleans teeth.
Can dress and undress all but difficult
buttons and laces.

5 years

Can use knife and fork.
Washes and dries hands and face.

Personal—Social and Play

3 months

Has begun to smile responsively.
Responds with pleasure to friendly
handling.
Holds rattle for short time.

6 months

Begins to find feet interesting.
Can reach for and grasp dangling toys.
May show some shyness with strangers.

9 months

Distinguishes strangers, may cling to known adult.
Plays peek-a-boo.

12 months

Shakes bell and puts objects in and out of box.
Likes to be with adults.
Demonstrates affection.

15 months

Pushes large wheeled toy around.
Throws objects onto the floor in play.
Closely dependent on familiar adult.

2 years

Imitates simple actions—'reading', brushing floor.
Will play alone but likes adult to be near.
Alternates between clinging and resisting.

2½ years

Prolonged domestic make-believe play.
Watches other children, may join in for a few minutes.
May throw tantrum when thwarted.

3 years

Generally more amenable.
Enjoys helping adult around the house or garden.
Joins in with other children.

4 years

Enjoys dressing up and dramatic play.
Can play alone but shows evident enjoyment when playing with others.
Building constructively with any materials to hand.
Understands turn-taking.
Shows concern for others.

5 years

Plans and builds in play.
Floor games may be quite complicated.
Chooses own friends and can play with appreciation of rules.

Appendix 2
For Further Reading

There are three major sources of further reading. The first is the large-scale **general text**, consisting of many chapters covering a wide range of topics. The three I quote below are all American and thus have a slant on the work taken to illustrate their points. They are:

Helen Bee, *The Developing Child*, Harper International.
James E. Birren, Dennis K. Kinney, K. Warner Schaie and Diana S. Woodruff, *Developmental Psychology, A Life-Span Approach*, Houghton Mifflin Co.
Elizabeth B. Hurlock, *Child Development*, McGraw-Hill Kogakusha.

The second is the single book on a more **specialised topic**. One such is:

Michael Rutter (ed.), *Scientific Foundations of Developmental Psychiatry*, Heinemann Medical Books. As the title implies, this considers child psychiatry from a developmental viewpoint.

Many others have been quoted in the main body of the text but readers might like to look out for the following paperback series:

Child Development series, Pan Books.
The Developing Child, Fontana/Open Books.
Essential Psychology, Methuen.
Penguin Science of Behaviour, Penguin Books.

The third is the **scientific journal**. There are many and they can usually be found only in college or university libraries. Among those to be looked for are:

British Journal of Developmental Psychology
Child: Care, Health and Education
Child Development
Developmental Psychology
Journal of Child Psychology and Psychiatry
Journal of Experimental Child Psychology
Journal of Genetic Psychology
Merrill-Palmer Quarterly

In addition, a number of other titles in the **Made Simple series** cover subjects that may be of interest to students of child development, including:

Childcare, by Claire Rayner
Psychiatry, by M. T. Haslam
Psychology, by A. Sperling and K. Martin
Social Services, by A. Byrne and C. Padfield
Sociology, by Jane Thompson

Name Index

Subject Index